T0384020

Minority Party Misery

Minority Party Misery examines the role of likely minority party status
on politicians' engagement in electoral politics. The main argument of
this book is that political actors pull back from electoral politics as it
becomes increasingly likely that they will be in the minority in a legislative body, particularly under the high levels of polarization that
accompany conditional party government. Politicians whose party will
be in the majority have a clear incentive to engage in electoral politics
because their preferred policies have a credible chance of passing if they
are in the majority. In contrast, it is generally difficult for minority party
lawmakers to get a hearing on—much less advance—their preferred
policies, particularly when the rules favor the majority party. Instead,
minority party lawmakers spend most of their time fighting losing battles against policy proposals from the majority party. Being left out can
take a psychological toll on politicians as individuals, causing them to
seek to avoid situations in which they are likely to continue to lose. To
establish the robustness of my theory, I examine an array of political
actors in various institutional settings. The first four chapters focus on
the U.S. House of Representatives, but later chapters examine the U.S.
Senate and state legislatures. Throughout the book, I generally find
support for my theory, although I find somewhat more nuanced results
for the Senate and state legislatures. The findings of this book have
important consequences for democratic governance, as highly qualified
minority party politicians may choose to leave office due to their dismal
circumstances rather than continue to serve until their party eventually
reenters the majority.

Jacob F. H. Smith was a Lecturing Fellow in the Thompson Writing
Program at Duke University when he wrote this book and is now an
Assistant Research Professor of Statistical Science and Political Science
at Duke University.

LEGISLATIVE POLITICS & POLICY MAKING

Series Editors

Janet M. Box-Steffensmeier, Vernal Riffe Professor of Political Science,
The Ohio State University

David Canon, Professor of Political Science, University of Wisconsin, Madison

RECENT TITLES IN THE SERIES:

Minority Party Misery: Political Powerlessness and Electoral Disengagement
JACOB F. H. SMITH

The Politics of Herding Cats: When Congressional Leaders Fail
JOHN LOVETT

Committees and the Decline of Lawmaking in Congress
JONATHAN LEWALLEN

Losing to Win: Why Congressional Majorities Play Politics Instead of Make Laws
JEREMY GELMAN

It's Not Personal: Politics and Policy in Lower Court Confirmation Hearings
LOGAN DANCEY, KJERSTEN R. NELSON, AND EVE M. RINGSMUTH

*On Parliamentary War: Partisan Conflict and Procedural Change in the
U.S. Senate*
JAMES I. WALLNER

*The Jeffords Switch: Changing Majority Status and Causal Processes
in the U.S. Senate*
CHRIS DEN HARTOG AND NATHAN W. MONROE

*The Committee: A Study of Policy, Power, Politics, and Obama's Historic
Legislative Agenda on Capitol Hill*
BRYAN W. MARSHALL AND BRUCE C. WOLPE

The Whips: Building Party Coalitions in Congress
C. LAWRENCE EVANS

Indecision in American Legislatures
JEFFREY J. HARDEN AND JUSTIN H. KIRKLAND

Electoral Incentives in Congress
JAMIE L. CARSON AND JOEL SIEVERT

Gendered Vulnerability: How Women Work Harder to Stay in Office
JEFFREY LAZARUS AND AMY STEIGERWALT

For a complete list of titles in this series, please see www.press.umich.edu.

MINORITY PARTY MISERY

Political Powerlessness
and Electoral Disengagement

Jacob F. H. Smith

University of Michigan Press
Ann Arbor

For questions or permissions, please contact um.press.perms@umich.edu

Published in the United States of America by the
University of Michigan Press
Manufactured in the United States of America
Printed on acid-free paper
A CIP catalog record for this book is available from the British Library.

Library of Congress Cataloging-in-Publication data has been applied for.

First published March 2021

ISBN: 978-0-472-07476-1 (Hardcover : alk paper)
ISBN: 978-0-472-05476-3 (Paper : alk paper)
ISBN: 978-0-472-12852-5 (ebook)

For my parents

Contents

List of Figures   ix

List of Tables   xi

Acknowledgments   xiii

Introduction   1

ONE A Theory of Minority Party Status   14

TWO I'm Out of Here! Minority Party Status and the
Decision to Retire from Congress   29

THREE How Does This Make Cents? Party Fundraising and the
Congressional Minority   54

FOUR Minority Party Status and the Decision to Run for Office   70

FIVE To Meddle or Not to Meddle? Minority Party Status,
Party Leaders, and Candidate Recruitment   88

SIX Political Ambition, Electoral Engagement, and the U.S. Senate   103

SEVEN Laboratories of Ambition? The Legislative Minority
in U.S. States   121

Conclusion   143

Appendixes

Appendix A: Notes on Interview Subjects and Methods   151

*Appendix B: Discussion of Data Collection for Campaign Finance Data
    in Chapter 3*   155

Appendix C: Detailed Discussion of Methods for Content Analysis   157

Notes   159

Works Cited   169

Index   189

Digital materials related to this title can be found on the Fulcrum platform via the following citable URL: https://doi.org/10.3998/mpub.11513438

List of Figures

Figure 2.1. Probability of minority party status by party, 1946–2018   37

Figure 2.2. Retirement by party, 1946–2018   39

Figure 2.3. Probability of minority party status and the decision to retire   42

Figure 2.4. Probability of minority party status and the decision to retire, 1956–1994   43

Figure 2.5. Probability of minority party status and the decision to retire, 1996–2018   44

Figure 2.6. Retirement and terms served in the pre-Reform era (1956–1974)   45

Figure 2.7. Retirement and terms served in the post-Reform era (1976–1994)   45

Figure 2.8. Probability of minority party status and the decision to retire among supersafe and supervulnerable members   47

Figure 3.1. Members of the likely minority are less likely to give to party (Random Effects Tobit Model)   67

Figure 4.1. Percentage quality candidates by party, 1946–2018   78

Figure 4.2. Probability of minority party status and quality candidate emergence   80

Figure 4.3. The role of region in the pre-Reform era   82

Figure 4.4. The role of presidential vote lean in the post-1994 era (1994–2014)   85

Figure 5.1. Recruitment attempt, seats where incumbent won with under 60 percent   99

Figure 5.2. Recruitment failure, seats where incumbent received
  under 60 percent in last election   100
Figure 6.1. Probability of minority party status by party, 1946–2018   111
Figure 6.2. Candidate quality by region and party   113
Figure 6.3. Candidate entry decisions in nonsouthern Senate seats,
  1958–1966   115
Figure 6.4. Senate retirement decisions, 1946–2018   116
Figure 6.5. Senatorial retirement decisions and age, 1994–2018   117
Figure 7.1. Minority party status and state legislative chambers
  in 2012 and 2014   130

List of Tables

Table 1.1. Four scenarios for the role of minority party status   24
Table 2.1. Models of legislative outcomes   36
Table 2.2. Probability of minority party status and the decision
    to retire from Congress   41
Table 3.1. Probability of minority party status and party money
    contributions   66
Table 4.1. Probability of minority party status and the decision
    to run for Congress   79
Table 5.1. Probability of minority party status and
    recruitment attempts   98
Table 5.2. Probability of minority party status and
    recruitment failures   99
Table 5.3. Results in 1994 models for probability of minority
    party status variable   100
Table 6.1. OLS model of Senate outcomes   110
Table 6.2. Senate candidate entry decisions   112
Table 6.3. Senate retirement decisions   117
Table 7.1. Models of state legislative outcomes in 2012 and 2014   129
Table 7.2. State legislative candidate entry in the 2012
    and 2014 elections   131
Table 7.3. Conditional party government and candidate entry   132
Appendix Table A.1. Summary statistics about interview subjects   153

Acknowledgments

Minority Party Misery grew out of my dissertation, which I started working on in early 2015. I was interested in how the overall competitiveness of legislative institutions, rather than an individual member's chances of winning alone, affected how politicians engaged with electoral politics. As the project evolved, I became especially interested in the minority party in legislative institutions. While I drew upon many works from political science in writing this book, two that were especially important in this project were Jack Pitney and William Connelly's *Congress' Permanent Minority? Republicans in the U.S. House* and Frances Lee's *Insecure Majorities*. These works' discussion of the poor conditions facing the minority party were crucial in guiding the development of my theory of minority party misery.

A great number of people and institutions were crucial in helping me write this book. First, I must acknowledge the Political Science Department at the University of North Carolina at Chapel Hill, where I completed my PhD, and the Thompson Writing Program at Duke University, where I received a postdoctoral fellowship that allowed me to complete this book project. At UNC, my advisor, Jason Roberts, and committee members Sarah Treul, Tom Carsey, Chris Clark, and Candis Watts Smith all provided important suggestions that improved this project. John Aldrich, who served on my committee, continued to provide feedback as my research mentor at Duke, reading the entire manuscript and providing extensive comments. Others, including Marc Hetherington, Michele Hoyman, attendees at the American Politics Research Group at UNC, and discussants at numerous conferences provided helpful suggestions that improved this book.

A number of family members and friends provided support along the way. My parents, Forrest and Monica Smith, instilled in me the value of education that allowed me to complete this book. My siblings, Joey and Heidi Smith, have been a constant source of mutual support and camaraderie. A number of friends deserve acknowledgment for their support. Jon Spiegler, Simon Hoellerbauer, and Josh Jansa provided both friendship and extensive feedback on this manuscript. I also had help from Gavin Riley, who helped collect data as my research assistant in the summer of 2016 and later coauthored a paper with me. Elizabeth Demers, my reviewers, and everyone I worked with at University of Michigan Press were incredibly helpful as I completed this book. It is impossible to list everyone who was supportive along the way, but this work would not have been possible without the help of countless others. All errors are my own.

Introduction

If a majority be united by a common interest, the rights of the minority will be insecure.

—James Madison, "Federalist 51"

They're *Not* Running (for Governor): Three Red State Senators and the 2016 Election

On September 9, 2015, Senator Heidi Heitkamp (D-ND) announced that she was not running for the newly open North Dakota governorship in 2016, thus robbing Democrats of a strong recruit for the office, yet pleasing national Democratic leaders at the same time (Pathé 2015b). At first glance, it seems strange to assert that Democrats would be glad that their strongest possible recruit was passing on a seemingly winnable race, but that was the reaction from national Democrats. Indeed, *Washington Post* political reporter James Hohmann tweeted that "Washington Democrats are popping champagne to celebrate Heidi Heitkamp's decision to stay in the Senate."[1]

To understand why Democrats had this reaction, one should consider the political context surrounding Senator Heitkamp's decision. After losing nine seats and their Senate majority in 2014, Senate Democrats appeared to face a narrow, but realistic, path to win a Senate majority in 2016, with seven Republican senators from states won by Barack Obama in 2012 up for reelection that year (Shepard 2015). If Senator Heitkamp had decided to run for governor of North Dakota, a recently passed law by the Republican-controlled state legislature would have required a special election in early 2017 to choose her successor, rather than allowing her to make an appointment to the seat (Nowatzki 2015). In a Republican-leaning state like North Dakota, this would have been an uphill battle for Democrats. In other words, a decision from Heitkamp to run for governor would have made it more difficult for Democrats to win the Senate majority in 2016.

Also underlying the reaction from national Democrats was the notion that majority control of the Senate is something worth having for a political party. Political scientists tend to portray the majority leader as weak in the Senate due to the empowerment of the minority party through procedural rules such as the filibuster (e.g., see Binder and Smith 1997; but also see Den Hartog and Monroe 2011 and Hanson 2014). However, Democrats' reaction to Heitkamp staying in the Senate, which made it more likely they could reassume majority party status in 2017, suggests that holding the majority is important as the majority began eliminating the 60 vote threshold for executive and judicial appointments (Hare, Poole, and Rosenthal 2014). The value of holding the Senate majority became especially clear in 2016 when Senate Republicans announced they would not hold hearings for any nominee that President Barack Obama picked for the open seat on the Supreme Court caused by the death of Justice Antonin Scalia (Everett and Thrush 2016).

While one might dismiss Heitkamp's decision and the ensuing reaction as anecdotal, this was not the first time a red state Democratic senator decided not to run for governor of their state in the early months of the 2016 election cycle. Earlier in 2015, Senators Claire McCaskill (D-MO) and Joe Manchin (D-WV) also announced that they would not run for open governorships in their respective states (Cheney 2015a, 2015b). Similar to North Dakota, West Virginia's legislature considered a bill that would use a special election to select Senator Manchin's replacement were he to have been elected governor, and the veto-proof Republican majority in the Missouri legislature could have passed a similar law if McCaskill had won the governorship (Cardosi 2015). Additionally, like Heitkamp's decision not to run for governor, national political reporters hailed these decisions as good news for national Democrats' hopes to win back the Senate majority (DeBonis 2015).

At the federal level, considerations of majority control do not apply exclusively—or even primarily—to the Senate. In 2016, however, observers generally viewed winning majority control of the House as out of reach for Democrats (House 2015). In a departure from their Senate counterparts,

House Democrats saw several of their incumbents in Republican-leaning seats opt to run for other offices in 2016 instead of seeking reelection, with Representatives Ann Kirkpatrick (D-AZ) and Patrick Murphy (D-FL) announcing their 2016 candidacies for the U.S. Senate in the second quarter of 2015 (Cahn 2015b). Given the options of potentially serving as part of a Senate majority, or—should they win reelection—continuing to be constantly outvoted as part of the minority in the House, these two legislators decided to run for the chamber where they seemed to have a higher probability of serving in as part of the majority party.

Considerations of majority control also do not apply solely to federal political institutions. Extensive variation exists at the state level in terms of the permanence of majority control of a single party and scholars have spent considerable time developing measures to examine this phenomenon (e.g., Ranney 1976; Holbrook and Van Dunk 1993; Hinchcliffe and Lee 2015; Curiel 2019). Relevant to the decisions of Senators Heitkamp, Manchin, and McCaskill, all three of their states' legislatures featured Republican veto-proof majorities.[2] While different from the decision to run for a legislative body, the relative powerlessness that would have accompanied the potential governorship of these three senators may have also played into their decision to remain in the Senate. Alongside the pressure from Senate Democratic leadership to remain in the upper chamber, the reality that they would have faced frequent veto overrides would have made service as governor much less gratifying. Thus, it seems that their decisions may flow directly from considerations about how to avoid the powerlessness of being in the political minority.

In this book, I examine the meaning of minority party status and its effect on electoral engagement. I theorize that the feeling of powerlessness that arises from minority party status causes politicians to disengage from electoral politics. I consider an array of political actors including incumbent legislators, political party committees, and prospective candidates, focusing on the U.S. House of Representatives, but also looking at the U.S. Senate and state legislatures. Discerning the nature of a link between minority party status and electoral engagement is crucial to understanding broader patterns of electoral competition in democratic politics and the condition of the political minority.

Concerns about the rights of the political minority date back to the American founding. Writing in "Federalist 51," James Madison expressed concern that the rights of the political minority would not be secure when facing a unified majority (Madison, Hamilton, and Jay [1787–88] 2003a). Madison felt that there were two ways to prevent this oppression. First, in a monarchy, having a ruler who was independent from the majority faction could guard against the whims of this group. Second, in a republic like the United States, breaking up the public into so many different groups that it was necessary to form ever-changing coalitions on each issue would prevent majority tyranny since the same interests would rarely align. Madison rejected the first of these two solutions, noting that it was highly possible that a sovereign ruler's views might align with those of the majority, thus tyrannizing the minority. Madison was much more optimistic about the second solution, arguing that American society would be "broken up into so many parts," so "the rights of individuals and the minority" were "in little danger from interested combinations of the majority" (Madison, Hamilton, and Jay [1787–88] 2003a, 321). While many of Madison's ideas on how to structure American democracy have stood the test of time, centuries later it is clear that one "interested combination" frequently dominates American politics: political parties. For much of American democracy, parties faced internal divisions, so coalitions of groups from each party dominated American politics; today, however, political parties often vote together as a bloc, following a trend of nationalization in American politics. Contrary to the belief expressed by Madison in "Federalist 10" that the structure of American government would form a "happy combination" of local and national interests, the "national object" of party has become increasingly salient in congressional decision-making (Madison, Hamilton, and Jaya [1787–88] 2003a, 77). In contemporary politics, the congressional majority often has the ability—and the desire—to trample the minority party, realizing some of Madison's worst fears. While creating an extended republic with elected leaders refining the views of their constituents solved many problems facing the early republic, he did not anticipate the level of partisanship that would exist in the modern Congress. In this book, I seek to establish the consequences for American democracy that arise from the majority party treading on the rights of the minority party in Congress.

Previous Literature on the Congressional Minority

An examination of minority party status begins by reviewing existing literature on the minority party. I begin with literature that focuses specifically on what it means to be part of the congressional minority party. This starts with Charles O. Jones (1970), who wrote a book studying the congressional minority of the early to mid-twentieth century. While his study is wide-ranging and covers many aspects of minority party status, particularly relevant to this study is his examination of the "minority party mentality" (Jones 1970, 170–74). Jones argues that minority party status is a source of frustration to new members, while members who are more senior accept the fact that they will not regain the majority and instead decide to pursue their own goals. Jones, however, does not discuss here what happens to a senior member who had served in the majority for much of their career and finally finds themselves in the minority. Within the scope of Jones's study, this scenario applies to a number of Democrats who won their seats in the FDR era and then experienced minority party status after the 1946 midterm election (and again from 1951 to 1955). Additionally, personal goals may make service in Congress worth it only to some members. While Mayhew (1974a) focuses on reelection to the exclusion of other goals, other scholars (e.g., Fenno 1978 and Rohde 1991) argue that members also focus on achieving what they view to be good public policy, as well as amassing power in the institution. These goals are often difficult—if not impossible—to achieve when one is in the minority. Thus, it seems that the unpleasantness of minority party status that Jones ascribes to new members may also apply under certain conditions to more senior members. Indeed, data he provides on the length of congressional service of Republican members from this era suggests that senior members may retire due to minority party status (Jones 1970, 173–74). Jones notes that Senate Republicans, who—despite being in the minority for much of this period—had real influence on public policymaking due to the empowerment of the minority party in Senate rules, served much longer in Congress than their House counterparts.[3] In total, Jones's study crucially establishes that a specific state of mind affects the members of the minority party in Congress, which may cause them to disengage from democratic politics.

More recently, Connelly and Pitney (1994) examined the Republican minority that persisted in the U.S. House from 1955 to 1995. While Republicans were the minority party for much of the period examined by Jones, "congressional Republican" was synonymous with "minority party" for the entirety of Connelly and Pitney's study. With Democrats characterized as the "party of government," Republicans struggled to recruit strong challengers and keep incumbents from leaving the House to advance their careers in this period (Connelly and Pitney 1994, 12). Consistent with Jones's observation from several decades earlier about retirement, Connelly and Pitney point out that, as of January 1993, only 32 of 176 Republicans (or 18 percent of the caucus) had served more than six terms in Congress. Most problematic for the minority is the fact that minority party status seems to compound upon itself. Reflecting their unfavorable circumstances, incumbent Republicans were not "hungry for a majority" and were generally unwilling to participate in party fundraising efforts (Connelly and Pitney 1994, 154). Increased retirements force the party to defend more open seats, which makes it harder to win the majority. Additionally, the loss of talented leaders who decide to leave Congress hurts the ability of the minority party to function well as an opposition party, affecting not only the minority party but also the quality of democratic governance more broadly. In total, Connelly and Pitney's study further underscores Jones's (1970, 170) observation of a "minority party mentality" and its ill effects. An important question that was impossible to answer at the time of Connelly and Pitney's study, however, is the extent to which their findings apply to minority party *Republicans* in the mid- to late twentieth century or the congressional minority *in general* across time. Even a long-serving Republican in this period did not ever serve in the majority and would not have had a reasonable expectation of ever doing so.[4] In examining a wider sweep of history and institutions beyond the U.S. House of Representatives, I seek to establish the generalizability of this result.

While much research on the minority party in Congress focuses on periods where one party is permanently in the minority, other scholars have examined how the sense of minority party status changed after the 1994 election, when Republicans won back the majority after four decades in the minority. Lee (2016) considered this question in her book on how party competition affects polarization in the United States. As with previous authors, Lee discusses the minority party mindset that prevailed among Republicans before 1994. For much of this period, Republicans worked with Democrats on policy, accepting agreements that tilted toward Democratic policy priorities in order to play a role in shaping the final agreement. This changed once Republicans felt they could be a majority. Lee contends that this outlook—at least among some Republicans—began to shift even before the 1994 change in power. After Senate control switched in the 1980 Reagan landslide, some Republicans began to believe they could potentially win the House majority relatively soon. Led by Representative Newt Gingrich (R-GA), who had begun to ascend through the ranks of House Republican leadership, some Republicans came to believe it was better to fight Democrats and hope to win the majority in the next election than make concessions in order to shape legislation. Eventually, this logic paid off as Republicans won the House majority for the first time in 40 years in 1994.

Once Republicans finally won the majority, a new approach set in for both parties. Lee argues that the belief that either party could win the majority increased polarization in Congress, with each party digging in to improve their position in the next election. For example, party leaders increasingly used votes to make a political point rather than expect these proposals to pass and actually become law. "Partisan message votes," as Lee (2016, 266) calls them, force members to cast votes on controversial issues that are designed to hurt their reputations and thus harm their reelection prospects (also see Egar 2016).

Other authors have similarly documented how the battle for House majority control has affected the behavior of members of Congress. Heberlig and Larson (2005, 2007, 2010, 2012, and 2014), have demonstrated that numerous aspects of what it means to be a member of Congress have undergone substantial changes in recent years since the House majority became more competitive following the 1994 election (also see Currinder 2003; Deering and Wahlbeck 2006; Green 2008).[5] These authors focus especially on the rise of fundraising on behalf of party efforts to win majority control. Parties now expect safe seat incumbents to help the party raise money by redistributing campaign or leadership PAC funds to party committees or directly to vulnerable members of their party. Heberlig and Larson (2012) find that advancement in the institution increasingly requires a commitment to raise money for the party. While other factors such as legislative loyalty and time commitments to the party are also important, when majority control is at stake it is crucial for members who want to receive or remain in important leadership positions to contribute financially to those races that are likely to make a difference in the battle for majority control. Indeed, even when Congress is in session, leaders expect members to spend about four hours a day on the telephone engaged in "call time," speaking with potential donors in order to raise money for upcoming races in vulnerable seats, or for overall party efforts in the case of safe seats (Grim and Siddiqui 2013).

Another crucial point of debate in previous literature on the minority party is the extent to which they can shape public policy and how this has changed over time. Jones (1970) devotes several chapters to the topic of when minority parties participate in policymaking in Congress. He argues that party disunity, as happened to Republicans in the 63rd and 73rd Congresses (1913–15; 1933–35) can particularly limit the ability of the minority party to shape debate (Jones 1970, 57). Other factors that limit the minority include the party of the president, legislative procedure, and the strength of leadership within the party. There are also times when the minority party plays an important role in policymaking. Jones discovers that presidential weakness, a close balance of seats between the parties

when the minority had recently been in the majority, and—paradoxically—
weak leadership in the minority party allow them to participate more in
policymaking efforts.[6] Jones (1970, 96) expresses surprise at his findings on
presidential power and minority party leadership. He explains this unexpected result by observing that minority parties rarely build their own
policies; instead, a strong majority party decides to "build majorities for its
own program" by including members of the minority party in the process
(Jones 1970, 97).

Given changes in Congress since the time of Jones's book, one should
also examine patterns of participation for minorities in more recent congressional sessions. Since Congress has become more polarized, other
research paints a more negative picture for the minority party. Connelly
and Pitney (1994, 70) note that Republicans did not know how bad things
would get in the first decade and a half of being the minority party as they
were able to participate in the policymaking process at first. A few decades
later, Democrats had almost entirely shut out Republicans from policymaking. As Rep. Bill Frenzel (R-MN) noted, "Republicans feel ignored because
they are ignored" (Connelly and Pitney 1994, 4; quote from Birnbaum
1987). Democrats largely agreed with this view, with Rep. Henry Waxman
(D-CA) noting that if there was a "unified Democratic position, Republicans are irrelevant" (Connelly and Pitney 1994, 4, quote from Hook 1986).
Generally, then, it seems the rise in party voting in the 1970s is crucial to
explaining the change in the role for the minority party. Indeed, Meinke
(2016) argues that the increase in the competitiveness of the congressional
majority, coupled with rising polarization, has resulted in an increase in the
size of party whip organizations in Congress. These organizations seek to
enforce party discipline in Congress, thus making it easier to shut out the
minority by pushing for consensus among majority party members. Further, Lee's research suggests that the use of devices such as "message votes"
may augment polarization beyond existing ideological disagreements, further diminishing the ability of the congressional minority to play a role in
policymaking (Lee 2009, 2016).

While conditions seem bleak for the contemporary minority party in
Congress, several recent authors dispute the view that minorities cannot
participate. Green (2015) argues that, due to the harsh conditions facing
the minority, they are more likely to become policy innovators. He uses
Newt Gingrich in the 1980s as an example of one such minority party
innovator, pointing out that he and other minority party Republicans were
able to bring new ideas to the forefront of debate. In terms of affecting
legislation, the minority party can occasionally win support for its amend-

ments, motions, or discharge petitions (Green 2015, 178–79). Minority parties can also play a role if the president is of their party, although this can be a somewhat frustrating experience if the president's copartisans in the minority dislike a deal cut with the majority party. In keeping with Lee (2016), however, Green acknowledges that the minority party typically uses its influence on the floor to advance its position in the next election rather than to influence policy. Clark (2015, 16) also examines this question, arguing that the minority party plays a role when there is "policy conflict and uncertainty." When there is not consensus among political elites, the minority party is more likely to be part of a winning coalition. One example that highlights how a lack of consensus in the majority party can result in the inclusion of the minority party in policymaking comes from the budget politics of the Obama administration. Republicans had a relatively narrow majority during this period (especially during 2013–15) and lacked internal consensus on a number of budget-related items, requiring Speaker John Boehner (R-OH) to make deals with Minority Leader Nancy Pelosi (D-CA) in order to obtain the necessary 218 votes to pass legislation keeping the government open and raising the debt ceiling. Clark also argues that uncertainty increases the likelihood that the minority will be involved in policymaking because reducing ambiguity makes it easier for members to achieve their goals of good public policy and reelection. When such uncertainty exists, the minority is less likely to obstruct the majority to serve these broader goals. The perspectives of Green (2015) and Clark (2015) are an important reminder that the minority still sometimes plays a role in influencing policy. Nevertheless, the congressional minority is highly restricted, a circumstance reflected by the fact that much of Clark's book focuses on the role of the minority party in state legislatures rather than Congress. Thus, while some conditions exist where the minority party is able to have its voice heard, they are still at an extreme disadvantage to the majority party in terms of influencing policy.

In addition to considering the effects of minority party status on policymaking inside Congress, I reflect upon how these poor conditions affect the minority's engagement in electoral politics outside the institution. Thus, in addition to examining literature about the minority party as a group, I draw upon literature that focuses on how politicians make individual decisions about whether to engage in electoral politics. I begin with Riker and Ordeshook's (1968) formalization of the political decision-making process, given as R=pB-C+D. In this formula, p relates to that political actor's own prospects for success and B relates to the personal benefits they derive from achieving that goal. Further, C denotes costs to that actor that arise from the action, while D signifies a sense of civic duty the politician may feel (Riker and Ordeshook 1968). This formalization suggests that personal considerations are foremost in the mind of politicians when they decide whether to take an action. Black (1972) extends this formula specifically to the decision to run for office, focusing on the potential benefits, costs, and the probability of winning for individual candidates. Going a step further, Rohde (1979) examines progressive ambition—the desire to win a more prominent elective office—among officeholders. While Rohde's study adds the consideration not only of *whether* to run for office, but *which* office to run for, the central consideration for a political actor is whether he or she is likely to win elective office. Aldrich and Bianco (1992) also build on Riker and Ordeshook's formula, examining a prospective candidate's decision to join a particular political party. As Aldrich and Bianco (1992, 105) note, at the center of this theory is "the assumption of (pure) office-seeking ambition." Like previous studies, the focus of a political actor's decision-making process is their individual goal of achieving elected office.

The same focus on individual electoral success is present in a variety of studies on the decision to run for Congress. Famously, Mayhew (1974a) posited that reelection was the proximate goal for members of Congress. For Mayhew, running for Congress was an individual endeavor, writing, "no theoretical treatment of the United States Congress that posits parties as analytic units will go very far" (Mayhew 1974a, 27). Even past studies that include a role for parties tend to focus on the goal of winning as resulting in a personal benefit for that member of Congress rather than the party as a whole. For example, Jacobson and Kernell (1983) examine how potential candidates respond to national conditions such as the state of the economy and level of presidential approval when making decisions about whether to run for office. These factors affect a party's overall prospects, but Jacobson and Kernell focus on how these conditions affect a candidate's own prospects for success in congressional elections. Studies such as Jacobson and Kernell's, written before the 1994 Republican Revolution, presuppose that Democrats will retain the majority, thus requiring further examination of how a competitive congressional majority affects electoral engagement.

Some studies conducted after the 1994 election have given closer attention to how candidate decisions to run for office benefit the party as a whole. Maestas et al. (2006) conducted a national study where they surveyed potential candidates to determine why they ran for office. They found that state legislators who were contacted by the party, and thus given the signal that there was a commitment to winning their district, seemed to have more ambition to run for Congress than those legislators who did not receive such a message. Although parties surely want as many of their candidates as possible to win, resources are scarce, which forces them to prioritize those seats that they are most likely to win so as to maximize their chances of capturing or keeping the majority. In keeping with this logic, Carsey and Berry (2014) posit that parties act to prioritize their chances of success when recruiting candidates to run for state legislatures. Parties want to nominate the strongest possible candidate to run for office, but when this is not possible, they suggest that a party tries to recruit a "sacrificial lamb" to maintain a presence in the district, perhaps setting them up for victory in the future. Although these studies pay closer attention to the goals of the party than previous research, the emphasis is still on a party's prospects of winning an individual seat, rather than their overall prospects for winning the majority in a particular election. While the focus of this literature is somewhat different from my study, this research, alongside that on the congressional minority, provides a good starting point for examining how the prospect of minority party status affects the electoral engagement of political actors. Next, I describe the methods I used to conduct my study and the plan of this book.

Data and Methods

This book makes use of a combination of regression analysis, content analysis of newspapers, interview research, and a case study. I conducted the interviews for this book in the summer of 2019. I conducted 17 interviews focused on politicians and staff at the state and national level. I used a combination of quota and purposive sampling to select interviewees. At the national level, I used these interviews to refine my theory; for state legislatures, these interviews allowed me more closely to examine retirement and candidate entry decisions by Democrats in the post-2010 era. Thus, I have a balance between Democrats and Republicans at the national level in my sample, but it skews more toward Democrats at the state level. A more in-depth discussion of my method is available in appendix A.

The datasets used in this book are a combination of data generously shared by others and original data collection efforts by myself. In the second and fourth chapter, I built upon the dataset compiled and generously shared by Gary Jacobson and Jamie Carson to look at congressional retirement decisions and candidate entry. This data is the basis for both statistical models and a case study in chapter 2 and my candidate entry models in chapter 4. I compiled the data on party fundraising used in chapter 3, but relied on previous data shared generously by Eric Heberlig and Bruce Larson as a guide (see appendix B). I carried out a content analysis of newspapers to examine party recruitment in chapter 5 (see appendix C) and collected data on Senate candidate entry in chapter 6. Gavin Riley, my research assistant and future coauthor, helped with data collection efforts to examine state legislative candidate quality in chapter 7 during the summer of 2016. By conducting an analysis using data from a variety of institutions and by using a mixed methods approach, I seek to establish the robustness of my findings.

Plan of the Book

Having considered previous perspectives on minority party status, I proceed to lay out my theory of electoral engagement by the minority party in chapter 1. I argue that political actors are more likely to compete for legislative seats when their party is likely to win the majority and more likely to disengage when doomed to the minority. My theory brings together research on political ambition, good public policy as a goal of members of Congress, conditional party government, and the psychology of winning and losing (e.g., Schlesinger 1966; Fenno 1978; Rohde 1991; Aldrich 2011; and Robertson 2012). In chapter 2, I apply this theory to congressional retirement decisions, considering Mayhew's (1974a) assumption that members of Congress want to seek reelection as long as possible. I argue that the goal of perpetual reelection is not always present when a member is unlikely to serve in the majority in the near future. Next, I develop an original measure of the probability that members will be in the minority in the next session of Congress. I subsequently conduct a statistical analysis of retirement patterns over time, as well as a case study of the 2018 election. This case study allows for closer examination of the record number of Republican retirements that occurred in this election cycle. Chapter 3 examines how minority party status affects party fundraising efforts, drawing heavily on the work of Heberlig and Larson (2012). I contend that legislators do not want to participate in these efforts and are less likely to put up with them when fated to be in the minority. In chapter 4, I look at candidate decisions to run for office, arguing that quality candidates are less likely to emerge when it is likely that their party will be in the minority. Chapter 5 examines how the prospect of minority party status affects party committee recruitment, using a content analysis of newspaper stories to test my theory. Finally, in chapters 6 and 7 I apply my theory to other political institutions, specifically the U.S. Senate (chapter 6) and state legislatures (chapter 7). While the institutional features of these chambers vary from the U.S. House, I posit that minority party status can still affect how members behave. Chapter 6 makes use of statistical analysis, while the evidence used in chapter 7 includes a combination of quantitative analysis and qualitative interviews. In the conclusion, I discuss the implications of my findings for American democracy, focusing on their consequences for voters and public policymaking. Conditions that lead to fewer quality politicians seeking office is of central concern to American politics. As noted by Schlesinger (1966), it is crucial to electoral democracy to have a plentiful supply of politicians who desire to seek elective office. Thus, this study seeks to answer a question that is central to the state of democratic politics.

ONE

A Theory of Minority Party Status

When Democrats lost their House majority in 2010, they immediately started to regroup to try to win back the majority two years later. With Representative Chris Van Hollen (D-MD) stepping aside as Democratic Congressional Campaign Committee (DCCC) chair, a new leader of the party's campaign arm had to be selected (Ferraro and Cowan 2010). Soon thereafter, Representative Steve Israel (D-NY) stepped up to run the committee, beginning an effort he referred to as the "Drive for Twenty-Five," which referred to the number of seats Democrats would need to gain in order to assume the majority after the 2012 elections (Halbfinger 2011). Democrats fell short, gaining a net of eight seats, but Israel decided to stay on as the committee chair for the 2014 cycle. After Democrats lost 13 seats in 2014, falling below their post-2010 level to the fewest seats held by the party since after the 1946 election, Israel stepped aside from the DCCC chair position. Nonetheless, Israel remained in Democratic leadership, with Minority Leader Nancy Pelosi (D-CA) creating a new position for him, the "Chair of the Democratic Policy and Communications Committee" (Brune 2014). Thus, Israel's future in Democratic politics still seemed bright, with some suggesting he could be a future House Speaker, when Democrats eventually won back the majority, or that he could become a U.S. senator (Kane 2016).

A year later, however, Israel shocked the political world by announcing he was retiring from the U.S. House—and national politics altogether—so that he could focus on his side career as a novelist. In a post-announcement interview, Israel attributed his retirement to the fact that the system was "beyond broken" and that he was unwilling to spend any more time "in a call room begging for money," referring to the fact that representatives spend much of their time on the phone trying to raise money to help win or retain the majority (Hulse 2016). As a member of the Democratic congressional leadership who consistently won reelection by solid margins, a member like Israel would both want to and be successful at continuing to win reelection to Congress (e.g., Mayhew 1974a; Fenno 1978; Rohde 1991). Yet, as Israel's interview comments suggest, while he may well have been able to win reelection, conditions in Congress were so miserable for him as a minority party member under extreme polarization that he decided continued service was no longer worth it.

In this chapter, I construct a theory to explain why politicians such as Israel who are likely to be in the minority may seek to withdraw from electoral politics.[1] The theory I present here is broad and meant to apply to a variety of aspects of contemporary electoral politics including (1) the decision of incumbent representatives to retire, (2) the participation of these members in congressional fundraising efforts, (3) prospective candidates' decisions to run for office, and (4) party committees' efforts to recruit their desired candidates to run for office. While members themselves typify this theory, it applies more broadly to those with an investment in who wins the congressional majority. Representative Israel is a particularly good example for this theory because of how closely his actions relate to three of the aforementioned behaviors: congressional retirement, party fundraising, and party committee recruitment efforts. In future chapters, I specifically apply my theory to each of these contexts, as well as to other legislative institutions in the United States.

First, however, I present a broad theory of electoral engagement. This theory relies on several key assumptions: (1) politicians are ambitious, (2), politicians care about enacting good public policy, (3) the unpleasantness of minority party status is not constant, and (4) politicians are human beings with emotions that affect their willingness to engage in activities. In this chapter, I corroborate and then build upon these assumptions in turn to construct a theory of political engagement as it relates to minority party status. My theory begins with a discussion of how ambition and a desire for good public policy meet to affect a politician's engagement in electoral politics.

Political Ambition, Good Public Policy, and Engagement in Electoral Politics

The decision about whether to engage in electoral politics naturally starts with an examination of political ambition. In his seminal work on the topic, Joseph Schlesinger (1966, 10) suggests that politicians can have one of three types of ambition: static, discrete, or progressive. Statically ambitious politicians want to serve their term and then leave politics, while a discretely ambitious politician wishes to continue serving in the office they currently hold for an indeterminate amount of time. Finally, a politician with progressive ambition wishes to rise to the next level of political office. Examples of ambitious politicians are abundant. As Schlesinger (1966, 2) notes, representative government relies on there being a plentiful supply of politicians seeking office, so this bountiful supply is good for democratic government. Data he provides for the period of his study demonstrates that the number of candidates for U.S. Senate or governor of their state often numbers in the teens or low twenties (Schlesinger 1966, 213–14).

It is not difficult to find examples to show that politicians are still ambitious today. The average tenure for members of the U.S. House has fluctuated between about eight and 10 years in recent decades, showing that at least some members intend to make a career out of service in the institution (Congressional Research Service 2019). Further, politicians may be even quicker to act on progressive ambition than in the past. In recent years, numerous first-term senators from both parties have run for president. Examples include Kamala Harris (D-CA) in 2020, Marco Rubio (R-FL) and Ted Cruz (R-TX) in 2016, and of course Barack Obama (D-IL) in 2008. The 2020 field also included a former cabinet secretary, Julián Castro, and numerous current and former House members. In 1960, Senator John F. Kennedy (D-MA)—who had served eight years in the Senate and six in the House—was accused of being overly ambitious and too inexperienced, which he overcame by being an exceptional candidate (Selverstone 2014). The view that Kennedy represents something of a gold standard among young, inexperienced candidates became clear in the famous interaction between vice-presidential candidates Dan Quayle (R-IN) and Lloyd Bentsen (D-TX) in the 1988 vice-presidential debate. In this debate, when Quayle noted that he had as much experience in Congress as had Kennedy, the Texan famously shot back "you're no Jack Kennedy" (Bierman 2016).[2] In other words, not just anyone with (what was then viewed as) minimal experience could run for president—or vice president. Yet in the twenty-first century, running for president with significantly *less* experience than Kennedy or Quayle is commonplace. Similarly, a number of first-term House members have run for the Senate in recent years including Jacky Rosen (D-NV) in 2018, Tom Cotton (R-AR) and Steve Daines (R-MT) in 2014, and Rick Berg (R-ND) in 2012. All of these representatives save Berg, who lost by a percentage point, were successful in their bids for the upper chamber. In an age where those with less experience attack politicians who spend long periods in office as insiders and part of the establishment, seeking to move up quickly may be the best strategy for these politicians to achieve their goals in office. As a whole, recent candidate entry patterns suggest that many ambitious politicians still desire to hold office and their best strategy is often to act quickly upon it.

Ambition theory relates closely to party theory, although Schlesinger (1966, 4–5) notes that even in countries where parties operate like teams (e.g., the United Kingdom), understanding individual ambitions within each party is still essential. At the same time, even in countries with weaker parties, such as the United States at the time of his book, parties are central for understanding political ambition because politicians will seek to advance their careers through one of the major parties (Schlesinger 1966, 119). He argues that the "structure of opportunities appears to be independent of the state of competition between the parties," although it does affect *which* offices are available to the parties (Schlesinger 1966, 197, also see 119–42). Put differently, the hierarchy of offices within each of the parties is broadly similar even though some offices are only available to one of the parties. For example, in the context of the U.S. House of Representatives, the top offices for the majority party are traditionally the jobs of Speaker, majority leader, and majority whip, while the minority party's top jobs are minority leader and minority whip. In one instance of party status clearly affecting the hierarchy of a party, when Democrats lost the House majority in 2010, they decided to create the office of assistant Democratic leader for outgoing Majority Whip Jim Clyburn (D-SC) so that he could remain in the leadership. This new position seemed to exist somewhere between minority whip and caucus chair, and Clyburn returned to the job of majority whip when Democrats regained the House majority in 2018. The assistant Democratic leader position remained, however, with DCCC chair Ben Ray Lujan assuming the position, which was renamed assistant Speaker (Caygle 2018). Broadly, however, Schlesinger's observation about the offices available to an ambitious politician being unrelated to the state of political competition holds.

Building on Schlesinger, I contend that the prospect of minority party status can affect the kind of ambition held by a politician. When a party is likely to be in the congressional minority, this limits the opportunities available to its members. There is one fewer top leadership position for the majority (other than for Democrats after 2010, with the addition of assistant Democratic leader), as the majority assumes the speakership. Further, minority party leadership positions are far less powerful than the comparable top positions for the majority party. Additionally, the majority party assumes all chair and subcommittee chair positions. While members of the minority party serve as ranking member, this is not the same as being a chair. Connelly and Pitney (1994, 4) provide an anecdote where Minority Leader Bob Michel (R-IL) notes that constituents reacted to being told that a member is ranking minority member by saying "Rank? Gee that smells." Although committee chairs are generally senior in the party, subcommittee chairs have a variety of levels of experience. Indeed, in the 116th Congress, leadership selected several first-term members to serve as subcommittee chairs. For example, on the House Oversight and Reform Committee, a panel that played a central role in investigating the Trump administration where an ambitious Democrat could make a name for themselves in the party, one of the six subcommittee chairs—Harley Rouda (D-CA)—was a first-term member (House Oversight and Reform Committee 2019). Furthermore, two of the other subcommittee chairs, Jamie Raskin (D-MD) and Raja Krishnamoorthi (D-IL), were in their second terms, while another first-term member, Katie Hill (D-CA), became the vice-chair of the full committee. Thus, valuable leadership positions are available to members as soon as their first term, but are only obtainable if one is in the majority party. Adding insult to injury, the majority party also controls access to meeting spaces in Congress, meaning that the minority is likely to have less desirable locations to plot strategy ahead of committee meetings (Hulse 2018).

Additionally, the likely majority party may receive electoral benefits *because* of its likely majority status. Members or candidates of the party likely to be in the majority can use that fact as a reason for voters to support their campaign. The argument made by these politicians is that, because they are likely to be in the majority, they are more likely to be part of negotiations on important pieces of legislation and be in a position to help their constituents. Based on this line of reasoning, voters risk having a representative looking in from the outside if they elect someone who is in the minority. An editorial by the *Missoulian* newspaper for the 2017 Montana special election to fill the seat held by former U.S. Representative Ryan Zinke (R-MT) after he became interior secretary serves as a good example of this logic. This editorial noted that part of the reason the paper chose Republican Greg Gianforte over Democrat Rob Quist was because Gianforte would be part of the majority party in Congress (Missoulian 2017).[3] Another advantage held by the majority party is in the area of fundraising. Access-driven donors seek to give to the party that they think will most be able to shape policy. In other words, they want to donate to the party or parties that they think have a decent chance of being in the majority in the next session of Congress (e.g., see Jacobson and Carson 2016, 92, and Gimpel, Lee, and Pearson-Merkowitz 2008).[4] This has a significant benefit for members of the majority in marginal seats who find that they have more access to financial resources than do their minority party counterparts. These two advantages make majority party members in competitive seats—many of whom are likely to have a short tenure in the body due to electoral turnover in these seats—more likely to believe that they will have the support necessary to make a career of Congress. In total, the majority party holds an advantage over the minority in terms of the ability of its politicians to further their ambitions.

When faced with the specter of minority party status, politicians have one of three options: (1) stick it out, (2) disengage from politics, or (3) seek a different, generally higher office.[5] The first option coincides with static ambition, the second with discrete ambition, and the third with progressive ambition. Importantly, disengagement could mean leaving politics altogether, or just scaling back one's efforts while remaining in office. Overall, I posit that minority party status makes it more likely that a politician displaying static ambition will become one with discrete ambition. More rarely, minority party status may ignite a nascent progressive ambition, causing a politician to run for a higher political office because the existing office is no longer desirable. For example, Rep. Chris Van Hollen (D-MD), long viewed as a potential future Democratic Speaker, decided to run for the Senate seat vacated by Barbara Mikulski (D-MD) in 2016 rather than waiting for party status to flip—and for existing leaders to retire (Draper 2013).[6] Van Hollen faced a competitive primary with Rep. Donna Edwards (D-MD); both of these representatives gave up safe House seats to run for the Senate, with the knowledge that one of them would be shut out of elective office altogether. Come January 2017, Van Hollen was a senator, but Edwards was a private citizen.[7] This third option, however, is only available to some political actors making some decisions; the DCCC cannot decide to start recruiting for Senate races or the presidential race because it is not able to win a House majority. They must decide to either recruit or not recruit for the House.[8] I mean this simply to be a comprehensive list of options that apply to at least one type of political actor examined in this book.

While holding office for the sake of holding office may be enough for some politicians, the goal of enacting what they view to be good public policy drives many to engage in electoral politics. In his landmark work on Congress, David Mayhew posits that members of Congress are "single-minded seekers of reelection," which he admits is an oversimplification, although not much of one (Mayhew 1974a, 5). In contrast, other scholars such as Fenno (1978) and Rohde (1991) argue that members of Congress also seek to enact what they view to be good public policy. To support this view, Rohde (1991) uses the example of the reform effort undertaken by liberal Democrats in Congress in the 1970s. Rohde (1991, 28–29) notes that pro-Reform members framed their argument in terms of how making reforms to the committee structure would allow them to make better public policy. Rohde also notes, however, that they only targeted the parts of the committee structure that made it difficult to achieve these goals, while keeping others in place that helped them achieve their other objectives of reelection and power in the institution.

A number of recent policy actions also provide evidence to suggest that members of Congress act in order to achieve what they view to be good policy, sometimes even at the expense of future electoral prospects. The effort to pass the Affordable Care Act in 2010, as well as the attempt to repeal it in 2017, both serve as examples of members acting in a manner that did not advance their career—or the standing of their party—but that they did anyway. The Affordable Care Act was polling poorly when Democrats voted to pass it in early 2010 and research shows that members of Congress who represented competitive and conservative-leaning districts who supported it were more likely to lose in 2010 (e.g., Brady, Fiorina, and Wilkins 2011; Nyhan et al. 2012). Yet Democrats voted to pass it because they believed it was good policy. For example, Earl Pomeroy (D-ND), who stood up in a Democratic caucus meeting to announce his crucial support for the bill, attributed his loss in 2010 to voting for the Affordable Care Act, but said that he did not regret voting for it (Hunt 2010; Jacobs 2013). Seven years later, Republicans faced similar opposition by the public to repealing the Affordable Care Act, but nonetheless pressed on. Also standing up in a caucus meeting to urge skittish members to vote "yes," Representative Martha McSally (R-AZ) famously urged Republicans to "get this f[-]ing thing done" (Werner 2017).[9]

The goal of achieving good public policy is significantly more difficult when one is in the minority. Members of the minority party are disadvantaged at every step of the legislative process. In committee, the minority party has fewer seats, making it difficult to block proposals they do not like. Additionally, the chair of that committee will only bring up a minority party proposal if it is also in line with his or her priorities. On the floor, the minority party is also at a significant disadvantage. As detailed by Sinclair (2015), the majority has a number of tools they can use, should they so choose, to shut out the minority. This has negative consequences for both passing their own policies and blocking those of the majority with which they disagree. In both instances, when the majority wants to pass something that will encounter significant opposition, they can structure the rules to their advantage (Sinclair 2015). Finally, the minority, by definition, has fewer members in the chamber, meaning that when 218 members of the majority party want to pass a policy on their own, they have the ability to do so. The relative advantages of the majority party in policymaking are apparent if one looks at legislative effectiveness scores, a metric of success in policymaking calculated by Wiseman and Volden (2014). In the period from 1973 to 2018, the average legislative effectiveness score of the majority was 1.44 compared to only 0.42 for the minority, a statistically significant difference.

If one cannot achieve policy goals in the House, one may decide to pursue them elsewhere, or simply give up and withdraw from electoral politics altogether. Such ventures can go far afield of politics. As mentioned previously, Steve Israel left Congress to write another book, while Bay Buchanan, once Treasurer of the United States under Ronald Reagan and a later a frequent advocate for Republicans on television, gave up on being a public voice for the GOP after Mitt Romney's loss in the 2012 presidential race and decided to become a realtor (Hulse 2016; Reeve 2013). However, minority party status does not always present the same obstacle to enacting one's vision of good public policy.

Conditional Party Government as a Precondition

Some minority parties participate more in policymaking efforts than others. As noted by Connelly and Pitney (1994), the ability of the congressional minority to participate in policymaking efforts declined substantially over the course of the 40-year period of Democratic control of Congress. This decline corresponds to the rise of conditional party government in Congress. Under the conditional party government theory of party influence, party leadership only exerts sway over the caucus when policy differences exist between the parties and there is "widespread policy agreement" within a party (Rohde 1991, 91; also see Aldrich and Rohde 2001; Smith and Gamm 2001; and Aldrich 2011). In the pre-Reform era, Rohde (1991, 6) argues that a "working coalition" existed between conservative southern Democrats and Republicans in committee. This coalition was able to amend proposals to make them more palatable for Republicans or block their passage altogether. The Rules Committee, chaired by conservative Representative Howard Smith (D-VA) for much of this period, played a decisive role in bottling up proposals. Additionally, these two groups were often successful when they worked together on the floor to defeat proposals (Polsby 2004, 12).[10] In the 1970s, particularly after the 1974 election, a number of changes advantaged the majority party, and particularly northern Democrats who began to dominate the party. Two of the most important changes affected the selection of committee chairs and the role of the Rules Committee. After the 1974 election, seniority no longer guaranteed one a chair position and the huge new class of Democratic freshmen—known as the "Watergate Babies" due to the role of the scandal in the election of the huge class of Democrats—forced chairs to interview in front of their class to keep their positions (also see Lawrence 2018). Several southern chairs lost their positions and others who narrowly survived got the message that they would need to be friendlier to progressive policy goals. At the same time, the Speaker obtained the power to appoint new members from his or her party to the Rules Committee and the ability to select its chair (Rohde 1991, 24–25). Thus, the coalition between southern Democrats and Republicans to bottle up legislation deteriorated. In total, these reforms made it so that the majority party would be more able to achieve its goals.

I expect that political actors are particularly likely to disengage from electoral politics when there is conditional party government. Minority party Republicans in the pre-Reform era had clear incentives to remain in Congress because they could work with southern Democrats to stop or modify legislation. After Reform, however, these incentives were gone. Instead, the majority increasingly ignored the minority party in committee and outvoted them on the floor. Returning to Connelly and Pitney (1994), this reality is why Republicans began expressing frustration several decades into being in the minority. Even though recent periods of minority status have not lasted as long as that for Republicans in twentieth century, the experience of the minority may be even more unpleasant. Lee (2009) found that under extreme polarization, parties increasingly oppose one another even on nonideological issues. As a result, even those minority party members who have nonideological goals are likely to experience frustration, prompting disengagement from electoral politics. Further, those looking to help elect more allies to Congress to achieve policy goals are also likely to be frustrated, wondering how much it matters that their party recruit strong candidates if they are perpetually in the minority.

At the same time, other perspectives on party government provide an important reminder that minority party status may be unpleasant even when conditional party government is not in place. Cox and McCubbins (1993, 2005) conceptualize congressional parties as acting like a cartel with the ability to control the agenda and thus determine the bills considered in Congress. In terms of negative agenda power, these authors note that even during the mid-twentieth century, when there were a substantial number of conservative southern Democrats in Congress, there is little evidence of this group siding with Republicans to pass an agenda (Cox and McCubbins 2005, 28–29).[11] Indeed, the final majority party roll rate—that is, where a majority of the majority party is on the losing side of a bill that passes—during this era closely approximates that in other periods (Cox and McCubbins 2005, 92–93). In other words, when southern Democrats and Republicans worked together, they did not generally work together to pass legislation where the two groups stood in opposition to the majority of Democrats.

Nevertheless, other evidence presented by Cox and McCubbins (2005) demonstrates that the House increasingly passed policy that was anathema to the minority party in the post-Reform period. Specifically, the data these authors provide on party rolls—that is, where a vote passes with the majority of members in a party voting in opposition—speaks to the worsening conditions for the minority party. Although the number of final passage *majority* party rolls (i.e., when a vote passed with a majority of the majority party voting "no") remained relatively constant over time, the number of final passage *minority* party rolls (i.e., when a vote passed with a majority of the minority party voting no) increased rapidly over the course of the late twentieth century. Between 1951 and 1975, an average of 15.5 minority party rolls occurred per Congress, representing an average of 20.1 percent of all final passage votes and 16.8 percent of all votes. In contrast, from 1976 to 1999 this number increased to an average of 43.6 rolls per Congress, or an average of 32.7 percent of final passage votes and 31.6 percent of all votes (Cox and McCubbins 2005, 92–93).[12] This evidence is consistent with my expectation that the minority party's experience in Congress is worse in the post-Reform era, which in turn prompts disengagement from electoral politics. Reflecting on the poor conditions of the minority under conditional party government—with the reminder from Cox and McCubbins that the minority generally faces significant disadvantages—the typology below (table 1.1) displays my expectations for electoral disengagement based upon whether a party is likely to be in the minority and whether there is conditional party government.

Psychological Foundations of Minority Party Misery

To this point, my theory of electoral disengagement has focused on broad goals for members, specifically political ambition and the ability to pass what a member views to be good public policy. To explain fully why minority party politicians decide to disengage from electoral politics, however, one should also consider the motivations of politicians as people. Despite some characterizations and portrayals in popular culture stating otherwise (e.g., the show *House of Cards*), politicians are human beings with emotions. In his 2006 book *Politicians Are People Too*, longtime *USA Today* White House correspondent Richard Bendetto shares his experiences of following politicians for several decades. Based on his observations, he maintains that politicians are like other people, having both strengths and weaknesses. Agreeing with this viewpoint, *NPR* commentator Scott Simon (2009) said of politicians: "If you prick them, they will bleed. If you pet them, they'll lick your hand. They're filled with anxieties, contradictions and duplicities, but I wonder what groups . . . are not." The inevitable health events that affect politicians and their families remind the American people of their mortality. Such events come into specific focus when a legislator's vote is crucial. The 2009 stimulus vote serves as a poignant example. Democrats held 58 seats in the U.S. Senate at this point, as the Minnesota U.S. Senate race that Al Franken (D-MN) ultimately won remained undecided. Securing the support of Senators Susan Collins (R-ME), Arlen Specter (R-PA), and Olympia Snowe (R-ME) gave Democrats 61 votes, one more than the needed number to overcome a Republican filibuster. On the final vote on the motion to proceed, however, Senator Ted Kennedy (D-MA) could not cast a vote due to declining health because of brain cancer that ultimately claimed his life in August 2009. Democrats had the exact number of votes needed, but Senator Sherrod

TABLE 1.1. Four scenarios for the role of minority party status

	Likely Minority Party	Likely Majority Party
Conditional Party Government	Minority almost completely shut out of policymaking; most miserable and most disengagement.	Majority able to achieve goals; least incentive to disengage.
No Conditional Party Government	Minority allowed to play some role in policymaking; somewhat miserable and some disengagement.	Majority able to use agenda control, but minority can block; some incentive to disengage.

Brown (D-OH) had to return home for a funeral after his mother died. To meet the 60-vote hurdle, Majority Leader Harry Reid (D-NV) held the vote open as the Obama administration had a government plane fly Brown back to Washington to cast the decisive vote (Koff 2009). The circumstances affecting Kennedy and Brown reminded the American people that politicians are not cogs within a machine, but human beings who are affected by their own and their family members' health.

Having highlighted the humanity of politicians, it follows to consider how political success and failure might affect their health. The psychology of winning and losing serves as a natural starting point for this examination, building upon the political science research previously discussed in this chapter. According to Robertson (2012), winning has positive effects on neurotransmitters in the brain, while losing has the opposite effect (also see CBS Sunday Morning 2013). Political parties have become increasingly like teams (Lee 2009), so research on the psychology of losing—which especially focuses on the effect of defeated sports teams on fans—is of relevance to this study. Bernhardt et al. (1998) examined the response of Italian fans to a soccer match that Brazil won on penalties, finding that their testosterone levels dropped an average of 27 percent, while Brazil fans saw an increase of 28 percent. More recently, Oliveira, Gouveia, and Oliveira (2009) found similar results when looking at the testosterone levels of winning and losing female soccer players in Portugal. Conversely, other psychologists argue that this response to losing is not universal and, even though the *average* loser experiences a decrease in testosterone, this response varies (e.g., see Archer 2006). In the context of electoral politics, Stanton et al. (2009) found that the 2008 election caused a decrease in testosterone for men who backed Senator John McCain (R-AZ), the losing candidate, while levels remained constant for supporters of Senator Barack Obama (D-IL) as he won. No change occurred among women who supported either candidate, further showing that this response varies across populations. Those who do experience reduced testosterone, however, are also less likely to participate in future competitions (Mehta and Josephs 2006). This response to losing for those who have reduced testosterone levels is consistent with neurochemistry, as testosterone levels have subsequent effects on dopamine (Robertson 2012, 115). Dopamine is a neurotransmitter that affects individuals' levels of motivation, so one would expect those with lower levels of dopamine to withdraw from contests where they might lose again (e.g., see Wise 2004; Morita et al. 2013).[13]

Losing can have other negative effects on health. Olsen et al. (2015) found that fans of losing New Zealand rugby teams were 2.6 times as likely to have hospital admissions due to heart arrhythmias. Further, Kloner et al. (2009) discovered that deaths due to cardiovascular events were higher following Super Bowl losses in the Los Angeles area when the local NFL team lost the Super Bowl in 1980 and *lower* when they won the Super Bowl in 1984. In total, this research establishes that losing has negative health effects and that these effects happen for competitors and fans alike. Since these studies come from a different academic discipline than political science, however, the next step is to connect this research with the lived experiences of political actors.

The negative consequences of losing fill the daily life of a minority party politician. From the perspective of ambition, the minority party politician misses the ability to chair committees and subcommittees. They cannot rise above a certain place in Congress. Similarly, the minority party loses the ability to enact good public policy, particularly under conditional party government. A minority party legislator has to go through the motions of proposing bills, knowing that they will never get a hearing, much less a successful vote. In the meantime, they are often on the losing side of votes on the majority's priorities, particularly on proposals on which there is meaningful division between the parties. Minority party members get to be in the majority in near-unanimous votes on uncontroversial proposals (e.g., renaming post offices), but on policy that divides the parties, they typically lose out under conditional party government because the majority party has taken affirmative steps to disempower the minority. The rare exception to this was the aforementioned example of when minority party Democrats frequently sided with Republicans during the Obama administration because Speaker John Boehner was unable to get enough Republicans to pass bills without the support of Democrats. However, this is not the typical experience for minority party members, and even in this period Democrats were typically on the losing side of votes. After Democrats retook control of Congress in 2018, many Republicans who first won their seats in or after the 2010 GOP wave faced their first experience in the minority. In giving advice to these members on how to handle the situation, longtime Representative Tom Cole (R-OK)—who served in the minority from 2007 to 2011—somewhat jokingly said, "Smoke a lot; drink a lot" (Hulse 2018).

One could expect that a political actor would react negatively to the prospect of frequent losing and may seek to do something about it. As noted above when discussing political ambition, the three options for electoral engagement are (1) stick it out, (2) disengage from politics, or (3) seek a different office. For a miserable politician who does not want to experience losing, options two or three may prove to be attractive options. When option one becomes untenable, they may decide that they need to disengage or move to a different context where they are likely to be more successful. Disengagement could include scaling back one's activities (e.g., fundraising less for the party) or withdrawing from the electoral arena altogether. Given that men are grossly overrepresented in Congress, Stanton et al.'s (2009) finding about men who supported John McCain, the losing presidential candidate in the 2008 election, is of particular relevance here, assuming this result among mass publics translates to political elites. As with sports and team fans, this effect is likely not to be limited to legislators themselves, but also to those working on their behalf. For example, I expect party committees seeking to recruit potential future legislators also to react negatively to the prospect of their party continually losing and perhaps recruit fewer candidates.

In total, the unpleasantness of minority party status is likely to affect a politician's calculations about whether he or she should engage in electoral politics. Returning to Riker and Ordeshook's classic formula for political decision-making, $R=pB-C+D$, the experience of minority party legislators has the potential to affect *both* the B term and the C term as one decides whether to engage in the electoral process.[14] The B term is less for members of the minority than the majority because they are not able to achieve positions of the same prominence. They also cannot expect to achieve the same amount of what they view as good public policy as the majority. Based on the psychology of losing, however, the minority also sees their C term increase. The cost of engagement is greater because their party is likely to experience loss more often than the majority, as the majority outvotes them and generally leaves them out of the policymaking process. Under conditional party government, the B term further decreases and the value of the C term increases. In total, then, one can expect the calculus of political decision-making to change based on the psychology of losing, making it less likely that the minority party engages in electoral politics.

Summary and Conclusion

Drawing upon an array of literatures, I construct a theory of minority party status in this chapter. My theory draws on ambition theory, arguing that politicians who are likely to be in the minority party have fewer opportunities available to them, making them less likely to want to engage in electoral politics. A similar logic is present for those who focus on enacting good public policy, as this task is difficult for those in the minority.

The disparity in policymaking power heightens under conditional party government, as members empower the majority to push the party to pass its agenda, which often comes at the expense of the minority. The psychology of losing also explains why politicians pull back from electoral politics because the unpleasantness of constant defeat often causes human beings to avoid such situations. In total, the costs of being in the minority are higher and the benefits lower than for a majority party member, making it more likely that a politician will participate less in electoral politics.

In the subsequent chapters, I apply and refine this theory to various contexts in the House of Representatives and other legislative chambers in the United States. The focus of this chapter is on the effect of minority party status in the U.S. House of Representatives, but the theory presented is broad and does not detail a specific activity. Its immediate application is to the activities of legislators—or potential legislators (i.e., prospective candidates)—who must decide the extent to which they will participate in electoral politics. That is the focus of the next three chapters. As research in psychology finds, the effects of losing are not limited to competitors themselves. Thus, I subsequently apply the theory to political party committees, which are centrally involved in the battle for majority control. The party committee chair is a member of Congress from that chamber and party, but donors and staff (among others) do not serve in Congress. Finally, I refine this theory as I seek to apply it to other legislative chambers.

As noted by Schlesinger (1966), having ambitious politicians seeking office is essential to the continued vitality of American democracy. First, the opposition serves an important role in presenting an alternative vision to voters in elections and in Congress. Without such an alternative vision, a majority may grow overly comfortable in its role and malaise may set in. Second, the minority party is, in a sense, the majority-party-in-waiting. If minority party members decide serving in Congress is not worth it, then this may sap the party of talent as members retire. When they do regain the majority, this presents a problem, as the party may have fewer talented leaders ready to take the reins of power. I begin my empirical examination with just this topic in the next chapter, looking at when minority party status increases the likelihood that a member of Congress decides to retire.

TWO

I'm Out of Here! Minority Party Status and the Decision to Retire from Congress

> There's a big wave coming. Sometimes you've got to get off the beach.
>
> —Retiring Rep. Charlie Dent (R-PA)[1]

On April 11, 2018, Speaker Paul Ryan (R-WI) stunned the political world by announcing his retirement from Congress (Martin and Burns 2018). Although Ryan faced a better-funded challenger than he had in years in Democratic steelworker Randy Bryce, most political prognosticators still rated Ryan as the solid favorite for reelection (Cook Political Report 2018).[2] In retiring, Ryan sent shockwaves of panic through the Republican establishment, which realized it could trigger additional retirements and further jeopardize the Republicans' majority—something he surely knew could result from his retirement decision. Nonetheless, Ryan decided he would leave Congress at the end of his term.

While Ryan's announcement was notable by itself, what made this decision particularly striking was the fact that dozens of other Republican retirements preceded it. All told, almost 40 Republicans—representing the largest percentage for any party caucus since World War II—announced their departure from Congress before the 2018 elections. These members ranged from prominent members like Ryan, Appropriations Committee Chair Rodney Frelinghuysen (R-NJ), and Financial Services Committee Chair Jeb Hensarling (R-TX), to lesser-known members such as Rep. Dennis Ross (R-FL), who announced his retirement the same day as Ryan to much less fanfare (Rakich 2018; Connolly 2018).[3] Like Ryan, three of these four lawmakers were favored for reelection at the time of their retirement announcement, the exception being Frelinghuysen, whose seat was rated a "Toss Up" by the *Cook Political Report*, but "Lean Republican" by *Sabato's Crystal Ball* (Cook Political Report 2018; Kondik 2018).[4] In contrast, fewer than 20 Democrats announced they would depart Congress at the end of their term.

Underlying these decisions, I argue, is the fact that these Republicans believed that it was likely that their party would lose control of Congress in 2018. For a party and chamber leader like Ryan, or a committee chair like Frelinghuysen, losing the majority would mean a loss of power. For all Republicans, losing the majority would mean their agenda would come to a halt. Thus, rather than experience the indignity of being relegated to the minority in the next session of Congress, these members decided to leave the institution altogether. Indeed, Republicans did lose their majority in 2018, with 13 open seats flipping to Democrats. Continuing a midterm election pattern that began in 1994, the president's party lost every open House seat that the other party had won in the previous presidential election (Crass 2018), demonstrating that retirement is both a symptom of the likely loss of the congressional majority and that it further increases the likelihood that a party will lose the majority.[5]

In this chapter, I examine how the probability that a member's party will be in the minority in the next session of Congress—as seemed to be likely for Republicans leading up to the 2018 election—affects the decision of individual members to seek reelection. I apply my theory of minority party misery to incumbent members of Congress, aiming to reconcile my expectations with those of David Mayhew in *Congress: The Electoral Connection*. I then create a measure of the likelihood of a member's party being in the minority and examine whether retirements increase in relation to this measure. Finally, I seek to put the record number of post–World War II congressional retirements in a broader context by conducting a case study of these retirements.

Still Single-Minded Seekers of Reelection? The Electoral Connection Meets Conditional Party Government

Still Single-Minded Seekers of Reelection?

In his seminal work on Congress, Mayhew (1974a) argued that members of Congress wanted to be reelected to the body as many times as possible and engaged in specific behaviors (i.e., advertising, position-taking, credit-claiming) designed to maximize their prospects for winning reelection. An important assumption underlying Mayhew's theory is that Congress is a desirable institution in which members wish to continue to serve; in other words, in keeping with Schlesinger (1966), Mayhew assumes that many members of Congress have *static ambition*. As evidence for this assumption, Mayhew (1974a, 15) points out that a congressional career comes with high pay and substantial prestige and that there are far more individuals who would like to serve in Congress than there are seats in the institution. Mayhew further assumes that members of Congress will *continue* to seek reelection (almost) in perpetuity, with other concerns (e.g., enacting good public policy) taking a back seat to the pursuit of reelection. Mayhew's examination focuses on individuals rather than parties, with him famously noting that "no theoretical treatment of the United States Congress that posits parties as analytic units [would] go very far" (Mayhew 1974a, 27).

When members do eventually decide to retire from Congress, previous literature focuses closely on individual electoral vulnerability as a cause of this decision.[6] Jacobson and Kernell (1983) find that members of Congress are more likely to retire when national political conditions (e.g., the state of the economy) are unfavorable for their party. Jacobson and Kernell (1983, 50) do briefly reference a member who is "concerned with his party's prospect of becoming the majority party" deciding to retire once they realize that this is not a realistic outcome for the foreseeable future. The focus of this chapter, however, is on how these conditions create individual reelection problems for members of Congress, which subsequently result in a decision to retire. Similarly, Stone et al. (2010) find that congressional incumbents who local activists rated as weaker were more likely to retire. Other studies (e.g., Hall and Van Houweling 1995; Mondak 1995) also focus on characteristics related to individual electoral prospects in predicting whether a member is likely to retire. In other words, when the goal of perpetual reelection is at risk, members reassess their decision to seek reelection.

Other studies that examine factors beyond an individual's own prospects for reelection focus on other factors specific to that member of Congress. In his 1978 study, Frantzich divides factors that might cause retirement into three categories: disability (e.g., age, poor health), desirability (e.g., lack of motivation, seniority), and electoral vulnerability. Cooper and West (1981) place heavy emphasis on member's disaffection within the legislative body, while also acknowledging a role for age, electoral vulnerability, and progressive ambition. Similarly, Fisher and Herrick (2002) find a relationship between job satisfaction and the decision to retire (also see Moore and Hibbing 1992 and Moore and Hibbing 1998). Fisher and

Herrick (2002, 454) contend that minority party status makes it hard to achieve policy goals and causes frustration, but that other factors ranging from constituency service to gaining publicity may make the job still worth it. Other scholars have examined a variety of other factors that relate to congressional retirement including gender, scandal, and disaffection with polarization, but age, seniority, and electoral vulnerability tend to be the most common variables that persist across these studies (e.g., Kiewiet and Zeng 1993; Theriault 1998; Lawless and Theriault 2005; Wolak 2007; Thomsen 2017). However, a variable may not necessarily have the same effect on retirement decisions across time. For example, Hibbing (1992) found that seniority negatively correlated with retirement decisions in the 1970s, but that there was a very slight positive relationship between this variable and retirement decisions in the 1960s. Similarly, while age often correlates positively with a decision to retire, Bullock (1972) noticed an increasing number of legislators who served numerous terms and did not depart voluntarily. Thus, even though actuarial realities push the correlation between age and retirement in a positive direction, the departures of senior members of Congress are often not voluntary and they may continue to run as long as their health allows. In other cases, opportunities may present themselves for a member to run for higher office that are specific to an individual, resulting in a House retirement as the member runs for another office such as the Senate (Copeland 1989).

Most important to my study, however, is the notion that disaffection or desirability plays a role in retirement decisions. While not exactly the same as my examination of how the probability of being in the minority affects retirement decisions, previous research suggests that elected officials may respond to unfavorable conditions by retiring from a legislative body. Connelly and Pitney (1994) speak more directly to the role of minority party status as a motivating factor in Republican Party retirements during the 40-year era of Democratic control of Congress. According to them, the inability to chair committees and the fact that ranking members' influence waned over the course of this period resulted in additional Republican retirements (Connelly and Pitney 1994, 134). They offer several specific cases of Republicans who decided to leave Congress rather than continuing to toil in the minority. Most strikingly, a number of members of Republican leadership decided to leave the chamber to advance their careers in other political institutions. Minority Whip Trent Lott (R-MS) decided to run for the U.S. Senate in 1988 rather than wait for the top Republican leadership position to open up; his successor, Dick Cheney (R-WY), similarly left the whip position only two years later to become secretary of defense in the

George H. W. Bush administration (Connelly and Pitney 1994, 113 and 134). Offering a different view, Murakami (2009) argues that ideology—and not minority status—is to blame for the greater number of Republican retirements. He argues that once Republicans gained the majority in 1994, one would expect Democrats consistently to retire at higher rates than Republicans (Murakami 2009, 224). However, unlike the previous period, the House majority was often quite competitive in this period, giving Democrats a hope of returning to the majority that their Republican counterparts in the previous era could not have realistically held. Overall, previous studies suggest a link *may* exist between minority party status and an increased likelihood of retirement, at least among Republicans in the era of Democratic control, but more research is necessary to establish this link fully. Thus, the next step is to apply my theory of minority party status such that it applies broadly to congressional minorities over time.

A Theory of Minority Party Misery and Congressional Retirement

The first test of my overall theory of how the probability of minority party status affects the engagement of political actors focuses on congressional retirement. In addition to a member's individual prospects of winning reelection, I theorize that congressional incumbents also account for their party's prospects for being in the minority after the next election when making their decision on whether to seek reelection. Consistent with Stimson, MacKuen, and Erikson (1995), I assume that elected politicians understand the direction of public opinion in the country between elections and what these opinion shifts mean for their party's ability to win the majority in the next congressional election. Through dispatches from their party's caucus leadership—as well as members conducting their own polling and reading the popular press—members will be able to paint an accurate mental picture of the direction of political winds. Speaking to the fact that politicians have a good sense of what is about to happen, one member I spoke to said a number of his colleagues decided to leave right before a majority flip because they were already "tired of this shit" and saw this as a good time to leave before things got even worse for them in the minority.[7]

Members heed their party's prospects for majority control for an important reason: it affects their ability to achieve important goals as a member of Congress. As with Fenno (1978) and Rohde (1991), I assume that members—in addition to goals such as winning reelection—seek to enact what they view to be good public policy. Thus, after assessing the direction of politics, incumbents who view it as likely that their party will be in the majority have a clear incentive to run for reelection because their preferred policies have a credible chance of passing. In contrast, it is generally difficult for minority party lawmakers to get a hearing on—much less advance—their preferred policies. Instead, minority party lawmakers spend most of their time fighting losing battles against policy proposals from the majority party. After almost 40 years of his party serving in the minority, Representative Bill Gradison (R-OH) summed up life in Congress by noting that "the sense of being in the minority is being left out" (Connelly and Pitney 1994, 5). Furthermore, as human beings, members of Congress are unlikely to enjoy the experience of constantly being on the losing side of issues. As psychological research establishes, losing can have negative effects on mood and health, making people try to avoid situations where they are likely to lose (Robertson 2012; CBS Sunday Morning 2013). Thus, an incumbent is likely to be deterred from running for reelection when their party is doomed to minority party status because of the emotional reaction they will have to constantly losing (e.g., being outvoted on bills, not getting to even vote on one's own proposals) that is a common occurrence when serving in the minority. One member of Congress I spoke to said that he saw a number of his colleagues walk away more quickly than he expected because of the stress and unpleasantness associated with minority party status.[8]

Because of this negative reaction, being stuck in the minority has the potential to affect a politician's political ambition, causing a static ambition to become discrete or providing the spark for a member with progressive ambition to take the next step and run for another office. Indeed, service in the minority may so degrade the experience for a member of Congress that, in recent years, several members fated to the minority have even decided to run for county-level office instead of seeking reelection. For example, Rep. Gloria Negrete McLeod (D-CA) mounted an unsuccessful bid for San Bernardino County commissioner rather than seek reelection in 2014, and Rep. Janice Hahn (D-CA) ran successfully for Los Angeles County supervisor in 2016 rather than seek another term in Congress (Cahn 2015a). For these members, the ability to make policy—even on the local level—was a more enticing prospect than continuing to serve in a congressional minority unable to pursue its policy goals. Others may choose to leave elective politics altogether. After Republicans lost the majority in 2018, Representative Tom Marino (R-PA) announced in early 2019 that he would be resigning from Congress to pursue a career in the private sector (Levy 2019). Similarly, soon after Democrats assumed the minority in 2011 Representative Jane Harman (D-CA) resigned in order to become the director of the Woodrow Wilson International Center for Scholars (Condon 2011).

The power of the minority to mold public policy varies, however, which is likely to influence how pleasant it is to serve as a minority party legislator, in turn affecting retirement rates. For example, in the less polarized era of the mid-20th century, minority Republicans frequently played a role in legislating. As Rohde (1991, 7) notes, "by the 1960s, the House was characterized by a system of committee government, dominated by a working coalition of southern Democrats and Republicans." In contrast, once an increased number of liberal Democrats won election to Congress in 1974 and empowered leaders to become more powerful under a system of conditional party government, the power of the minority greatly decreased (Rohde 1991). Nevertheless, despite the fact that the minority party had some power before conditional party government took hold, the majority party still had the ability to control the agenda. Even in this period, Cox and McCubbins (2005, 29) note that Republicans were typically unable to join with southern Democrats to push their own agenda, instead mostly just stopping northern Democrats or amending their proposals to be somewhat more favorable to conservative interests.

In total, I expect that members who are likely to be in the minority in the next session of Congress are more likely to retire than members who are likely to be in the majority. At the same time, minority party members will be especially likely to retire in an environment of conditional party government given that their ability to influence policy diminishes further than when the minority is allowed to play some role in affecting policymaking.

Constructing a Measure of the Probability of Minority Party Status

Before testing this theory, the next step is to construct a measure of the probability of minority party status, the key independent variable in this study. To build this variable, I begin by building OLS models that are similar to those commonly used to forecast congressional elections (e.g., Jacobson and Carson 2016). Since voters tend to evaluate congressional candidates through the lens of how they view the president, the dependent variable in these models is the percentage of seats won by the president's party in that year's congressional election (see Campbell 1993). To account for how national tides may help or hinder the president's party, independent variables measure the president's approval in the first Gallup Poll after

May 1 of the election year and the change in real disposable income from the second quarter the year before the election to the second quarter of the election year.[9] I also include a variable indicating whether it is a midterm election because the president's party tends to lose seats in midterm years, while fewer seats tend to shift between the parties in presidential years (Campbell 1993).[10]

Table 2.1 displays this model. Each of these variables attain statistical significance at the 95 percent level. OLS model coefficients are straightforward to interpret—a one-unit increase in an independent variable translates to an increase in the dependent variable of the amount of the coefficient. Thus, a 1 percentage point increase in previous seats held by the president's party translates to a 0.78 percentage point increase in seats won in the next election, while a 1 percentage point increase in presidential approval results in a 0.127 percentage point increase in the number of seats held by the president's party. It is important not to make direct comparisons of the magnitude of coefficients for different variables as they may be on a different scale. Finally, it is worth noting that the adjusted R^2 value in an OLS regression helps explain the amount of variation in the dependent variable explained by the variables in the model, with a slight penalty for the number of variables included in the regression. In this model, these independent variables explain 80 percent of the variation in seats held by the president's party, which is a relatively high amount.

After constructing this model, I obtain predictions for the probability that the minority party will win the majority in the next election. Specifically, I use postregression predicted values to obtain estimates of the probability that the president's party will win more than 50 percent of the seats

TABLE 2.1. Models of legislative outcomes

Variable	U.S. House (1946–2018)
Previous Seats	0.780*
	(0.078)
Approval	0.127*
	(0.051)
Change in Income	1.093*
	(0.287)
Midterm	−5.416*
	(1.344)
Intercept	0.769
	(4.687)
Adjusted R^2	0.800
N	37

*$p < 0.05$; dependent variable measures percentage of seats won. Summary statistics in appendix.

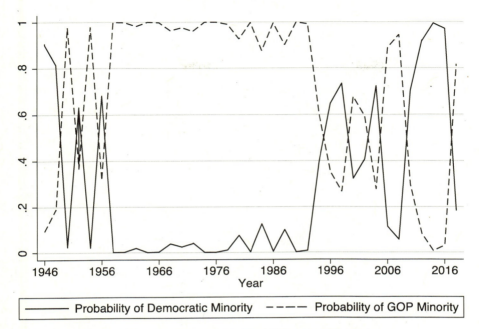

Figure 2.1. Probability of minority party status by party, 1946–2018

in the House. For the president's party, one minus this probability serves as an estimate of how likely it is that their party will be in the minority in the next session of Congress. For the party not holding the White House, this probability serves as an estimate that they will be in the minority.

Figure 2.1 displays how these probabilities have fluctuated over time. In some cases, a party's probability of being in the minority fluctuates substantially over time, although it was consistently low for Republicans in elections occurring in the 40-year period of Democratic control of the House from 1955 until 1995. Similarly, competitiveness was low for Democrats in 2012, 2014, and 2016, before rising markedly for the 2018 midterm election.

One objection to this measure is that it is more complicated than (for example) looking at the size of a legislative majority, a variable commonly used by scholars to indicate the competitiveness of congressional majorities (see Lee 2016). An advantage of this new measure, however, is that it takes into account both the *level* of seats for a party and the *direction* of the seat swing that is likely to take place in the next election. For an election such as 2002, where Republicans held a majority of fewer than 10 seats, looking only at seat level exaggerates the prospects of a flip in majority control since President George W. Bush's residually high approval after the September 11th attacks mitigated the usual seat loss for the president's party in midterm elections. Additionally, my new measure correlates much more strongly with whether or not the majority actually flips in a legislative election. The correlation between this variable and whether the majority flips in the next election is 0.74 while the correlation between seat margin and whether or not the majority flips is a paltry -0.26.[11] Furthermore, if one limits the sample to House elections occurring after Republicans won the majority in 1994, there is actually a *positive* correlation of 0.5 between seat margin and flips in majority party status (i.e., the majority is *more* likely to flip when the majority is not narrow). My measure has a 0.75 correlation with the probability of a majority flip. Two of the three majority flips that occurred during this period, in 2006 and 2010, happened when Republicans and Democrats controlled their largest number of seats since regaining majority control. Republicans also had a relatively large majority for the period when the House flipped in 2018. As exogenous, one-time events have the potential to affect election outcomes, one would not necessarily want a measure of competitiveness to correlate perfectly with whether a majority flip occurs, but a good measure of competitiveness should still correlate strongly with changes in majority control of an institution.

Analyzing Congressional Retirement Decisions in the U.S. House of Representatives

Dependent and Control Variables

Having created my focal independent variable, I next construct my main models. To test my expectations, I use random effects logistic regression models to analyze data on congressional retirements since 1946.[12] I use random effects models to account for the panel structure of the data, with incumbents reoccurring in the data each election year while they are in office. In these models, the dependent variable measures whether an incumbent decides to seek reelection. As displayed in figure 2.2, the retirement rate for the parties has fluctuated over time. For the 1946–54 period, when congressional majorities were competitive, the retirement rate of the parties varied substantially from election to election. In contrast, in the elections from 1956 to 1994, when Democrats were the assumed majority, Republicans consistently had a retirement rate higher than that of Demo-

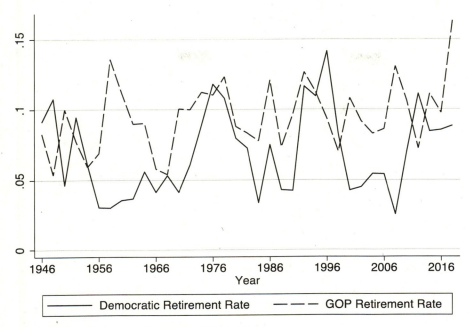

Figure 2.2. Retirement by party, 1946–2018

crats. In only two elections in this period (1976, 1982), did Democrats have a higher retirement rate; both parties saw a noticeable spike in 1992 in the midst of the House Banking Scandal. After the 1994 Republican Revolution, the Democratic retirement rate increased dramatically in the next congressional election in 1996 once the party no longer had a stranglehold on majority control. Since then, both parties have seen elections in which a higher proportion of their members retired. Republican retirements spiked in 2006, when they lost the majority, as did Democratic retirements when they lost the majority in 2010. Finally, the Republican retirement rate in 2018 (16.3%) was the highest retirement rate for a party in the dataset; only those of Republicans in 1958 (13.6%) and Democrats in 1996 (14.1%) come close. Each of these elections represents a turning point in congressional elections, first when the permanence of the Democratic majority was beginning to set in, and second after Republicans ended it 40 years later, ushering in an era of an oft-competitive majority.

In addition, I include a number of control variables in my models. In keeping with previous research suggesting the role of personal factors, I include a measure of a district's presidential vote compared to the nation as a whole in the most recent presidential election. Members who believe that they might be vulnerable to defeat in the next election may retire rather than face a tough reelection campaign. I also incorporate a measure of the number of terms served and a member's age (measured as years between birth and the year of the election). Members who have served for many terms in Congress may face burnout and decide to retire, while those who are older may retire for health reasons. I also control for whether the seat has been redistricted since the last election since a member could potentially have thousands of new voters in their district (or may be double-bunked with another incumbent), making them more likely to retire. Additionally, in keeping with Thomsen's (2017) research on how polarization has increased moderate members' likelihood of retirement, I include a measure of ideological extremism by comparing an individual member's DW-Nominate score to the mean for their party in that Congress.[13] Given the lack of competitiveness in southern congressional elections and the fact that during the Solid South era, members from the South sought to build seniority in order to serve as committee chairs, I include a dummy variable for whether the seat is located in the South. Finally, I add year dummies to account for the effect of trends over time. I run models over the entire period (1946–2016), as well as several subperiods, in order to examine the role of conditional party government on congressional retirement. Additionally, I include models with the subset of the districts that are the *safest* and the *least safe* for incumbent members in order to examine whether my theory applies to a broad range of seats.

Results

In table 2.2, I display the results of the first random effects logit model over the entire period.[14] In keeping with expectations, my measure of the probability that a party will be in the majority in the next Congress is statistically significant and positive, providing evidence to support my hypothesis that members will be more likely to retire when it is likely they will be in the minority in the next session of Congress. Logistic regression coefficients are less straightforward to interpret than OLS coefficients, so I provide estimates of the predicted probability of retirement as the prospects that a member's party will be in the minority increases (holding other variables at their means). Substantively as the probability from minority party status increases from "0" (essentially guaranteed to be in the majority) to "1" (all but guaranteed to be in the minority), the probability of retirement increases from 6.4 percent to 10.6 percent (see figure 2.3). As the standard deviation of this independent variable is 0.4, such a change is only slightly more than a change from one standard deviation below the mean to one standard deviation above the mean. Several control variables also attain significance in this model. In keeping with previous research, members who represent more electorally vulnerable seats in terms of presidential vote are more likely to retire than those who represent safe seats. Additionally, seniority and age positively correlate with the decision to retire; a positive relationship between moderation and likelihood of retirement falls short of significance.

To examine the effect of the expectation of minority party status on retirement rates over time, I then subset the data into the three major eras of House elections since World War II: the competitive era of congressional elections from 1946 to 1954, the generally uncompetitive era of congressional elections from 1956 to 1994, and the more competitive era from 1996 to the present. In the second and third eras, the probability of minority status is positive and significant and it falls just short in the model from 1946 to 1954 (p = 0.059).[15] It is of particular interest that there is a similar relationship in the generally uncompetitive 1956–94 era and the much more competitive era from 1996 to the present. In the 1956–94 period, an increase in the probability of minority party status from "0" to "1" trans-

TABLE 2.2. Probability of minority party status and the decision to retire from Congress

Variable	Random Effects Logit Model
Probability of Party in Minority	0.557*
	(0.076)
Presidential Vote Lean	−0.022*
	(0.003)
Terms	0.070*
	(0.009)
Age	0.010*
	(0.004)
Redistricted Seat	−0.030
	(0.145)
Ideological Extremism	−0.298
	(0.219)
Seat in South	−0.024
	(0.071)
Constant	−3.231*
	(0.276)
N	15,060
Log-likelihood	−4,096.752

*p < 0.05, dependent variable measures whether member retires

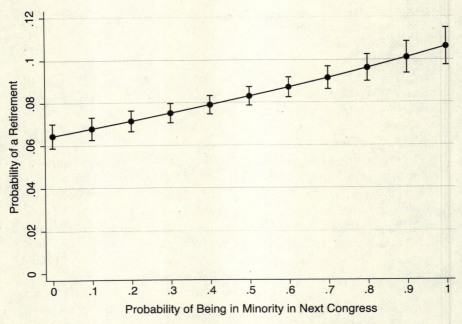

Figure 2.3. Probability of minority party status and the decision to retire

lates to a rise in the probability of a retirement from 6.1 percent to 10.6 percent (see figure 2.4). Similarly, in the 1996–2018 period, this change results in a growth in the probability of retirement from 8.2 percent to 11.7 percent (see figure 2.5).

Next, I break down the period from 1956 to 1996 further into two 20-year periods to test my second expectation on the role of minority party status based upon whether conditional party government is present. Initially, one might not expect a significant result in the first 20 years of this period due to the lack of conditional party government. Certainly, one might not expect there to be a substantively large effect compared to other periods. However, a model for the pre-Reform era (1956–74, see online appendix table 2.4) still shows the probability of being in the minority to be statistically significant; substantively, an increase from assured majority to assured minority status translates to a change in the probability of a retirement from 4.9 percent to 9.5 percent. To explain this result, I look to the role of seniority for each party in the pre- and post-Reform House. Similar to Jacobson and Kernell (1983, 50), I suggest that this result may be an artifact of the retirement of a number of senior Republicans in the

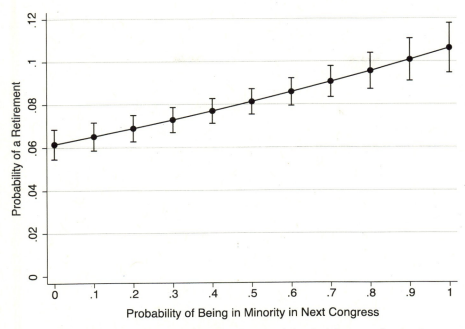

Figure 2.4. Probability of minority party status and the decision to retire, 1956–1994

1950s and '60s who came to realize that the party would not hold a majority again in their lifetime. These members then retired once they realized that they would never achieve their aspiration of being a committee chair or chamber leader. At the same time, majority party Democrats came to the realization that they could hold leadership positions as long as they were alive and in Congress since the majority was all but guaranteed. Thus, continued service for Democrats became a more enticing prospect than in the competitive period of the mid-1940s to early 1950s.

To examine this potential explanation, I run two additional models (both pre- and post-Reform) that include an interaction between my measure of probability of minority party status and the number of terms served by a member in both of these models (see online appendix table 2.5). Interaction terms allow one to examine if the effect of an independent variable on the dependent variable is conditional on the level of some *other* independent variable. In this case, I expect that the effect of the probability of minority party status on the dependent variable depends on whether a member is likely to be in the minority (which, in this case, essentially means they are a

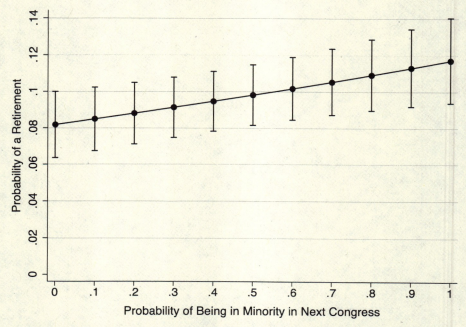

Figure 2.5. Probability of minority party status and the decision to retire, 1996–2018

Republican), or whether they are likely to be in the majority (i.e., typically a Democrat). After running this model, I find that the interaction between the probability of being in the minority and that member's number of terms served in the pre-Reform period is statistically significant, while the competitiveness measure no longer attains significance. In this period, a member who is guaranteed to be in the minority sees their probability of retirement increase from 7.4 percent to 12 percent as the number of terms served increases from being a first-term member to having served 10 terms in the body. In contrast, for members guaranteed to be in the majority (i.e., Democrats), the probability of retirement actually *decreases* slightly for senior members, dropping from 5.7 percent for a first-term member to 4.4 percent for a 10-term member. Since senior members tend to be older and one would expect an increase in the probability of retirement over time, this noteworthy finding demonstrates the allure that now-permanent majority status had for senior Democrats. It is worth noting, however, that at each number of terms served, a member of the expected minority is more likely to retire than is a member of the prospective majority party. This result is consistent with the explanation that although service in the

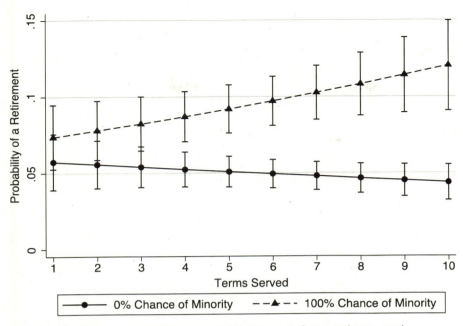

Figure 2.6. Retirement and terms served in the pre-Reform era (1956–1974)

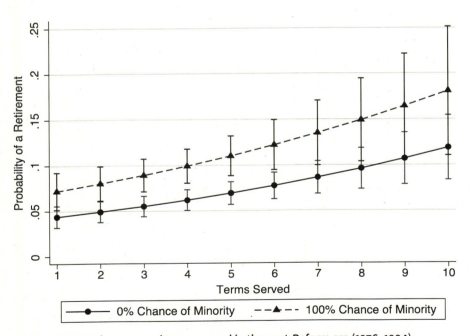

Figure 2.7. Retirement and terms served in the post-Reform era (1976–1994)

minority is more unpleasant under conditional party government, the lack of agenda power always makes it less pleasant than being in the majority (Cox and McCubbins 2005).

In contrast, in the post-Reform era, when Democrats still had control of Congress (1974–94), the interaction between the probability of minority party status and number of terms served is not significant. In this model, both parties see an increase in retirements as the number of terms served increases, with the probability of minority party status variable attaining significance. In this era, seniority relates to an increase in retirements without regard to whether a member is likely to be in the minority in the next session of Congress.

Additionally, I examine retirement patterns in both safe and marginal seats to see if my result is merely an artifact of vulnerable incumbents retiring so *they* can personally avoid electoral defeat (e.g., see Jacobson and Kernell 1983). Returning to Mayhew, one might expect safe seat incumbents regardless of party to continue to seek reelection as long as possible. While a vulnerable incumbent may decide not to seek reelection due to the unattainability of the goal—or the unpleasantness associated with attaining that goal eliminating any net utility—a safe seat incumbent does not need to worry about these costs. Thus, I ran several models on the subset of incumbents deemed to be the safest based upon several cutoffs (see online appendix table 2.6). First, to determine vulnerability I use the definition provided by Mayhew (1974b) in his examination of the "vanishing marginals." Using both definitions of marginality provided in Mayhew's article—winning with at least 55 percent of the vote in the prior election and winning with at least 60 percent of the vote in the previous election—I find that the probability of minority party status is still associated with an increased probability of retirement. While this is one good measure of vulnerability, another—particularly relevant in the modern era—looks at how a district's presidential vote compares to that of the nation as a whole. Thus, I also fit a model with the subgroup of districts where the presidential vote for the incumbent party is at least 5 percentage points more favorable than that of the nation as a whole. Again, the probability of minority party status relates positively with the decision to retire. Finally, I include a model for ultrasafe seats—those for which the incumbent won reelection with at least 60 percent in the last election *and* the presidential vote—is at least 5 percentage points more favorable than that of the nation as a whole. Once more, the probability of minority party status is significant. As displayed in figure 2.8, an increase in this variable from "0" to "1" (i.e., from assured majority status to sure minority status) is associated with an increase in the probability of retirement from 5.8 percent to 8.7 percent. In total, these results demon-

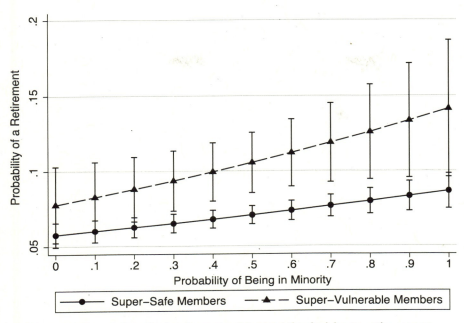

Figure 2.8. Probability of minority party status and the decision to retire among supersafe and supervulnerable members

strate that safe seat incumbents consider their party's prospects for majority party status when deciding whether to seek reelection.

Next, I examine the retirement decisions of vulnerable incumbents. These retirements are particularly important to examine because their seats represent particularly ripe targets for pickup by the other party. Using both Mayhew marginal seat cutoffs, I find that the probability of minority party status relates positively with retirement decisions for both the 55 and 60 percent cutoffs. Next, I look at districts whose presidential vote is *less* favorable for the incumbent party than that of the country as a whole; incumbents in these districts are also more likely to retire when it appears likely that their party will be in the minority in the next session of Congress. Finally, I examine those districts that are 55 percent Mayhew marginal seats and meet the presidential vote cutoff.[16] The variable measuring the probability of being in the minority is again significant; an increase in this variable from "0" to "1" is associated with an increase in the probability of retirement from 7.8 percent to 14.1 percent. Consequently, those incumbents whose decision to retire most drastically hurt their party's chances of winning or retaining the majority are also more likely to retire when their party's prospects look the worst. Notably, as displayed in figure 2.8, a vulnerable incumbent with a 0 percent chance of being in the minority is actually slightly *less* likely to retire than a safe incumbent who is all but guaranteed to be in the minority, further demonstrating how minority party status pushes even the safest legislators to leave Congress. The highest retirement rate, however, is among vulnerable members who are the most likely to be in the minority. These legislators must endure tough campaigns only to end up in the minority if they survive, making retirement more likely.

Are Effective Minority Party Legislators Willing to Remain?

A final analysis I conducted examined whether the most effective minority party legislators, as measured by Wiseman and Volden (2014), were willing to remain in Congress. Their data looks at the years from 1974 to 2018. It may be the case that minority party legislators who are able to achieve some modicum of success in Congress are willing to continue serving in the institution. At the same time, those legislators who are unable to achieve any success, despite their best efforts, may choose to retire.[17] I carried out this analysis in two ways: by interacting legislative effectiveness with competitiveness and by interacting legislators' rank within their own party with effectiveness to account for the fact that the majority party typically has higher levels of legislative effectiveness. Control variables remained the same as in previous models. In both cases, I obtained a null result, suggesting that being an effective minority party legislator does not mitigate the negative experiences associated with being in the minority. Effective legislators may choose to retire when relegated to the minority because, despite their relative effectiveness, they are still unable to achieve the successes that would be possible in the majority. At the same time, ineffective legislators in the minority may choose to stay because lobbying firms and others who may hire former members of Congress may not be especially interested in employing those who did not find success in Congress. Before offering some thoughts on the broader implications of the statistical findings in this chapter, I first discuss a case study of the large number of Republican retirements in 2018 and consider the legislative effectiveness of those Republicans who retired.

A Case Study of Republican Retirements in 2018

The statistical evidence in the prior section demonstrates that there is a clear pattern for when incumbents are likely to decide to retire. In this section, I conduct a more in-depth examination of a single case, the 2018 congressional election. This congressional election is of particular relevance because, as mentioned previously, the retirement rate for Republicans in this year was the highest for a single party in the post–World War II period. Thus, I will proceed with this examination, first setting the stage of this election and then examining the pattern of retirements and then discussing how this context relates to Republican retirement decisions.

Following the 2016 election, Democrats were initially shocked and demoralized by the election of President Donald Trump, but a broad social movement soon sprung up to push back against his presidency. On January 21, 2017, the day after his inauguration, millions of Americans descended upon Washington (and across the country) for what became the first Women's March to protest the Trump presidency in one of the largest protests in American history (Chenoweth and Pressman 2017). A significant number of other large protests soon followed as the self-described resistance sought to counter President Trump on actions ranging from the repeal of the Affordable Care Act to his conduct in office. The opponents of Trump soon turned to the electoral process, supporting candidates running in a number of congressional seats vacated mostly by Trump appointees (Cottle 2018). While Republicans held most—although not all—of these seats in special elections, they were typically by reduced margins (Silver 2018). Further indicating the mood of the country, President Trump's approval rating—which started his presidency at about net even—languished at historic lows throughout his presidency (Wilson 2018). While somewhat higher approval ratings on the economy likely prevented his overall approval rating from falling to the depths that President George W. Bush's approval fell to at the height of the Great Recession, Trump's average approval never climbed back above the mid-40s in his first two years (Liesman 2018).

Thus, all else equal, one would expect the 2018 midterm elections to not be good for Republicans. Going back to the model of legislative outcomes presented in table 2.1, many of these factors pointed to a poor midterm outcome. The mere fact that 2018 was a midterm suggested that Republicans would lose a large number of seats, which was heighted by the fact that President Trump had a low approval rating. Somewhat mitigating likely losses was the relatively good economy and the fact that the size of the Republican majority was relatively large, but the overall trend was unfavorable to Republicans. Indeed, the out-of-sample prediction for this model gave Democrats about an 80 percent chance of winning the House, a number similar to that in Nate Silver's "classic model" in much of the fall of 2018 (FiveThirtyEight 2018).

While this model suggested that there was a high probability that Republicans would lose the House, other 2018-specific factors cut both ways. Favoring Republicans' ability to keep the House was the fact that Democrats started with a historic disadvantage due to gerrymandering after the 2010 census and the fact that their voters tended to cluster in super-Democratic districts in cities (Wasserman 2017). At the same time, Republican members received a reminder about their party's poor prospects almost every day. In 2017, the then-daily Gallup tracking poll provided bad headlines of low approval for the president on a frequent basis, as did special election results and early models of the 2018 midterms (Golshan and Nilsen 2018; Shepard 2018; Silver 2018). While the Stimson, MacKuen, and Erikson (1995) assumption of elites knowing the direction of public opinion applies broadly, the nature of the media environment in 2017–18 suggests that Republicans incumbents may have been reminded of this more frequently than some of their predecessors who did not serve in an environment of 24-hour cable news, Twitter, and daily tracking polls. In addition to these factors related specifically to majority control, the political environment of the Trump presidency made continued service untenable for some Republicans. Retiring Republican U.S. Representative Ryan Costello (R-PA) summed up the feelings of many Republicans House members when he proclaimed that "all I do is answer questions about Donald Trump" (Sanchez 2018). Similarly, Washington Republican Party chair Chris Vance attributed the retirement decision of outgoing Representative Dave Reichert (R-WA) in part to Trump (Hyde and Aegerter 2017). For Republican members—most of whom did not want President Trump to win the Republican primary in 2016—continued service in Congress during a Trump presidency would not be particularly enjoyable even if they kept the majority. Not all members who retired were Trump opponents, but this certainly seemed to be a factor for some. Many of these members also faced young Democratic challengers who were able to use social media to raise large sums of money and paint the incumbent as being an out-of-touch insider. Overall, then, it seems that factors unique to 2018 were a net negative in making Republican members want to stay in the House. Thus, I contend that the systematic factor of likely minority party status set the stage for a large number of retirements, but conditions specific to 2018 also supercharged the number of retirements.

In reviewing which Republican members decided to retire in 2018, it is clear that individuals representing a varied array of districts decided to retire. Of the 39 who decided to retire, 5.1 percent represented Mayhew marginal seats at the 55 percent cutoff, but 25.6 percent did at the 60 percent cutoff. The wide disparity between 55 and 60 percent marginal seats here is reflective of the fact that Republicans drew a large number of districts after the 2010 census designed to give the party somewhat large—but not overwhelming—victories in order to maximize the number of seats held by the party. At the same time, 17.9 percent represented seats where Hillary Clinton performed better than she had nationally. Some representatives, such as Representative Ileana Ros-Lehtinen (R-FL), who won a special election in 1989 and then served 14 full terms, were senior members of the Republican caucus, while others, like two-term Representative Dave Trott (R-MI), were newcomers to Congress. Some members, like 88-year-old Representative Sam Johnson (R-TX), were elderly while others, such as 42-year-old Ryan Costello (R-PA), whose district became substantially more Democratic when the Pennsylvania Supreme Court ruled the existing map for the state to violate the state constitution, were much younger. A number of legislatively effective Republicans decided to retire in 2018, including Ed Royce (R-CA), who ranked second in the GOP caucus; Bob Goodlatte (R-VA), who ranked sixth in the party; and Gregg Harper (R-MS), who ranked thirteenth. While Royce and Goodlatte were term limited chairs, Harper could have remained as House Administration Committee chair if he had not retired and Republicans had kept the House. Other Republicans ranked lower in effectiveness also retired, such as Trey Gowdy (R-SC), who ranked 225th, and Pat Meehan (R-PA), who ranked 237th, further illustrating that being an effective legislator does not seem to correlate closely with minority party retirement decisions. Presumed minority party status acts as a blunt instrument, removing some poor legislators, but also taking away some of those who are most effective for whom having static—or progressive—ambition would be of benefit to the polity. In total, while the Republicans retiring in 2018 were many, they represented a wide array of types of districts, providing further support to the models presented in the previous section, which showed that retirement under conditions of likely minority party status cuts across many different types of districts.[18]

Conclusion

The results presented in this chapter demonstrate a clear link between the probability that a party will be in the minority and the decision of an incumbent to retire in a wide variety of situations. This result, however, does not happen for exactly the same reason in every period examined in this study. In the early part of the 40 years of Democratic control, this result is largely an artifact of the fact that senior Democratic members were enticed to remain in Congress much longer than their Republican counterparts. In contrast, once majority party leadership gained more power in the mid-1970s, the experience for a minority party member became more unpleasant, prompting an increase in retirements. The results in this chapter also show that incumbents from a wide variety of districts retire when it is likely their party will be in the minority in the next session of Congress. That seemingly safe incumbents decide to retire under such conditions suggests that service in Congress as a minority party member might not always be desirable, and even if a member could win reelection through the Mayhewian (1974a) activities of advertising, position-taking, and credit-claiming, it may not be worth it to do so. Members with static ambition see their desire to serve in office wane, while those with progressive ambition may decide to make the leap to the next level sooner than they would have otherwise.[19] This result suggests that the reelection concern is one of several concerns for politicians and that they also care about gaining power in the institution and enacting good public policy (Fenno 1978, Rohde 1991).

An important consequence of these results is that the implication that the House majority is—or is not—in play has the potential to heighten or dampen the prospects of a change in the House majority. When a party is in the minority and it seems unlikely that they will win the majority (e.g., for the GOP in the mid-late 20th century) an attitude of malaise may set in, causing more incumbents to retire and thus causing the minority party to lose their incumbency advantage in more open seats (Connelly and Pitney 1994). At the same time, when it looks like a majority is likely to flip—as was the case for Democrats in 2010 and Republicans in 2018—more incumbents may retire, making a change in party control more likely. Indeed, some of the Republican incumbents who retired in 2018, such as Representative Dave Reichert (R-WA) and Frank LoBiondo (R-NJ), had weathered the waves of 2006 and 2008, and their decision significantly worsened the party's prospects of winning their seats, which in turn increased the probability of a flip in majority control. Expectations then become reality, as incumbents who fear their party is likely to be in the minority retire will make minority party status a little more likely with each retirement.

Further, these retirements rob the minority party of some of their most talented politicians. In terms of legislative effectiveness, minority party status seems to act as a blunt instrument, removing effective and ineffective legislators alike. As noted by Schlesinger (1966), it is crucial to electoral democracy to have a plentiful supply of politicians who desire to seek elective office. In democratic politics, it is critical for the minority party to supply an alternative vision from the majority party in order to give voters a choice and force the majority party to articulate its program to compete for support in the electorate. Additionally, when the minority party eventually becomes the majority, it is important to have highly qualified leaders ready to take the helm. Thus, the link established here between a party's electoral prospects and the decision to retire may have more wide-ranging consequences that go beyond that specific election and affect the quality of democratic governance for years to come.

THREE

How Does This Make Cents? Party Fundraising and the Congressional Minority

I don't think I can spend another day in another call room making another call begging for money. I always knew the system was dysfunctional. Now it is beyond broken.

—Retiring Representative Steve Israel (D-NY),
as quoted by Hulse (2016)

An hour and a half is about as much as I can tolerate. There's no way to make it enjoyable.

—Representative Reid Ribble (R-WI),
as quoted by Grim and Siddiqui (2013)

Representative Alexandria Ocasio-Cortez (D-NY) made history in Congress for a number of reasons. The youngest woman ever to win election to Congress, Ocasio-Cortez gained a national following after defeating Rep. Joe Crowley (D-NY), the fourth-ranking House Democrat in party leadership, in a June 2018 primary (Watkins 2018). In early 2019, Ocasio-Cortez became a prominent voice for progressive causes in Congress, advocating policies ranging from the Green New Deal to single-payer health insurance. Further, her advocacy for progressive causes extended to the operation of *Congress itself*. For example, consistent with her view that employers should pay their workers a living wage, the first-term Democrat announced that she would pay her staff salaries of at least $52,000 a year

(Akin 2019). Another decision by Ocasio-Cortez that caught the attention of political observers was her choice not to participate in call time, the practice of devoting considerable time to calling donors in order to raise money for one's own campaign or for one's copartisans, if one represents a safe district.

Ocasio-Cortez declined to participate in call time because she argued that it takes time away from other crucial functions of members of Congress. In one tweet, Ocasio-Cortez noted that she spent the time "sitting through committee hearings," which she argued was worthwhile because it enabled her to learn more about public policymaking (Ocasio-Cortez 2019b). Additionally, Ocasio-Cortez stated that she also uses the time "to personally follow up on casework" her office was working on; for example, her office was dealing with a problem with mail delivery where some of her constituents were only receiving mail once every two or three days (Ocasio-Cortez 2019a, 2019c). Ocasio-Cortez's eschewing of call time sets herself apart from the vast majority of members of Congress who spend hours each day on this task; indeed, a report from early 2013 noted that incoming first-term Democrats were told that they should devote at least four hours each day to the task (Grim and Siddiqui 2013). Given the importance of the policymaking and constituent service functions of Congress, one might expect these tasks to dominate congressional behavior, but leadership told new members to expect to devote at least twice as much time to call time while in DC. Even when in their districts, the expectation was that members would spend at least three hours each day on fundraising tasks (Grim and Siddiqui 2013).

Despite the near universality of this practice, party fundraising is widely hated by members of Congress. In addition to taking time away from policymaking, members of Congress of both parties broadly view party fundraising as being miserable. As the opening quotes to this chapter suggest, this distaste is broadly shared by members of Congress across the political spectrum (also see Helderman 2012 and Grim and Siddiqui 2013). While the parties do not agree on much, hatred of party fundraising runs deep among politicians from an array of ideological perspectives.

The fact that party fundraising takes time away from other crucial functions of Congress and members do not even enjoy it raises the question of why incumbents do it in the first place. Typically, previous literature focuses on electoral security in one's own district and a member's desire to maintain or gain a leadership position, among other factors, in explaining member engagement in fundraising efforts (e.g., see Currinder 2003; Deering and Wahlbeck 2006; Green 2008; Heberlig and Larson 2012).

Building on that literature, in this chapter I argue that the probability that a party will be in the minority in the next session of Congress also plays an important role in the extent to which members engage in party fundraising. I begin by applying my theory of minority party misery to the context of party fundraising and then test this expectation using data on party fundraising since 1990. Finally, I discuss the normative implications of my findings, considering the fact that—paradoxically—the ability to influence policymaking by becoming part of the majority requires one to disengage from policymaking in order to raise money for the party. Additionally the task of party fundraising requires members to seek out donors who are unlikely to be representative of the American public as a whole. Those who typically give to campaigns are wealthier than the average American, more ideologically extreme, and clustered in a narrow set of zip codes (Francia et al. 2003; Gimpel, Lee, and Pearson-Merkowitz 2008; and Johnson 2012). Thus, in presenting a solution to party fundraising, one should consider the effects of such a solution to the quality of representative government.

The Most Miserable Task: What Makes Members Willing to Fundraise?

A Short History of Party Fundraising

A rich literature exists on campaign finance and fundraising in the context of congressional elections. As with most aspects of being a congressional candidate, fundraising was an individual endeavor in the 1970s. Raising adequate funds is important for both scaring off tough challengers and, in theory, surviving a well-financed challenge (Box-Steffensmeier 1996). Jacobson (1978) notably found, however, that challenger campaign spending has a greater effect on congressional election outcomes than does incumbent spending. Puzzlingly, incumbents who spend more do *worse* in congressional elections because those who spend more do so *because* they face tougher challengers. Nevertheless, these incumbents would have likely done even worse had they not spent any money; fundraising and spending money allows these incumbents to mitigate some, but not all, of the effects of the expenditures of a well-financed challenger (Jacobson 1978, 476–77). Further, Green and Krasno (1988) argue that, when correcting for several biases including candidate quality and interaction effects, incumbents reap a significant advantage when spending large sums of money.

An incumbent in a tough race during this period was largely on their own and could not expect much help from the DCCC or the National Republican Congressional Committee (NRCC) if they faced a difficult race.[1] Between 1974—when the data first became available due to the Federal Election Campaign Act of 1974 (FECA)—and 1980, no more than 5 percent of House Democrats' total receipts came from the party and Republicans' total varied from between 7 percent and 13 percent (Magleby and Nelson 2010, 108). Following amendments to the FECA in 1974, Congress also gave parties the authority to make coordinated expenditures on behalf of candidates. The NRCC was more aggressive on that front at first, with the DCCC not making any coordinated expenditures in 1978, compared to $2.7 million (in real 1988 dollars) by the NRCC (Magleby and Nelson 2010, 112).

Starting in the 1980s, national parties became somewhat more involved in party fundraising. Magleby and Nelson (2010, 108) show that the percentage of total receipts for candidates that came from the parties was relatively constant over this decade. However, party coordinated expenditures increased dramatically. House Democratic coordinated expenditures (in real 1988 dollars) increased tenfold over the course of the decade, while Republicans—who had gotten an earlier start—saw their coordinated expenditures almost double by the end of the decade (Magleby and Nelson 2010, 112). Additionally, even though total party committee receipts to candidates did not dramatically change, party committees—especially the DCCC—became more discerning about *which* candidates they financed in the 1980s. Before 1982, Democrats gave the same amount to every candidate, but DCCC Chair Tony Coelho (D-CA) started to focus on financing candidates in competitive races. Although overall Democratic Party receipts to candidates remained relatively constant, Democrats in competitive races saw their party financing increase even as those in safe or uncontested seats saw a drop in party funding (Magleby and Nelson 2010, 118–23).

The parties also began to help candidates fundraise more effectively for their own campaigns in the 1980s. According to Herrnson (1988, 71), party organizations started helping candidates hold fundraising dinners or other events and had major party officials make fundraising requests on candidates' behalf. The latter innovation rose out of the fact that Senate Republicans had made the maximum legal contributions to their candidates and still had money left over. To get around this problem, the party began suggesting that its donors give directly to candidates. Other advances made by party committees in the 1980s included the rise of direct mail appeals, making lists of supportive PACs and giving them to candidates, and arranging meetings between candidates in tough races and PAC leaders (Herrnson 1988, 71–73). Furthermore, party synchronization with PACs also included so-called PAC-grams, whereby a party would send a PAC a message listing the races where they were encouraged to get involved (Herrnson 1988, 74). Parties—particularly Democrats—also sent messages about which candidates from the other party to *not* support (Herrnson 1988, 77; also see Connelly and Pitney 1994 and Magleby and Nelson 2010). The 1980s marked a transition period for party involvement in congressional campaigns as they expanded the number of activities in which they engaged.

While fundraising involvement from party committees increased somewhat in the 1980s, it skyrocketed in the 1990s. The Republican Revolution of 1994 served as a critical pivot point for party involvement as both parties saw that neither party could take majority control for granted. Kolodny and Dwyre (1998) argue that the parties' legislative goals became more aligned with their electoral efforts as each party proactively sought to coordinate with other political actors including PACs, members of Congress, and national committees to a degree that was unprecedented to that point in order to win the House majority. While coordination increased in the 1990s, total party committee financial activity barely changed following the Republican Revolution (Jacobson and Carson 2016, 93). Rather, party committee spending began to increase dramatically in 2004, the first cycle governed by the Bipartisan Campaign Reform Act (BCRA). BCRA banned the use of "soft money," spending that parties engaged in on behalf of candidates purportedly for "party-building" and "get-out-the-vote" activities that really allowed them to help candidates without having to comply with the FECA's restrictions and limits (Jacobson and Carson 2016, 80; also see Kolodny and Dwyre 2006 and La Raja 2008). BCRA raised contribution limits, allowing parties to raise more "hard money" that was governed by FECA regulations. In response, parties increased the amount of hard money that they raised. After BCRA, independent expenditures by party committees rose dramatically as a legal alternative to the now-banned soft-money "party building" activities (Jacobson and Carson 2016, 80 and 90). In total, the late 1990s and early 2000s featured momentous changes to campaign finance law that required parties to raise more money in order to carry out their objectives.

With party financial demands now growing, the parties needed new ways to raise more money. Increasingly, party committees not only assisted vulnerable incumbents and credible nonincumbents in winnable seats but also asked safe seat incumbents to contribute to these efforts. In a series of articles that culminated in their 2012 book, Heberlig and Larson examined the causes and implications of the rise of party fundraising in Congress in this period (Heberlig and Larson 2005, 2007, 2010, 2012, and 2014; also see Heberlig, Hetherington, and Larson 2006). They attribute this rise in party fundraising to the close seat margins between the parties in Congress and the belief that majority control was now at stake in every election cycle. Members who wish to attain greater power in the institution through assuming a chamber or committee leadership post were especially vigorous in their efforts to fundraise for the party (also see Currinder 2003; Deering and Wahlbeck 2006; Green 2008; and Cann 2008). Considerable variation exists, however, in the amount that members contribute to party fundraising efforts in a given year and over time. Relevant to a study of minority party status, members contribute less as the size of the majority in the chamber expands (Heberlig and Larson 2012). In this chapter, I build on this analysis to incorporate both the seat level *and* direction of political forces in a given election. Thus, this chapter focuses on the anticipation of being in the minority as a cause of declining involvement in party fundraising efforts.

Minority Party Misery and the Avoidance of Party Fundraising

Incumbent officeholders must consider how involved they will be in raising money for their party's efforts to win majority control of their legislative institution. All else equal, I assume that incumbent legislators view contributing to party fundraising efforts to be a costly task that is not pleasant and that they will not engage in such efforts unless they have some sort of incentive to do so. This assumption relies on numerous quotes from former and current legislators who universally express distaste with such efforts. Interviewees I spoke to also expressed distaste toward the task of party fundraising. Beyond these examples, previous research demonstrates that telemarketers, whose job is quite similar to the "call time" component of party fundraising, have low job satisfaction and high turnover (Whitt 2006). Thus, some incentive must exist in order for legislators to be willing to engage in party fundraising efforts.

Political ambition plays an important role in the extent of members' engagement in party fundraising efforts. Based upon one's type of ambition, however, the amount of effort one puts into party fundraising is likely to vary. First, members who wish to maintain their current positions in the House (i.e., those with static ambition) are likely to contribute the most to party fundraising efforts. As established in prior literature (e.g., Heberlig and Larson 2012), those who seek leadership positions in the House, or want to keep the ones they already have, are likely to contribute heavily to these efforts. These members have a clear incentive to contribute, as the outcome of the next election determines whether they will be Speaker of the House or minority leader, or whether they will be a committee chair or just a ranking member. Further, members who do not hold especially high leadership posts may still be pushed to contribute by party leaders who want to put their party in the best possible financial position for the next election cycle. Members who anticipate spending a substantial amount of their careers in the House contribute to party fundraising efforts in order to avoid the wrath of party leaders. Therefore, it seems likely that a baseline level of party fundraising exists each year based upon the expectations of party leaders. Conversely, members who have either discrete or progressive ambition are less likely to contribute to party fundraising efforts. These members' time in the House is limited so they do not fear the same repercussions from party leaders. Additionally, these members reap fewer rewards from winning the majority. They obviously cannot become a committee chair if they leave Congress.[2] Furthermore, those with progressive ambition often face a competitive race to win their next office, so they cannot spare their time or money to help with party fundraising efforts on the way out of Congress. Overall, then, one would expect the statically ambitious politician to contribute most to the party's goal of winning or maintaining the majority.

Conditional party government was an important precursor to the birth of party fundraising. That party committee involvement in congressional fundraising began in the 1980s and ramped up in the 1990s and 2000s is no coincidence. Heberlig and Larson (2012) use cartel theory to explain the rise of party fundraising, arguing that parties use their agenda powers to create incentives for members to participate in party fundraising, but conditional party government could also explain this phenomenon. In the pre-Reform era, members would have viewed it as laughable for party leaders to ask them to contribute to party fundraising efforts. With each person looking out for themselves, there was no team attitude among members, who knew that it was "sink or swim" for each member (with Democrats presumably keeping the majority). Liberal members helped bring about reforms to empower party leaders in the 1970s, but party fundraising began to take off in the 1980s. Magleby and Nelson (2010, 106) attribute this to the 1980 House election, where Republicans did not win a majority, but did win enough seats to join more often with conservative Boll Weevil Democrats to enact parts of President Reagan's agenda. Democrats did not lose their majority and the agenda powers that came with it, but they felt more threatened, realizing that in order to win floor votes it was crucial to have a sizable majority in order to offset the fact that many of their southern members often voted with Republicans. Similarly, Republicans saw that they now could increase their relevance by cutting into Democrats' majority. Indeed, party committee spending among Republicans in this decade was much greater than that of Democrats (Connelly and Pitney 1994, 139).[3]

The effects of a narrowed Democratic majority were still less negative than those of the party losing the majority altogether, so party fundraising did not really take off until after the 1994 Republican Revolution. At this point, majority control was more competitive and the ideological differences between the parties were clear. While party leaders pushed members to contribute, rank-and-file members allowed this practice to continue. For example, after Democrats won the House majority in 2006, some of their members began to lag behind on fundraising as the 2008 election cycle drew near. According to Nir (2008), a *Roll Call* article at the time reported that Democrats were $14 million behind in party dues and that Speaker Nancy Pelosi and other party leaders convened a meeting to convince members to donate.[4] Perhaps the most convincing call for members to contribute was not from these party leaders, but from Representative Chet Edwards (D-TX). Edwards, who represented a conservative-leaning seat in Texas, announced that—despite the fact he was in a tough reelection battle of his own—he would contribute $100,000 to party fundraising efforts. With this action, members from safer districts than Edwards (i.e., most of the caucus) could hardly question party leaders' requests for contributions. Put simply, regular members condone and even *encourage* party leaders' efforts to get recalcitrant members to contribute because party fundraising helps obtain or keep the majority, which benefits all members.

Party activists also encourage party leaders' efforts to get rank-and-file members to contribute. At the start of the 111th Congress, David Nir (2009) of the *Swing State Project* blog (now *Daily Kos Elections*) noted that Chris Bowers of the now-defunct liberal blog *OpenLeft* led an effort to get Democrats to pay their party dues.[5] Heading into the 2010 election cycle, Democrats had a huge majority in the House of Representatives, but dwindling poll numbers. As a result, many House Democrats began to stockpile their own war chests rather than contribute to the party (Allen 2010). In response, a number of progressive bloggers ramped up their efforts to get disobedient Democrats to donate. These Democrats wanted party leaders to be *more* aggressive in putting pressure on Democrats.

David Nir wrote:

Personally, I feel like we've seen an insufficiently partisan spine over at the D-Trip, ever since Chris Van Hollen took over last cycle. SSP readers are well aware of the treachery perpetrated by Red-to-Blue chair Debbie Wasserman-Schultz in 2008, which Van Hollen permitted under his watch. This cycle, Van Hollen's apparent refusal to engage in bare-knuckled tactics to shake money out of his caucus is inexcusable. Rahm Emanuel would never have abided this. (Nir 2010)[6]

In total, then, it is not just party leaders who push their caucus members to contribute; rather, the party as a whole empowers leaders to take this action. Such a pattern is wholly consistent with conditional party government, where members enable leaders to make rules changes in the chamber and enforce party discipline. While the party authorizes its leaders to encourage fundraising for the party, members' individual efforts may vary.

Members whose party is fated to be in the minority in the next session of Congress have little incentive to become involved in party fundraising. Legislators broadly agree that the tasks associated with raising money for the party are unpleasant. Additionally, as noted by Representative Ocasio-Cortez, these tasks take time away from other important parts of representatives' jobs.[7] Thus, members are likely to participate only when there is some benefit from engaging in this activity. For a party that is likely to be in the majority, contributing is likely to advance one's chances of gaining a leadership spot such as a committee chair position (e.g., see Heberlig and Larson 2012). If majority control is competitive and each party has a reasonable chance of being in the majority, incentives exist to contribute because each donation makes it slightly more likely that one's party will be in the majority. Nevertheless, the parties typically offset each other's fundraising, so although a party does not want to fall behind the other party, they are often unable to use increased fundraising to gain an electoral advantage because the other party also raises substantial funds (Roberts, Smith, and Treul 2016). At the same time, members in a party with relatively equal chances of being in the majority or minority do not know if their contributions might land them a committee chair slot or merely a ranking member position. For a party that seems fated to be in the minority, the likely outcome is clearer. Members in this situation know that majority party offices including the speakership and committee chair positions are unavailable. At the same time, rank-and-file members know that they are unlikely to be able to advance their goals of good public policy. For these members, the costs of engagement in party fundraising efforts are more likely to exceed the benefits than for a member of the likely majority party. The value of winning a few more seats in the chamber, but not the majority, is less of an incentive to contribute than is winning the majority outright when faced with the unpleasantness of having to spend hours in a call room. This is not to say that these members will totally avoid contributing, but their drive to contribute is likely to diminish as prospects for majority party status dim. Top party leaders (i.e., the Speaker, party leaders, and whips) are less likely to scale back the effort they put into fundraising in order to avoid panic from breaking out in the party and because their caucus may blame them if they scale back their efforts and the party underperforms expectations in the next election. However, these leaders may face challenges in convincing donors to contribute to their party's financial efforts, so they may receive fewer contributions when in the minority.

In general, legislators who are likely to be in the minority face a tougher task in convincing access-focused donors to contribute. Connelly and Pitney (1994, 136) detail how 1980s DCCC Chair Tony Coelho pushed business leaders to donate to Democrats and not Republicans because Democrats "were going to be a majority for a long time" and these businesses would have to interact with the Democratic-controlled Congress "whether they want[ed] to or not." Coelho's pitch was largely successful. As Barber (2016) found, PACs tend to target their donations toward gaining influence and access in Congress, so it follows that these business leaders would focus their donations toward Democrats in order to maximize their sway in Congress. This example also suggests that the task of party fundraising is more difficult for minority party members under conditional party government because donors know that the minority party is unable to deliver most of its policy goals. In the past, minority party members could often get aid for businesses in their district by working with the majority. As polarization increased, however, these businesses came to fear repercussions from the majority if they donated to the minority party. Finally, as electoral conditions worsen for the presumptive minority party, relatively more of these members—and fewer presumptive majority party members—will be involved in competitive contests themselves than are members of the majority. This forces them to focus on their own reelection campaigns rather than help the party as a whole. In 2010, some of the troubles Democratic leaders faced in getting their members to contribute likely stemmed from the fact that many Democrats, such as Ike Skelton (D-MO), Jim Oberstar (D-MN), and Gene Taylor (D-MS), faced their first tough challenges in decades and had to focus on their (ultimately unsuccessful) reelection campaigns.

Overall, I expect minority party members under conditional party government to be less likely to contribute to party fundraising efforts than those who are likely to be in the majority. There is likely to be some base-level expectation from party leaders to contribute, so I expect *some* party fundraising still to occur throughout this era regardless of minority party status. Nonetheless, due to the unpleasantness of party fundraising relative to the benefits, the increased difficulty of the task, and the necessity to focus on their own races, I expect the likely minority party to fundraise less than the majority.

An Analysis of Party Fundraising in the U.S. House of Representatives since 1990

To examine the relationship between the prospect of minority party status and party fundraising, I use campaign finance data from the Federal Election Commission since 1990. Like Heberlig and Larson (2012), I look at three types of party fundraising: candidate-to-candidate giving (i.e., where candidates give directly to other candidates), candidate-to-party giving (i.e., where candidates give to the DCCC or NRCC), and giving from leadership PACs run by members of Congress to congressional candidates.[8] I aggregate these three sources of funding together to represent a candidate's total commitment to party fundraising efforts as my dependent variable, measured in real 2018 thousands of dollars.[9]

My main independent variable, as in the previous chapter, is the measure of how likely it is that a party will be in the minority in the next session of Congress. In this period, the value of this variable fluctuates substantially; the mean value is 0.476, which indicates that control of Congress was generally competitive in this period. However, its standard deviation is 0.35, demonstrating that a wide range of values were typical in this period. Indeed, these three decades of party fundraising saw uncompetitive elections such as 1990, 1992, 2008, and 2014 where one party seemed fated to be in the minority, while also seeing competitive contests such as 2000, where each party stood a decent chance of winning control of the chamber.

I control for various factors that are likely to relate to a member's commitment to party fundraising. Previous literature (e.g., Heberlig and Larson 2012) indicates that members in leadership roles are more likely to contribute to party fundraising efforts. Thus, I include a dummy variable that measures if a member is in top chamber or party leadership and another indicating if they are a committee chair or a ranking member.[10] I also control for the competitiveness of a member's seat in Congress using the presidential seat lean variable from the previous chapter, as members who are more electorally secure may feel more able to focus on party fundraising efforts as opposed to their own reelection campaigns. Additionally, I account for the fact that members elected in special elections after the start of that Congress did not serve an entire term by employing a measure of the percentage of the term a member was in Congress.[11] I also control for the member's ideological extremity compared to their party caucus, as moderate members may feel less compelled to contribute to party fundraising efforts as their policy goals are likely to be less disadvantaged by being in the minority than is the case for their more ideologically extreme colleagues. Similarly, members who are retiring—either voluntarily or through losing their primary—may also see fewer direct benefits to winning the majority and thus contribute less to party fundraising efforts, so I include a dummy variable measuring if a seat is open. Finally, I include year dummy variables to account for time trends in the data. These dummy variables also help account for the fact that the campaign finance regime in place differed greatly over this period. Early in this period, soft money donations were unrestricted, while from 2004 to early 2010 BCRA was in effect. Later, the Supreme Court loosened campaign finance restrictions with the *Citizens United* and other subsequent decisions.

To substantiate the robustness of my results, I test my theory using several models. Since the data has a panel structure (i.e., the same representatives occur multiple times in the data over time), I use a fixed effects model.[12] To model campaign finance outcomes, scholars often use tobit models because "contributions are censored at zero" (Heberlig and Larson 2005, 613, citing Long 1997; also see Heberlig and Larson 2012, among others). Due to the panel structure of the data, I use a random effects tobit model (see table 3.1 for both models).[13]

In both models, my measure of likely minority party status attains statistical significance. In the fixed effects model, as the probability of being in the minority increases by the equivalent of 10 percentage points, a member's contributions to party fundraising efforts decrease by about $4,000. An increase in the minority party variable from one standard deviation below the mean, when a member's party is virtually certain to be in the majority, to one standard deviation above the mean, where they are highly likely to be in the minority, results in a $27,000 decrease in party fundraising efforts, from about $153,000 to $126,000.[14]

The results of the random effects tobit model are broadly similar. As displayed in figure 3.1, a member whose party is all but guaranteed to be in the majority raises more than $100,000 (in real 2018 dollars), while a member who is fated to serve in the minority raises under $60,000. In both models, most of the control variables attain significance in the expected direction with two exceptions: the variable measuring the proportion of term served does not attain significance in the fixed effects model and ideological extremity is not significant in the random effects tobit and is actually negative in the fixed effects model. This result may suggest that the most extreme members feel distant from their party's priorities and as a result do not feel an impetus to help the party's efforts to win the majority. The year fixed effects variables show a clear increase in party fundraising over time, with a particularly large substantive jump in 2004 and again in 2006, the first presidential and midterm cycles in which BCRA was in effect. This result is consistent with the fact that parties had to lean more heavily on their members to fundraise as soft money became illegal. Finally, consistent with Heberlig and Larson (2012), the presidential seat lean variable is positive and significant in both models. This result speaks to how members address the collective action problem they face in choosing whether to participate in party fundraising efforts or focus on their own reelections. For both of these groups, contributions decrease as the probability of being in the minority increases. Safe members are more willing to endure the

TABLE 3.1. Probability of minority party status and party money contributions

Variable	Fixed Effects Model	Random Effects Tobit
Probability of Party in Minority	−40.385*	−43.764*
	(10.458)	(10.413)
Party or Chamber Leader	1,842.933*	1708.033*
	(46.377)	(40.744)
Committee Leader	78.609*	120.165*
	(15.106)	(13.797)
Percentage of Term Served	20.249	230.404*
	(64.951)	(65.765)
Presidential Vote Lean	2.100*	2.785*
	(0.856)	(0.590)
Ideological Extremism	−305.025*	−40.755
	(118.977)	(44.719)
Open Seat	−78.977*	−87.793*
	(12.573)	(12.383)
Constant	−58.875	−367.165*
	(65.935)	(67.103)
Overall R^2	0.332	—
Log-Likelihood	—	−40,043.770
N	6,484	6,484

*$p < 0.05$, dependent variable measures total party fundraising contributions

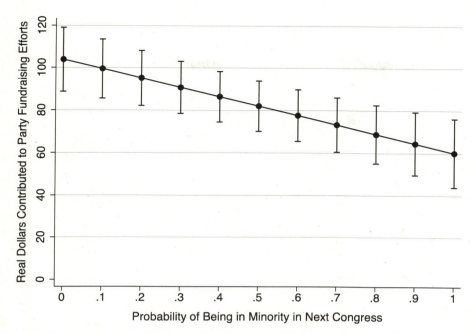

Figure 3.1. Members of the likely minority are less likely to give to party (Random Effects Tobit Model)

unpleasantness of party fundraising efforts when they might actually be in the majority after the next election. Similarly, those in marginal seats may divert some of their attention from their own reelection campaigns to help their party when the probability of being in the minority is low.

In total, I find strong support for my expectation that those members who are likely to be in the minority will raise less for party fundraising efforts.[15] Previous quotes from members make clear that they generally do not enjoy fundraising for their party because activities like call-time are unpleasant. When majority party status seems likely, members may be willing to put up with this task. When they are almost certain to be in the minority the futility of their efforts sets in and they stop performing this chore. Furthermore, some donors may be harder to convince that a contribution is worth it when one's party has little optimism of winning the majority, making party fundraising efforts even more unpleasant under such conditions. As a result, the likely minority party, already going into the election at a disadvantage, faces an even steeper climb to win the majority because they will have less money to win competitive contests. Thus, minority party status results in lower party fundraising, but it also has the potential to perpetuate minority party status as a party is less able to wage the vigorous campaigns needed to win swing districts.

Conclusion

A troubling implication of the results presented in this chapter is that many members who are in a good position to affect policymaking are likely to spend more of their time raising funds to win the majority. Members who are part of a majority that is likely to continue into the next Congress are, at least theoretically, the most able to focus on long-term policy efforts to address serious problems. Yet my results show that these members are the least likely to feel the freedom to pull back from party fundraising efforts. As noted by Rep. Ocasio-Cortez, members have to decide to prioritize their time, making decisions between whether to prioritize committee hearings, constituency service, or party fundraising (Ocasio-Cortez 2019b). Each hour spent on party fundraising means that members have to devote less time to the other functions of Congress, contributing to a decline in the time deliberating bills in committee and reducing the number of bills deliberated on and ultimately passed through the textbook committee process. As a result, the loss of committee time due to party fundraising may also contribute to the increase in omnibus legislation and legislation that reaches the floor without going through committee after originating with party leadership.

Several potential solutions exist to reduce the amount of time that members must spent raising money for their party. For the most famous members who have a strong following on social media, Rep. Ocasio-Cortez offers a potential solution that may mean that these members do not have to choose between policymaking and party fundraising. Following the DCCC's decision in early 2019 to punish firms that help primary challengers to candidates, Ocasio-Cortez encouraged her Twitter followers to pause their donations to the party and instead tweeted out links to specific Democratic incumbents who represented electorally competitive seats. In fewer than two hours, the first-term Democrat was able to raise more than $30,000 for these Democrats (Edmondson 2019). Put in context, this amount represents more than 10 percent of the average party fundraising for an incumbent in the *entire cycle* in 2018. Other members with a high profile on social media could theoretically replicate these efforts, although most representatives have far fewer followers on social media than Rep. Ocasio-Cortez. Furthermore, party leaders and other members would have

to view these efforts as equivalent to traditional forms of party fundraising or the member may risk losing party support and their chance to win
leadership positions and accrue other party-related benefits.

Other solutions may exist that could apply more broadly to members.
One solution, offered by Norman Ornstein, is to ban fundraising while
Congress is in session, as is the case in many state legislatures (Ornstein
2011). Such a reform proposal could force members to focus more on policy, although any reform effort would have to take steps to prevent members from shirking duties in their constituencies while not in session and
to prevent leaders from further limiting the number of days in session.
Another reform proposal, put forth by unsuccessful presidential candidates
Lawrence Lessig in 2016 and Senator Kirsten Gillibrand (D-NY) in 2020
is to give each voter a tax-funded "democracy voucher" that they could use
to donate to candidates of their choice (Kliff 2018; Zhou 2019). A benefit
of this approach is that members would have incentive to appeal to the
entire electorate as moderate and ideological extreme voters alike would
have the same amount to give. While some members would surely see
merit in appealing to the most extreme voters, there likely would be stiff
competition for these donors, making a strategy focused on getting more
moderate donors to contribute rather than have their voucher go unspent
a preferable strategy for many legislators. Thus, this approach could potentially reduce both the time spent on party fundraising and reduce the sway
of extreme donors at the same time.

Until the passage of these reforms, however, incumbents are fated
to continue toiling away at party fundraising efforts. That likely minority party status relates to lower rates of party fundraising should not be
read as a solution to the problems associated with party fundraising, but
rather both a symptom and further cause of minority status. Combined
with the evidence relating to the decision to retire in the previous chapter,
the analysis presented here shows that likely minority party status affects
the behavior of legislative incumbents. As these individuals have the most
direct experience with being in the minority in Congress, they represent a
logical, albeit somewhat easy test of my theory. In the next two chapters, I
go a step beyond incumbents to look at how the unpleasantness associated
with minority party status affects *potential* candidates and party committees
in order to examine the true extent of the feelings of powerlessness associated with being in the minority.

FOUR

Minority Party Status and the Decision to Run for Office

In 2000, a crucial election in Florida came down to fewer than 600 votes. Early on election night, returns had been favorable for the Democratic candidate, but the Republican candidate, confident he would win, refused to concede. Indeed, after the tabulation of all returns, he was ahead and his lead held up after a machine recount in Broward, Palm Beach, and Miami-Dade Counties (Associated Press 2000). The Democratic candidate requested a hand recount in Miami-Dade County, although the Republican called for Democrats to "accept the will of the people" (Eilperin and Vita 2000). After exhausting the campaign's options to contest the result, the Democratic candidate ultimately conceded to the Republican (Eilperin and Dewar 2000).

While the above vignette sounds a lot like the 2000 presidential race in Florida, it actually describes *another* competitive election in Florida that also had national importance: the congressional election in Florida's 22nd District between incumbent Clay Shaw (R-FL) and former Florida House Speaker Pro Tempore Elaine Bloom (D-FL).[1] The 2000 congressional elections represented a credible opportunity for Democrats to win back the House of Representatives for the first time since losing control in 1994, and the party recruited a number of politically experienced candidates—whom Jacobson (1989) designates as "quality" candidates—to challenge Republican incumbents and run for open seats.[2] These candidates seek to run for Congress when their party is most likely to gain seats and they are more likely to win congressional elections than are political amateurs, so the recruitment of these candidates was a good sign of Democrats' ability to gain seats in the 2000 election (Jacobson 1989). While some of the quality candidates who ran in 2000 won seats in Congress, such as State Senator Adam Schiff (D-CA), former U.S. Representative Jane Harman (D-CA), and Huntington Town Board member Steve Israel (D-NY), others, such as Bloom, Fanwood Mayor Maryanne Connelly (D-NJ), State Representative Lauren Beth Gash (D-IL), and Orange County Commission President Linda Chapin (D-FL), narrowly lost to Republicans (Eilperin 2000).[3] Ultimately, Democrats netted two seats in the 2000 election, leaving Republicans with a narrow 222–213 majority.[4]

Democrats ran far fewer quality candidates the next two election cycles. With President George W. Bush possessing a high approval rating after the September 11, 2001 attacks and the country recovering from the 2001 recession, Democratic prospects for House control in 2002 were below the norm for a midterm with a Republican president. Two years later, economic conditions—and President Bush's approval rating—were decent, if not at the heights of 2002. In many of the districts discussed above, Democrats failed to run quality candidates in one or both of these years. In Florida's 22nd District, Democratic county commissioner Carol Roberts ran with much acclaim in 2002, but she was defeated as Republican Governor Jeb Bush won a landslide reelection over Democrat Bill McBride (Bushouse and Man 2002). In 2004, Democrats initially planned to run Wilton Manors Mayor Jim Stork for the seat, but he had to bow out of the race in the fall due to a heart condition. Democrats made entreaties in seeking to recruit a number of other politically experienced candidates, including Representative Peter Deutsch (D-FL), who represented a neighboring district and had lost a primary for U.S. Senate, as well as State Senator Ron Klein (D-FL). Both of these candidates, as well as entrepreneur Jeremy Ring, turned down the party (Advocate 2004). Democrats ended up running political operative Robin Rorapaugh as their candidate, who lost by more than 20 percentage points (Associated Press 2004). That Democrats were stuck with an inexperienced candidate in this district was representative of a broad pattern in 2002 and 2004: even in swing districts where a strong Democratic candidate could potentially win, the party often lacked a politically experienced candidate to run in the seat in one or both of those years.

Conversely, Democrats ran a stronger slate of politically experienced candidates in 2006, as President Bush's approval rating fell to the mid-30s amid rising casualties in Iraq. In Florida's 22nd District, State Senator Ron Klein (D-FL), who party leaders asked to run after Jim Stork bowed out in 2004, finally made a successful bid for the seat.[5] Other quality candidates in swing seats where Democrats had run politically inexperienced candidates in one or both of the 2002 and 2004 elections included State Representative Linda Stender (D-NJ), Vanderburgh County Sheriff Brad Ellsworth (D-IN), and Former U.S. Representative Ciro Rodriguez (D-TX), among others (Hernandez 2007).[6] With their strongest class of politically experienced candidates since 2000, Democrats won control of the House of Representatives in 2006.

Candidates who run for Congress face a cost-benefit analysis to decide whether it is worth it to run. Previous studies portray potential candidates as being progressively ambitious, seeking to move up the opportunity structure when a credible opportunity to win a seat presents itself (e.g., see Ordeshook and Riker 1968; Black 1972; Rohde 1979; Aldrich and Bianco 1992). However, Democratic recruitment successes and failures from 2000 to 2006 suggest that a party's *overall* prospects for majority control may play a role in whether a quality candidate emerges. In swing districts, a strong candidate has the potential to break through in a relatively neutral or slightly unfavorable year for their party, as was the case for Democrats in 2002 and 2004.[7] Yet Democrats ran relatively few quality candidates in such seats in the interim between 2000 and 2006, suggesting that it may not be worth it to run for a candidate likely to end up in the minority. In this chapter, I examine how the prospect of minority party status affects quality potential candidates' decisions on whether to run for Congress. I begin by briefly discussing existing theories about the decision to run and build on these by discussing how likely minority party status factors into this process. Subsequently, I test my theory using data from congressional elections since 1946. I then focus specifically on House elections in the competitive, partisan era following the Republican Revolution. I find that likely minority party status results in fewer quality candidates in competitive seats, while quality candidates are generally unlikely to run in safe seats for the other party regardless of the political atmosphere. Finally, I discuss how scholars may need to revise existing definitions of candidate quality in light of the 2016 and 2018 congressional elections.

A Theory of the Decision to Run for Quality Prospective Candidates

Which Factors Affect Candidate Entry?

When considering whether to run for office, prospective candidates face numerous potential considerations that they must weigh when deciding if the time is right to seek to satiate their ambition for higher office. Previous examinations of the decision to run have generally focused on individual factors, which include a candidate's gender, their economic status, and their ideological fit with their party (Lawless and Fox 2010; Thomsen 2017; Carnes 2018). Scholars have also given considerable attention to a candidate's prospects for winning a seat in Congress. Any signal that an incumbent may be weak, either due to their performance in office or the competitiveness of their seat, can serve as a sign to a prospective challenger that they have decent prospects for winning the seat and should consider running (e.g., see Hetherington, Larson, and Globetti 2003; Stone and Maisel 2003; Carson 2005; and Gordon, Huber, and Landa 2007). Prospective candidates clearly want to maximize their chances of winning and are less likely to run if they are unlikely to realize the ambition to win a seat in Congress by running that cycle (Stone, Maisel, and Maestas 2004).

National political conditions also have the potential to affect candidate decisions on whether to run for Congress due to their downstream effects on individual races. Famously, Jacobson and Kernell (1983) examined how the national political climate affected quality candidates' decisions on whether to run for Congress. They found a party tended to field a higher proportion of candidates with political experience, which they designated as quality candidates, when political conditions are good for the party and field far fewer of these candidates when conditions are poor. Jacobson (1989) later tested this theory using data from congressional elections from 1946 to 1986. He again found that national factors such as the state of the economy and presidential approval affected whether quality challengers emerge, with more running when these conditions favor the candidate's party.

While these studies have a similar focus to this chapter, a key difference exists. These studies focus on the prospects of success for individual candidates, while this chapter examines how the overall success of a party in winning a congressional majority affects individual decisions to run. Even if a party is likely to have a good election, this does not mean that they are necessarily likely to win the majority. For example, numerous individual Republicans were able to win seats in Congress as Ronald Reagan won landslide presidential victories in 1980 and 1984, but the party still fell far short of winning a majority. A potential Republican candidate who considered running for Congress in one of these years knew that, even if they won, they would not be in the congressional majority.

When considering the decision to run for Congress, a crucial distinction exists between quality candidates (i.e., those who have previously held elective office) and political amateurs. Studies consistently show that quality candidates win at a higher rate than do political amateurs (e.g. Jacobson and Kernell 1983; Jacobson 1989). Lazarus (2008) argues that there are two main reasons why politically experienced candidates are more likely to win than are amateurs. First, experienced challengers have greater resources at their disposal to run successful campaigns. These candidates know how to raise the funds necessary to wage a competitive campaign, giving them a leg up over those who have never run a successful campaign. Second, experienced candidates self-select into more winnable races. Numerous other studies have found evidence of this selection effect (e.g., Fowler 1979; Banks and Kiewiet 1989). Indeed, Maestas and Rugeley (2008) argue that this selection effect is actually the cause of much of the disparity in funds raised between experienced and inexperienced candidates because these candidates run in the most competitive districts where donors are most likely to contribute to their campaigns.

A third advantage that politically experienced candidates have over inexperienced candidates is some level of existing name recognition in the district. Incumbents can develop a "personal vote" whereby constituents support them because of positive personal qualities or due to activities in office such as constituent service, conferring positive name recognition on the incumbent (Cain, Fiorina, and Ferejohn 1987). Additionally, incumbent officeholders are able to advertise their names in conjunction with official activities they perform while in office (Smith and Weinberg 2016). Because their constituencies often overlap with the congressional district in which they hope to run, those holding other offices have the potential to mitigate this advantage by drawing a similar benefit from the office they currently hold and transferring it to the congressional race. Carson et al. (2011) find that state legislators are more likely to run for Congress if their legislative district overlaps substantially with the congressional district they hope to represent. This indicates that risk-averse state legislators are well aware of the fact that incumbent legislators hold substantial electoral benefits, running only when they feel that they can effectively offset these advantages. Overall, existing research demonstrates that politically experienced, or quality, candidates are especially mindful of their chances of winning the next election when deciding if they should run. This stands in contrast with political amateurs who are often less calculating or may greatly overestimate their chances of success (Maisel 1986).

Given the success rate of quality candidates relative to their politically inexperienced counterparts, they are a natural subset of office seekers to examine in this chapter. These candidates are more electorally successful than are political amateurs (Jacobson and Kernell 1983; Jacobson 1989), so party leaders are likely to seek out these candidates. Thus far, the literature has established that these candidates are less likely to run when they have a low chance of winning the seat in the next election. I extend this logic to argue that they are also less likely to run when their party has a low chance of winning the majority.

Minority Party Status and the Decision to Run

The political opportunity structure of American politics relies on the fact that state legislators, mayors, and county officials want to serve in the House of Representatives. For many state, county, and local officials, a seat in the House of Representatives is the logical next step to advance their political careers. While state legislators, particularly those in party leadership, can advance to the Senate, this is relatively uncommon.[8] Similarly, while a mayor of a large city—such as Anchorage Mayor Mark Begich (D-AK) in 2008—is sometimes able to win a Senate election, this is also uncommon. In most cases, cities represent only a small percentage of a state's population—indeed, Anchorage's population as a percentage of its state total was second only to New York City in the 2010 census.[9] These officials could perhaps seek a statewide office in state government, but if they want to pursue their career in federal office then the House of Representatives generally seems to be the logical next step.[10] As Schlesinger (1966) argues, this is a feature of a healthy democratic system. By seeking high office, these politicians give voters more choices that are credible in elections and force incumbents to wage campaigns that are more serious in order to remain in office. Thus, their candidacy for the House potentially serves to benefit both their career and the health of American democracy at the same time.

I expect the calculus of the decision-making process to change when a prospective candidate views it as unlikely that they will be in the majority should they win a seat in Congress. Like incumbent legislators, prospective candidates with political experience are likely to consider their party's prospects for being in the majority, alongside their own prospects, when deciding whether to run for Congress. As experienced politicians, these prospective candidates may know what being in the minority party in a legislative body is like. For state legislators, this experience is direct as they have either experienced being in the minority or see how their colleagues in the other party cope with the experience.[11] County and local officials may have less experience with partisan politics, but the factionalism that often develops due to parochial concerns in localities may give them some taste of what losing—or winning—feels like in politics.[12]

Having some knowledge of the status of the minority, I expect that these officials' desire to run will diminish when prospects for their party to win the majority appear grim. These prospective candidates know that they will be able to get little done in Congress should they win. As first-term members, their role in policymaking is generally likely to be minimal, but this lessens further when they are in the minority. Beyond playing a direct role in policymaking, first-term members of the majority have the opportunity to preside over the House floor and gavel votes to a close. While undoubtedly a tedious task after a while—special circumstances aside (Rovner 2019)—new members may bask in the attention and can send clips of themselves looking powerful back to their districts to aid their reelection campaigns or increase their national stature (Law 2019). Further, since the majority party is generally unlikely to call a vote unless they are likely to win it, presiding over votes in the House should generally give members experience with winning, setting them apart from the experience of the minority. Based on the assumption that quality potential candidates should have some idea of the different experiences of the congressional majority and minority, as it becomes more likely that a party will be in the minority, I expect that they will field fewer quality candidates.

Under conditional party government, prospective candidates who are likely to serve in the House minority have even less incentive to run for Congress. The day-to-day experience that these members have overflows with the unpleasantness associated with losing (Robertson 2012). Given the spread of conditional party government to subnational government (Aldrich and Battista 2002), these quality potential candidates are likely to be well aware that they will have difficulty seeing their policy goals enacted in Congress in this environment and that instead they will spend most days fighting losing battles to stop the other party's proposals.

Service in the House minority under conditional party government may be so unpleasant that it may alter the political opportunity structure. Indeed, when a prospective candidate views the House majority as being out of reach, they may decide to run for a different office rather than seek election to Congress. For example, former Lieutenant Governor Sheila Simon (D-IL) decided against a run for Illinois' 12th District in 2016 to seek election to the Illinois State Senate—a body in which Democrats enjoyed a sizable majority—in a district that was far more Republican-leaning than Illinois's 12th District (Cahn and Gonzales 2015; Koziatak 2016; Daily Kos Elections N.d.). In other words, Simon decided that she would rather face a tougher general electorate in order to win a seat in a state legislative majority instead of running in a somewhat more favorable one to win a seat in the House minority.[13] Ultimately, she lost by more than 20 percentage points, an ignominious outcome for someone with Simon's political stature.

Overall, I expect that the party not currently holding a seat in Congress is less likely to have a quality candidate as its nominee when they are likely to be in the minority in the next session of Congress. I do not make any prediction as to *which* quality candidate will or will not run, but rather expect that a party is more likely to lack such a candidate when they are likely to be in the minority in the next session of Congress. As with my expectations in chapter 2, I expect generally to find some disparity between the parties due to the way in which agenda control empowers the majority (Cox and McCubbins 1993, 2005). Nevertheless, I anticipate that this difference should grow under conditional party government because the experience of the minority party becomes even more miserable under such conditions.

Testing the Theory, 1946–2018

To test the effect of the prospect of minority party status on potential candidates' decision to run, I use data on candidate quality since 1946.[14] My dependent variable measures whether the candidate from the party not currently holding a seat has previously won elective office. Figure 4.1 displays how the percentage of quality candidates has varied over time. While Republicans had nearly as many quality candidates in the early 1950s when the majority was competitive, once Democrats began their 40-year reign in the House they consistently fielded candidates with political experience in a larger proportion of seats they did not control than did Republicans. Once control of the House majority again became more competitive after the 1994 Republican Revolution, Democrats no longer had the wide edge in fielding quality candidates that they had for the previous four decades. A curious pattern develops in the two most recent congressional elections: Republicans saw their percentage of quality candidates fall in both 2016 and 2018 and Democrats, despite a good year for the party, ran quality candidates in a lower proportion of seats in 2018 than they had in 2016. I explore this phenomenon in more depth later in this chapter.

I begin my analysis by constructing a model where the dependent variable measures whether a party not holding a seat in Congress fields a

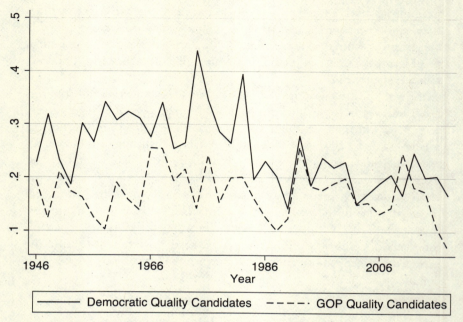

Figure 4.1. Percentage quality candidates by party, 1946–2018

quality candidate. This group of candidates includes both challengers and candidates from that seat's out-party in open seat races. This analysis is similar to the retirement analysis in the second chapter, but is an important extension because it allows me to test the full reach of my theory, showing that minority party status may not just affect those legislators who are currently in the body but also prospective legislators considering whether to run. As with the second chapter, in which I examined retirement decisions, I use random effects logistic regression models to account for the fact that incumbent members reoccur in the data. In all of the models, the focal independent variable is my measure of the probability of minority party status. Since the focus of this chapter is on the challenging party, rather than incumbents, I subtract the value for the measure used in the previous two chapters from one so that this measure represents the probability that a successful out-party candidate would be in the congressional minority. My control variables are similar to those used in previous chapters. Specifically, I control for the presidential vote lean, whether the incumbent in a seat is retiring, if the incumbent is in their first term, the total number of terms served by the incumbent, whether redistricting took place in the seat since the last election, the incumbent's ideological extremity, and if the seat is located in the South. I also control for whether the incumbent is in their first term because these incumbents are often among the most vulnerable since they have yet to develop a strong incumbency advantage and therefore attract stronger opposition.[15] I include the extremism variable in this model because ideologically extreme incumbents are more vulnerable than those with views more in line with their seats, providing an opportunity for an enterprising challenger to exploit their record to win the seat (Canes-Wrone, Brady, and Cogan 2002).

My first model examines the entire period from 1946 to 2018. In keeping with expectations, I find that the probability of minority party status relates significantly to whether a quality candidate emerges. Specifically, as the probability that a quality candidate would be in the minority (should they win the seat) increases from "0" (i.e., practically guaranteed to be in the majority) to "1" (i.e., all but assured to be in the minority), the probability that a quality candidate emerges falls from 24.4 percent to 18.3 percent (see figure 4.2). Several control variables also attain significance in this model. First-term members and those who are ideologically extreme are

TABLE 4.1. Probability of minority party status and the decision to run for Congress

Variable	Random Effects Logit Model
Probability of Party in Minority	−0.464*
	(0.067)
Presidential Vote Lean	−0.069*
	(0.003)
Retiring	1.275*
	(0.077)
First-Term Member	0.567*
	(0.068)
Terms	−0.038*
	(0.008)
Redistricted Seat	0.015
	(0.110)
Ideological Extremism	0.433*
	(0.218)
Seat in South	−0.985*
	(0.079)
Constant	−0.570*
	(0.178)
N	15,060
Log-likelihood	−6,659.391

*$p < 0.05$, dependent variable measures whether candidate from party not holding seat is quality candidate

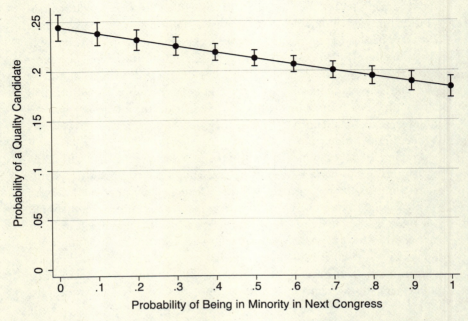

Figure 4.2. Probability of minority party status and quality candidate emergence

more likely to face quality candidates; seats without an incumbent seeking reelection also see more quality candidates run. In contrast, the total number of terms served, the presidential vote lean, and whether the seat is in the South relate negatively to the probability of the party not holding the seat running a quality candidate.

Next, I look at whether different patterns exist in the pre-and post-Reform periods. In the pre-Reform period, one might expect to see a smaller drop-off in the percentage of seats featuring quality candidates as minority party status becomes more likely. With the majority party less favored by the rules than after conditional party government took hold, a prospective candidate from the likely minority party could see a path for influence should they win election to Congress. To examine whether this is the case, I include a model for the first half of Democrats 40-year stint in the House majority (1956–74, see online appendix table 4.1). I focus on this period because it features both (1) a general sense that Democrats were likely to remain in the majority, but also (2) an ability for minority party Republicans still to play some role in policymaking. While one might expect to see a smaller decline in candidate quality when comparing the likely majority party to the minority than in other eras, there is actually a statistically significant and substantively large decrease in the percentage of quality candidates who ran as the probability of being in the minority increases from "o" to "1".[16]

To explain this result, I consider the lack of political competition in the American South during this time frame. Frequently in this period, Republicans not only lacked a quality candidate, they lacked a candidate altogether. Further, the array of *potential* quality candidates in a seat was often rather meager as southern Republicans lacked strong party organizations to recruit and support candidates, holding few state and local offices (Aldrich 2000; Aldrich and Griffin 2018). Republicans first became competitive in presidential elections in the region, then started winning Senate and House elections, then other statewide races, and then won offices further down the opportunity structure. Indeed, even today, a half a century after Nixon's Southern Strategy, there are still vestiges of the Democratic Solid South at the state and local level. For example, as of mid-2019, 24 county sheriffs in Alabama were Democrats, almost twice as many as the number of counties Hillary Clinton carried in the state in 2016.[17] This included Colbert County, which Donald Trump won with 67 percent in 2016, and Franklin County, where he took almost 79 percent. Given the top-down nature of the Republican takeover of the South, there simply was not a large supply of quality candidates to run for Democratic-held seats during this era. At the same time, if a seat fell into Republican hands, there was a seemingly endless supply of Democratic talent to run in order to win it back for the party. Following this pattern, after Democrats lost five of the eight seats in the Alabama U.S. House delegation in 1964 as Barry Goldwater surged in the South, two years later the party ran quality candidates in all but one of these seats in an effort to win them back.[18]

To correct for the possibility that the warped ambition structure of the South in this era may be affecting my results, I include another model where I interact the competitiveness measure with the region of the seat (see online appendix table 4.1). Indeed, there is a huge contrast between the results for the North and those for the South (see figure 4.3). In the South, seats where a potential candidate is likely to be in the majority should they win (i.e., Democrats) frequently feature quality candidates, while those where the candidate is likely to be in the minority (i.e., Republicans) see very few quality candidates run. In the North, however, this drop-off is more modest, as the probability of a quality candidate drops from 31.2 percent for the likely majority to 26.1 percent for the expected minority. This decrease is slightly more modest than that for the entire period.

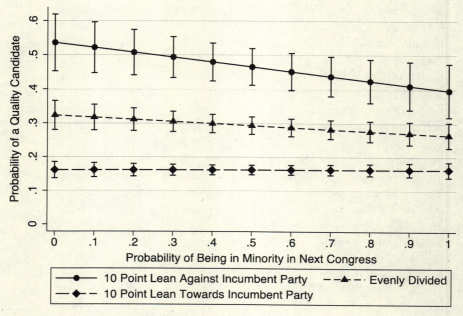

Figure 4.3. The role of region in the pre-Reform era

To add an additional point of comparison, I conducted the same analysis for the second half of the 40-year period of Democratic control (1976–94) after rules changes made due to conditional party government disempowered the minority. In this period, the interaction between region and probability of minority party status falls just short of significance at the 95 percent level (p=0.056). This result demonstrates that the ambition structure of the rest of the country began to exist in the South in this period as party competition in the South started to approximate that in the rest of the country (Aldrich and Griffin 2018). Further, the decline in candidate quality in this period outside the South is substantively larger in this set of seats than in the previous 20 years, falling from 27.9 percent to 19.4 percent as the probability of minority party status increases from "0" to "1." In total, these results are consistent with those in chapter 2 for incumbents. A quality prospective candidate is generally less likely to run when they would almost certainly be in the minority, but this effect heightens in the presence of conditional party government as the ability of the minority party to play a role in policymaking decreases.

A Closer Examination of 1994–2018

Since the 1994 Republican Revolution, intense competition and a deep divide between the parties have defined congressional elections. Thus, an examination of this period allows one to see whether the effect of conditional party government varies when politicians do not believe that minority party status is permanent. Duplicating the noninteractive model used in previous sections, I do not find a significant relationship between the probability of minority party status and quality candidate emergence (see online appendix table 4.2). Initially, it may seem as though minority party status does not have the same effect in this competitive environment as it did during the uncompetitive era when Democrats held the majority for 40 years.

If one considers how polarization has changed the structure of competition in recent congressional elections, however, a clear link between minority party status and quality candidate emergence appears in a specific subset of seats. In recent congressional elections, the link between presidential vote share and congressional outcomes has grown substantially (Jacobson and Carson 2016). The correlation between presidential vote and congressional election outcomes has grown from 0.75 in 1994 to 0.97 in 2018 (Jacobson 2019). Prospective quality candidates are likely to know the connection between presidential vote in the seat in which they would run and their own prospects for winning a seat in Congress. In recent years, state and even local elections have felt the sway of presidential politics (Hopkins 2018). In 2017, Democrats swept county row offices in Chester County, PA, a suburban Philadelphia county that had swung from a narrow Mitt Romney win in 2012 to a more than 9 percentage point win for Hillary Clinton in 2016.[19] In explaining how his party went from holding only one county office before the election to sweeping every office on the ballot in 2017, Chester County Democratic Party chair Brian McGinnis said, "'Donald Trump was on the ballot. . . . Whether or not his name was there, he was on the ballot'" (Rellahan 2017). Thus, one can assume that prospective quality candidates have at least some understanding of the fact that their prospects depend at least to some extent on the presidential lean of a seat. Indeed, although the overall percentage of quality candidates has declined in recent years, there has actually been an *increase* in quality candidates since 1994 in seats with a presidential lean favoring the party not currently holding it, from 30.7 percent in 1994 and before to 36.7 percent in the subsequent years. A strong candidate might be able to overcome a 5 percentage point lean to the other party. Under most circumstances, they cannot prevail in the face of a 25-percentage point presidential vote advantage for the other party, even in wave election years like 2018.[20]

Based on the new realities of competition in recent election years, I ran another model, in which I included a variable where I interacted the probability of minority party status with presidential vote lean. What I found provides some answers to the role of likely minority party status in this era, while raising some additional questions. In the entire period from 1996 to 2018, the interaction term does attain significance, but it falls just short of significance in a model for 1996–2016 (p=0.084), and attains significance in a 1996–2014 model. There are two important takeaways from this set of results. First, it seems that when elections are highly nationalized, for at least much of the time, quality candidate emergence in the most competitive districts (i.e., those in which a quality candidate could potentially win) does depend on whether it is likely that a candidate would be in the minority should they win the seat. In the 1996–2014 model, for a seat that leans against the incumbent's party by 10 percentage points—that is, one that leans *toward* that of a prospective challenger—a quality challenger emerges 53.6 percent of the time when they are all but certain to be in the majority, with this number falling to 39.7 percent when minority party status is all but certain. The decline is a more modest 32.3 percent to 26.5 percent in evenly divided seats, while no meaningful difference exists in seats that lean toward the incumbent's party by 10 percentage points. This suggests that prospective quality candidates in the most winnable seats for the party not currently controlling them respond to whether their party is likely to be in the minority.

Second, however, it is important to consider whether existing definitions of candidate quality still apply in the era of Trump. In the model for the full period, the interaction did not achieve significance. Furthermore, if one looks at figure 4.1 above, the patterns of quality candidate emergence do not really fit well with the theory presented in this chapter. In 2016, Democrats ran quality candidates in 20.3 percent of seats held by Republicans, while 10.7 percent of seats held by Democrats featured a quality Republican candidate. This represented a substantial decline for Republicans, who ran quality candidates in 17.4 percent of seats held by Democrats in 2014, even though their odds of holding the majority did not differ substantially across these two years. One might expect a slight drop for Republicans given that they had already gained a number of the most competitive seats held by Democrats in 2014, but this decline is noteworthy. Even more strangely, in 2018, both Republicans *and* Democrats saw their ranks of quality candidates atrophy. Republicans ran quality

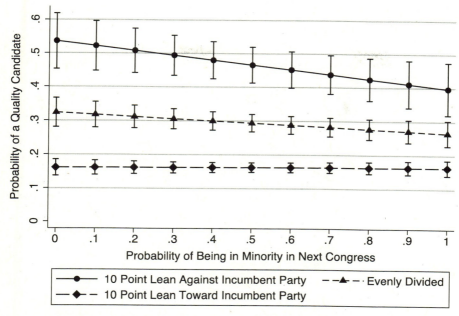

Figure 4.4. The role of presidential vote lean in the post-1994 era (1994–2014)

candidates in only 6.8 percent of seats held by Democrats—the smallest percentage for any party in the period—and Democrats ran quality candidates in only 16.7 percent of seats held by Republicans. That Republicans would run fewer quality candidates than in 2016 is unsurprising given that it was fairly likely that they would lose their majority in 2018, although the record-setting low percentage is noteworthy and may at least in part be related to distaste among established politicians that President Trump leads the party. There may have been little desire among these establishment Republicans to serve in Congress with Trump in the White House. Even more surprising, however, is that *Democrats* ran fewer quality candidates in 2018 than in 2016, when they had very little chance of winning the majority. Typically, one would expect an increase in quality candidates when a party's prospects of winning the majority improve, as happened for Democrats in 2006 compared to 2004.

The limited research that exists on the 2016 and 2018 congressional elections suggests that previous experience in elective office may be declining as a marker of candidate quality. Using data from the political betting website PredictIt, Riley and Smith (2018) found an increase in the number of political amateurs who won nominations in 2016 as it became more likely that Donald Trump would win the Republican nomination. In fact, a slight majority of candidates who flipped seats in 2016 did not have previous experience in elective office. Further, Porter and Treul (2018) found that more Republicans without political experience defeated ones with experience in primaries than is typical in 2016 (also see Treul and Porter 2018).

In 2018, several Democrats without political experience defeated candidates who held elective office in primaries including Amy McGrath in Kentucky's 6th District, who defeated Lexington Mayor Jim Gray and Haley Stevens in Michigan's 11th District, who defeated State Representative Tim Greimel. In McGrath's case, a viral announcement video allowed her to gain recognition around the country and raise significant amounts of money from grassroots activists (Kurtzleben 2017). Additionally, in many cases Democratic candidates who were recruited and heavily touted by the party did not have political experience, with the party particularly excited about female veterans such as Mikie Sherrill in New Jersey's 11th District and Chrissy Houlahan in Pennsylvania's 6th District (Mistler 2017). Going forward, new definitions of candidate quality may need to be developed should the patterns of 2016 and 2018 continue, although Carson and Hitefeld (2018) found that candidates who fit the traditional definition of quality still won more frequently than amateurs in 2018.[21] Thus, in forming any new definition, it may be best not to discard the traditional Jacobson definition, but to build upon it. For the time being, another approach to getting around the changing nature of candidate quality is to look at candidate quality from the perspective of the party and their candidate preferences. Chapter 5 of this book, which looks at party committee recruitment, employs this approach.

Conclusion

In total, the evidence presented in this chapter demonstrates that a link exists between whether a party is likely to be in the minority in the next session of Congress and whether they field a quality candidate in the next election. This result has important implications for the ambition structure in American politics because if an elected official determines that service in Congress is not desirable, then they may seek to hold a different office or may remain in their existing office for a longer period of time. When their party is unlikely to be in the congressional majority, this may mean that the next rung of the ambition ladder for a state legislator is not Congress.

Instead, they may choose to amass power in their existing state legislative body or perhaps run for a statewide office.

These results also have important implications for voters and the choices they have in elections. Given the success of quality candidates compared to political amateurs in flipping seats under normal circumstances, a voter is more likely to have two credible options to choose from when a quality candidate contests a seat for Congress (Jacobson and Carson 2016; Banks and Kiewiet 1989). Furthermore, having a credible opposition party candidate run makes it more likely that voters can hold an incumbent to account during a campaign if a scandal occurs or they begin to ignore the desires and preferences of their constituents. Thus, a lack of strong opposition may insulate incumbents from the dangers they face from an electorate's ability to serve as a "rational god of punishment and reward" (Key 1964, 568) when it seems likely that their party will be in the majority and they do not face a quality challenger.

Finally, the results of this chapter do come with several caveats. As previously discussed, the nature of what it means to be a quality candidate may be changing in the age of Trump. An important assumption made in this chapter is that a candidate with political experience who emerges as a party's nominee is a strong candidate and is desirable to the party. While this is often the case, it does not always hold. In the next chapter, I more closely examine these caveats by looking at candidate emergence from the perspective of party committees. This allows for a closer look at when candidates whom a party views as high quality decide to run for Congress.

FIVE

To Meddle or Not to Meddle?
Minority Party Status, Party Leaders,
and Candidate Recruitment

Democrats' success in recruiting their preferred candidate to regain Illinois' 12th District could not have been more different in 2016 and 2018.[1] Having lost the longtime Democratic seat to Republicans in 2014, the party immediately started to regroup to try to win it back the next cycle. In 2016, however, three major candidates who Democratic Party leaders favored—former Lieutenant Governor Sheila Simon, State Representative Jay Hoffman, and St. Clair County State's Attorney Brendan Kelly—all passed on the race (Cahn and Gonzales 2015). Instead, Democrats were left with lawyer C. J. Baricevic, a political novice who was outspent 2 to 1 by first-term incumbent Mike Bost (R-IL), who ultimately defeated Baricevic by a margin of 54.3 percent to 39.7 percent (Open Secrets N.d.; New York Times 2017b). Two years later, however, Democrats had much more success in obtaining their desired candidate, with Brendan Kelly announcing his candidacy in early July 2017 (Martin and Burns 2017; Hundsdorfer 2017). Kelly, a Navy veteran who won reelection unopposed as state's attorney in the district's largest county in 2016, remained a top choice of Democratic leaders and immediately proved to be a strong fundraiser (Bustos 2017). Kelly ultimately lost to Bost by 6.2 percentage points (51.6 to 45.4 percent), but this race was viewed as such a crucial one that the *New York Times* included it in its first set of "live polls" of House districts and then polled it a second time.[2]

While a single example such as this is anecdotal, other congressional seats saw a similar divergence in candidate recruitment from 2016 to 2018. For example, Democratic State Senator Jennifer Wexton declined requests to run against Representative Barbara Comstock (R-VA) in 2016, but ran against Comstock two years later (Pathé 2015a; Schneider 2017). Similarly, former state representative Paul Davis (D-KS) rebuffed party entreaties to run for Kansas's 2nd District in 2016 but then decided to run for the seat in 2018 (Ryan 2015; Schneider 2017).[3] These examples represent a broader pattern in my data for these two years, as Democratic recruitment attempts failed 63 percent of the time in 2016, compared to 33 percent of the time in 2018.[4]

In this chapter, I argue that prospects for House control play an important role in candidates' willingness to respond to party appeals for them to run for office. These candidates see their party's prospects for winning the majority and respond by entering more frequently when it looks like their party has a good chance of winning the majority and all the benefits that come with it. However, party-favored candidates are less likely to run when it looks like their party will be in the minority. The focus of this chapter is similar to the previous chapter in that it focuses on candidate entry, but different in that it seeks to examine these decisions from the perspective of party committees. The Democratic Congressional Campaign Committee (DCCC) and National Republican Congressional Committee (NRCC) play a crucial role in recruiting and funding congressional candidates, helping to ensure that the party has a strong candidate to run in marginal seats held by the other party and in open seats. When a party does not field its strongest candidate for office in a potentially winnable seat, this denies the voters in that seat a true choice in the subsequent election. Further, failed recruitment attempts have upstream effects as the party not holding that seat faces a more difficult path to winning the majority. Thus, the outcomes of individual recruitment attempts have broader consequences for America's electoral democracy.

When to Recruit? How Minority Party Prospects Affect Party Recruitment

The Role and Actions of Party Committees

I begin by considering the role parties play in electoral politics, focusing specifically on how party committees fit within this system. Historically, parties were conceptualized as having a "tripartite" structure, consisting of the "party-in-the-electorate, the-party-in-government, and the party-as-organization" (Aldrich 2011, 11; Curiel 2019; also see Key 1964; Sorauf 1964; and Hershey 2009). Each of these components is crucial for parties to achieve their various goals. For Aldrich (2011, 19), parties represent a means to "solv[ing] problems that current institutional arrangements do not solve and that politicians have come to believe they cannot solve" alone. Specifically, parties help to police the large number of ambitious politicians who wish to run for office, support their favored candidates' efforts to win elections, and help guide their policy decisions once in office. A political party has many component parts (e.g., see Herrnson 2009), but especially important to a party's efforts to win and maintain control of Congress are chamber-specific party committees (i.e., for the House the DCCC and NRCC). Having existed since at least the 1860s when the NRCC sought to elect northern Republicans and begin to build the party in the South (Kolodny 1998, 24), these committees play an especially important role in addressing two of the three problems raised by Aldrich: regulating the number of candidates seeking office and subsequently helping these candidates win election to Congress.[5] Parties serve as a gatekeeper of sorts by determining *who* can run for office (Matthews 1984, 562–63). Rather than conceiving of elections as the only mechanism for selecting officials, in Matthews's conceptualization they are the last stage of a multistage process that previously includes the recruitment of candidates by party leaders.

Parties face a Goldilocks situation with candidate entry: they do not want too many candidates to run for a single seat, nor do they want too few.[6] In some cases, numerous ambitious politicians seek to run for an office and a party committee's job is to convince some of them to drop out in order to avoid a contentious primary that saps party resources and makes it more difficult to win the general election (Kenney and Rice 1987, but see Lazarus 2005). In other cases, the party may lack anyone they see as a credible candidate. For example, in Nevada's 3rd Congressional District in 2016, Democratic leaders saw numerous prominent politicians such as State Senate Minority Leader Aaron Ford and former Nevada Secretary of State Ross Miller decline to run before finally convincing synagogue president (and now U.S. Senator) Jacky Rosen to run (Pathé 2016). It is worth noting, however, that five other Democrats ran besides Rosen (Thomas 2017). The party did not see these five as credible candidates, so they continued to search to find a better candidate until they convinced Rosen to run.[7]

While sometimes a party has numerous races in which they face a glut of candidates, other times they have many races where they have too few. Notably, in the 40-year era of Democratic control of the House, scholars often focused on the poor state of Republican recruitment, which stemmed from their permanent position in the minority. Connelly and Pitney (1994, 12–13) noted that House Republicans blamed their recruitment woes on the weak condition of the party in state and local government, giving them a limited bench from which to draw candidates. Further, they argue that Democrats' status as the "party of government" in this period gave them a recruitment advantage and that demands from local conservative activists for issue purity hampered those candidates who did run (Connelly and Pitney 1994, 12–13). While not explicitly stated here, it may also be the case that moderate candidates, anticipating difficulty winning over these activists after seeing what happened to others who ran, may have also decided not to seek office in the first place. As noted by Herrnson (1988), party committee recruitment has potential costs, as the national party may come into conflict with local party officials or activists if they seek to recruit a different candidate than the one locals prefer. This could potentially harm the party's chances of winning the seat in November. While Republicans were often unable to recruit their desired candidates in this period, it was not always for lack of trying. Herrnson (1988, 49) argues that Republicans' recruitment operation became more robust than that of Democrats in the 1980s, but that Democrats had more success in recruiting their preferred candidates. This finding fits with Connelly and Pitney's observation that Democrats' position of power gave them a clear advantage in recruiting candidates.

Party committees especially seek to recruit candidates to run in competitive districts, beginning these efforts immediately after the previous election (Herrnson 1988; Kazee and Thornberry 1990). Even in marginal seats, it is worth noting that active recruitment efforts were relatively limited in this period. In a survey of congressional candidates in the 1982 elections, Kazee and Thornberry (1990, 68) found that only five of the 35 they interviewed had been actively recruited, compared to 20 who decided to run all by themselves, and eight whose decision to run fell somewhere in between these two extremes. Unsurprisingly, in this survey, those whom party leaders recruited tended to have a previous history of party involvement of some sort.

Recent literature on party recruitment finds some important similarities with previous studies. In a survey of state legislators, Maestas et al. (2006) find that recruitment for Congress is more likely to take place when the legislator represents a marginal district or serves in a professional legislature, both markers that they may have the experience and political skill necessary to wage a competitive congressional campaign. Hassell (2016 and 2018) adds to the literature on party recruitment by constructing a new measure that looks at a candidate's fundraising sources based on overlap between party committee and candidate donors. Hassell also conducts interviews with party elites, finding that perceived strength in the general election is an important factor in recruiting candidates. One crucial difference with the pre-1994 era, however, is the increased number of cycles in which majority control is competitive, a topic that receives some attention from Hassell (2018, 14 and 165), but generally has not been a focus of previous studies on recruitment. Now, having established what party committees are and what they do, the next step is to consider how the prospect of minority party status affects their actions.

Explaining Party Committee Recruitment Patterns

Party committees face a difficult calculus when deciding whether to try to recruit a candidate for a race. As discussed previously (e.g., see Herrnson 1988), a party runs the risk of creating conflict between federal, state, and local party organizations when they decide to get involved in recruitment efforts. In some cases, the national party may annoy local activists who see them as swooping in and imposing a candidate on a district when the national party views the local choice to lack the campaign skills or financial acumen to win the general election. For example, local party activists in the San Joaquin Valley of California expressed frustration with DCCC efforts to recruit candidates to run in California's 10th and 21st Districts in 2016, potentially winnable seats held by Republican members of Congress that had gone for President Obama in 2012 and later went for Hillary Clinton in 2016. Doug Kessler, a local Democratic Party official, expressed frustration with the DCCC, saying that the local party wanted "some say who a candidate is" and that they wanted to "have people who respect and understand the Valley and do not dictate to us" when choosing candidates (Ellis 2015).

At other times, the divide between national and local party activists may arise on ideological grounds, as was the case in Texas's 7th Congressional District in 2018. In this district, the DCCC decided that Democratic candidate Laura Moser was too liberal for the seat, which Hillary Clinton narrowly won in 2016 after the district was won by Mitt Romney by more than 20 percentage points four years earlier.[8] The DCCC went so far as to release opposition research against Moser. This caused a negative response from local activists, potentially even *helping* Moser attain a spot in the May runoff election with eventual winner Lizzie Pannill Fletcher. After this incident, to avoid further conflict, the DCCC decided not to get involved in the runoff that took place between Moser and Fletcher (Bowman 2018; Voorhees 2018). Thus, before a party decides to involve itself in recruitment efforts, it needs to determine that the benefits of recruiting its preferred candidate outweigh these potential costs.

Additionally, a party committee may get involved when they feel there are too many strong candidates contesting a race in order to avoid a costly primary and to prevent wasting talent on a single race. A good example of when such an effort took place comes from the 2018 contest for Florida's 27th District. This Miami-based seat had gone for Hillary Clinton by about 20 percentage points in 2016 and was left open by Representative Ileana Ros-Lehtinen's (R-FL) decision to retire (Caputo 2018a). The primary field included a plethora of ambitious Democratic politicians including former (elected) Judge Mary Barzee Flores, State Representative David Richardson, and State Senator José Javier Rodríguez, whom the DCCC had recruited for the race (Hagen 2017). A few months later, however, former Health and Human Services Secretary Donna Shalala entered the race and became the frontrunner. Only one of these politicians could win the seat, so ultimately the party was able to convince some of them to switch races.[9] Rodríguez, the initial DCCC pick, decided to remain in the Florida Senate, giving Democrats a better chance of winning that chamber (Caputo 2018b).[10] Barzee Flores soon thereafter entered the race in Florida's 25th District against Representative Mario Diaz-Balart (R-FL), giving Democrats a credible recruit for another potentially winnable seat (Daugherty 2018). Richardson remained in the House race, running as a progressive alternative who was critical of Shalala—who became the establishment choice—and the DCCC as a whole. Indeed, Richardson's campaign manager, Sam Powers, was quoted in *Roll Call* stating that he was "not really afraid of the Democratic establishment in this race or of pissing off the DCCC" (Pathé 2018). While Richardson was not able to take the nomination from Donna Shalala, she won by only 5 percentage points, causing speculation that she was a weak candidate for November (Caputo 2018b). In total, party involvement in this race was able to channel some of the party's talent into other races, but it also exposed ideological fissures. Thus, it seems clear that there are generally some costs for a party committee to get involved in a race both when they are trying to get a candidate to run and when their goal is to get a candidate *not* to run, so such a decision is not taken lightly.

Several other key assumptions underlie the logic of party recruitment in congressional races. First, one assumes that party involvement will make it more likely that a desired candidate will run. Given the potential cost of engaging in a race, a party will want to have some sort of return on its investment. Indeed, Broockman (2014) found in an experiment that candidates who are encouraged to run are more likely to do so (also see Preece and Stoddard 2015). Second, another important assumption is the fact that getting involved will actually help candidates win the election. While some risk of party involvement backfiring certainly exists, as in the case of the Moser/Fletcher race in Texas, Dominguez (2011) finds that partisan endorsements are generally helpful in congressional primaries. While Dominguez examines endorsements beyond those of party committees—including elected officials and interest groups—these sorts of endorsements tend to flow to candidates when they have support from the party. Importantly, I do *not* assume that parties recruit candidates in every race. As noted by Kazee and Thornberry (1990), many candidates are "self-starters," or their decision to run arises from a combination of their own desire to run and efforts from the party to convince them to enter the race. Overall, I assume that the party will sometimes seek to recruit candidates when they feel that the likely payoff from recruitment exceeds the potential costs that come from engaging in the primary.

My initial conjecture was that a party might be less involved with recruitment when they looked likely to be in the minority in the next session of Congress. Given the potential costs of annoying party activists and the potential difficulties in convincing candidates to run in a bad year, engaging in recruitment may not be worth it. My expectation here changed, however, after the interviews I conducted for this book. One interviewee noted that bad recruitment can be a "self-fulfilling prophecy," so parties still need to recruit in bad years. Another interviewee who worked closely with a party committee said that parties asked the same people to run in bad years as in good years, but they were more likely to say "no" when prospects for the majority were poor. Further, a third interviewee noted that Democratic candidates seemed to "come out of the woodwork" in 2018. In other words, the party needed to push these candidates to run less vigorously because ambitious politicians, seeking to move up, were ready to run when conditions looked good for their party. This does not mean that recruitment is unnecessary for a party in a good year (e.g., 2018 for Democrats), but rather that it may be less like pulling teeth than it is in a bad cycle (e.g., 2014 for Democrats). In total, then, I expect party recruitment to—somewhat paradoxically—be more prevalent in years when the party is *less* likely to be in the majority. A party committee may especially have to recruit candidates to run in marginal seats in years when they are unlikely to be in the majority. Even in a bad year, a party might be able to win a handful of these seats; for example, Democrats gained a few marginal seats in 2016. Additionally, the lack of a credible nominee is likely to be embarrassing for the party and can compound upon itself in other races as potential candidates see their party doing poorly.

In contrast, I expect that a party's ability to convince candidates to run will decrease as it becomes more likely that they will be in the minority in the next session of Congress. Interview subjects universally stated that recruitment was harder in such years. Several mechanisms are likely to be at play in this process. First, there is likely to be a selection effect because the party is most likely to *need* to ask candidates to run in bad years for their party. Second, in good years, candidates may already have a seed planted in their mind that they should consider running. Party engagement provides the final push that allows that ambition to grow.[11] When asked to run, candidates are also likely to consider what might happen should they win the election. One potential congressional candidate I interviewed said he briefly thought about running and the thought of winning the election was an even bigger deterrent than the thought of losing because of the unpleasant experience he expected in the minority should he have won. For a candidate such as this, an appeal from the party is unlikely to be successful because of the candidate's negative expectations about life in the minority. Finally, variation in recruitment success is likely to be the most noticeable in marginal seats because parties seek to recruit the most serious, ambitious politicians for these seats. These politicians do not want to risk a loss in a bad year. At the same time, many of these candidates can still win in a relatively tough environment for the party. For example, Democrats were still able to win seats like Nevada's 3rd and 4th Districts and New Hampshire's 1st District, among others, in 2016. However, some candidates who believe they could win a marginal seat might instead prefer to run for another political office where they would not be in the minority, turning back party requests to run.

Under conditional party government, I anticipate a magnification of this effect. As discussed in previous chapters, members of the minority party have an increasingly negative experience under such conditions, having less input into the process and losing to a party at which they are at ideological odds more often. Thus, the likely minority party will have to push harder to recruit candidates for marginal seats in tough years under conditional party government. These potential candidates, seeing the negative experiences of those in the minority, are subsequently more likely to say "no" under such conditions.

Examining Party Recruitment Using a Content Analysis of Newspaper Articles

To test my expectations, I conducted a content analysis of newspaper articles from four leading publications that cover Congress: *Roll Call*, *CQ Weekly*, the *Washington Post*, and the *New York Times*. Content analyses of prominent newspapers have been used in a number of important studies in political science in order to examine media attention of politically relevant topics (e.g., see Baumgartner, De Beof, and Boydstun 2008). Atkinson, Lovett, and Baumgartner (2014) find that coverage of high-salience topics, or ones that have regular spikes in attention, is relatively consistent across media organizations, while those with low coverage that lack such spikes exhibit idiosyncratic patterns of coverage. As a topic, candidate recruitment is likely to have a spike in coverage in the months before the filing deadlines for Congress every two years. While of low interest to general audiences, this topic is of high salience to those who read publications that focus closely on the inner workings of Capitol Hill. Thus, I did not limit my search to a single publication, including several that focus specifically on Congress (*Roll Call*, *CQ Weekly*) and others that have large budgets relative to other publications in the industry, allowing them to cover a wide array of stories including candidate recruitment (*Washington Post*, *New York Times*).

To carry out my content analysis, I constructed a search string of terms that were likely to relate to party recruitment.[12] With this search string, I was able to narrow the articles I examined to those that were most likely to relate to recruitment efforts. I then read the newspaper articles that the search string identified as being potentially relevant to see if they mentioned a candidate recruitment effort. I then coded two variables for every congressional district in each two-year election cycle to indicate (1) whether a recruitment effort took place, and (2) if there was a recruitment attempt, whether it was successful.[13]

When to Run? Testing the Decision to Run with an Alternative Measure of Candidate Quality

First, I use this data to examine whether a party waged a recruitment attempt in a seat in the 1990–2018 congressional elections. I again employ a random effects logistic regression model to conduct this analysis. My dependent variable measures whether any articles my search string flagged as being potentially relevant mentioned a recruitment attempt from the party committee of the party not currently holding the seat. The focal independent variable is my measure of the probability of minority party status, measured in the same manner as in the previous chapter (i.e., a value of "0" indicates a prospective candidate is all but assured to be in the majority if elected to Congress, while a value of "1" indicates almost certain minority party status). I include the same set of control variables as in the previous chapter that examined candidate emergence.[14] Given the potential for recruitment efforts to be more frequent in marginal seats, I also include models for seats that are likely to be more competitive based upon several measures.[15] Drawing on my results from the previous chapter on candidate entry, quality candidates are less likely to enter marginal seat contests in this period when their party is likely to be in the minority. This finding suggests that a party may have to make a tougher sell in bad years and still may come up short.

My findings reported in table 5.1 demonstrate that in the most marginal seats, party recruitment efforts increase as it becomes more likely that the party will be in the minority. In a model of House races from 1990 to 2018, there was a positive but nonsignificant relationship between the probability of minority party status and the occurrence of an out-party committee recruitment attempt. As figure 5.1 shows, this relationship moves toward statistical significance once one looks at the most marginal seats. For those seats where the incumbent party's presidential candidate performed no more than 10 percentage points better than their national average, the variable measuring the probability of minority party status still falls well short of significance (p=0.126), but it comes closer for a 5 percentage point cutoff (p=0.054).[16] However, for those seats in which the incumbent received under 60 percent of the vote in the previous election, the focal independent variable becomes statistically significant. For these seats, when the party not currently holding the seat is all but assured to be in the majority, a recruitment attempt is mentioned to have occurred 7.7 percent of the time. Conversely, when the party not holding the seat is almost certain to be in the minority, these publications mention an attempted recruitment in 13.1 percent of seats. As observed, these results indicate that party committees do indeed devote more effort to trying to recruit candidates in seats narrowly decided in the last election in years where it seems likely that the party will be in the minority.

The results of my analysis become even stronger when I look specifically at the post-1994 era, when party control of the House switched frequently (see table 5.3). Party committees ramped up their activities in this era and it became expected that the party would recruit more candidates. Thus, inaction in a bad year had increased potential of creating a death spiral for the presumptive minority party, resulting in the party winning even fewer seats than expected. Indeed, I find some evidence of there being a 1994 threshold effect after running four models with a term that interacts the probability of minority party status and a dummy variable measuring whether the election took place after 1994.[17] In all four models, the interaction term is positive and it attains significance in the 60 percent threshold model; it also falls just short in the model for all seats and those where the party's presidential candidate performed no more than 10 percentage points better than their national vote share.

Next, given that a party engaged in a recruitment effort for a seat, I examine whether the recruiting party was successful at landing their favored nominee when an article mentioned a specific name of a preferred recruit.[18] Using the same set of control variables, I find mixed results, but ones that are somewhat clearer in the most marginal seats. For all seats and for those with the 10 percentage point cutoff for presidential vote lean, the

TABLE 5.1. Probability of minority party status and recruitment attempts

Variable	All Seats	Presidential Vote Lean under 10	Presidential Vote Lean under 5	Previous Incumbent Percentage under 60
Probability of Party in Minority	0.209	0.308	0.489	0.676*
	(0.172)	(0.201)	(0.254)	(0.277)
Presidential Vote Lean	−0.048*	−0.059*	−0.066*	−0.072*
	(0.008)	(0.126)	(0.017)	(0.016)
Retiring	0.770*	0.711*	0.753*	0.400
	(0.172)	(0.196)	(0.230)	(0.289)
First-Term Member	0.472*	0.672*	0.865*	0.387
	(0.169)	(0.189)	(0.230)	(0.238)
Terms	−0.019	−0.005	0.019	−0.026
	(0.018)	(0.020)	(0.023)	(0.033)
Redistricted Seat	−0.345	−0.250	−0.211	−0.428*
	(0.355)	(0.407)	(0.450)	(0.553)
Ideological Extremism	−0.391	0.010	0.685	0.699
	(0.537)	(0.589)	(0.705)	(0.785)
Seat in South	−0.245	−0.436*	−0.334	−0.432
	(0.152)	(0.178)	(0.217)	(0.245)
Constant	−3.034*	−3.110*	−3.713*	−2.821*
	(0.279)	(0.318)	(0.423)	(0.524)
N	6,037	3,279	1,991	1,627
Log-likelihood	−1,322.944	−882.957	−587.294	−496.345

*p < 0.05, dependent variable measures whether party committee attempts to recruit candidate

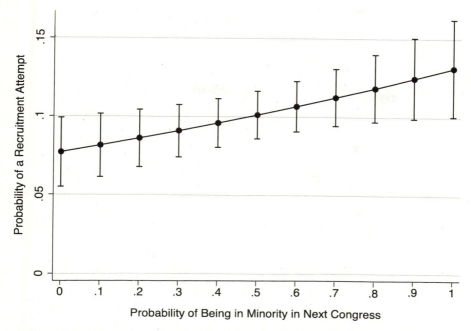

Figure 5.1. Recruitment attempt, seats where incumbent won with under 60 percent

TABLE 5.2. Probability of minority party status and recruitment failures

Variable	All Seats	Presidential Vote Lean under 10	Presidential Vote Lean under 5	Previous Incumbent Percentage under 60
Probability of Party in Minority	−0.023	0.315	1.163	1.494*
	(0.390)	(0.440)	(0.619)	(0.638)
Presidential Vote Lean	0.006	0.014	−0.004	0.021
	(0.015)	(0.024)	(0.034)	(0.029)
Retiring	−0.437	−0.653	−0.687	−0.829
	(0.379)	(0.443)	(0.524)	(0.688)
First-Term Member	0.348	0.293	0.468	0.591
	(0.351)	(0.367)	(0.454)	(0.467)
Terms	−0.025	−0.011	−0.035	0.107
	(0.035)	(0.037)	(0.046)	(0.063)
Redistricted Seat	0.971	2.041	2.482*	2.836
	(0.803)	(1.137)	(1.230)	(1.474)
Ideological Extremism	−2.101*	−1.916	−1.933	−3.050
	(1.060)	(1.190)	(1.348)	(1.589)
Seat in South	0.473	0.051	−0.346	0.021
	(0.285)	(0.349)	(0.449)	(0.029)
Constant	−0.233	−0.341	−0.929	−1.153
	(0.537)	(0.581)	(0.846)	(0.897)
N	374	266	190	161
Log-likelihood	−233.721	−162.210	−109.068	−91.044

*p < 0.05, dependent variable measures whether party committee recruitment attempt fails

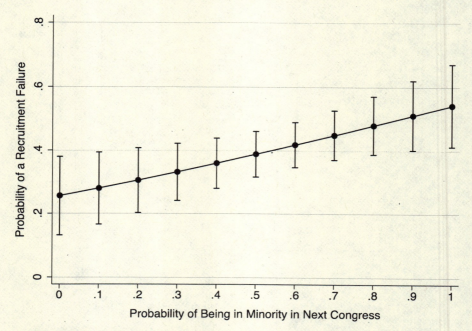

Figure 5.2. Recruitment failure, seats where incumbent received under 60 percent in last election

TABLE 5.3. Results in 1994 models for probability of minority party status variable

Dependent Variable	All Seats	Presidential Vote Lean under 10	Presidential Vote Lean under 5	Previous Incumbent Percentage under 60
Recruitment Attempt	*	*	**	**
Recruitment Failure	NS	NS	**	**

Dependent variables measure (1) whether party attempted to recruit candidate and (2) whether party failed to recruit; **p < 0.05, *p < 0.10, NS = Not Significant; controls were the same as overall models. See online appendix for full models.

coefficient for the probability of minority status does not attain significance. It does, however, come closer to significance for the 5 percentage point cutoff (p=0.06), and it attains significance for those seats in which the incumbent won with under 60 percent of the vote in the previous election. For these seats, going from all-but-guaranteed majority status to assured minority status results in an increase in the probability of a failed recruitment attempt from 25.6 percent to 54.2 percent. These results suggest that, at least for some of the most marginal seats, a party's preferred nominee responds to a party's prospects for minority status. These results should be interpreted with some caution due to a relatively small number of cases, but they provide at least some initial evidence for my expectations. As with the attempted recruitment models, I find stronger results in the post-1994 era, with two of the three measures of marginality, suggesting increased responsiveness to likely minority status in recent years (see table 5.3).

Conclusion

This chapter provides several important contributions to the study of quality candidate emergence and its implications for competition in congressional elections. First, the analysis conducted in this chapter allows for an examination of how likely minority party status affects the emergence of candidates whom the party views as being of high quality. While many desired party recruits fit the usual definition of quality candidates (Jacobson 1989), that is, those who have previously won an elective office, sometimes parties attempt to recruit strong candidates who do not fit this definition. An interviewee who worked closely with a party committee said that, from the perspective of the party, a quality candidate is someone who is able to raise the necessary funds to contest a seat, has a plan to win, and can network. For this interviewee, these candidates also have a story they can tell to voters, and can show that have done something and are able to fix problems. While a state legislator or county commissioner may fit this description, these are not the only backgrounds from which a party might seek to draw candidates. These results show that, in at least some marginal seats, potential candidates whom the party seeks out respond similarly to likely minority party status as do quality candidates as defined by Jacobson.

Second, the results in this chapter suggest that party committees play an important role in ensuring competitive elections. Since the 2016 elections, activists in both parties have given a bad name to the so-called establishment. However, my first set of models shows that this "establishment" seeks to ensure that more voters in marginal districts have a real choice between credible candidates. Furthermore, while promoting the competitiveness of individual races, these actions may also yield unanticipated downstream effects. Skittish incumbents may decide not to retire or continue fundraising for the party as they see their party committee still pushing to win the majority. At the same time, the fact that the second set of models shows that party committees often fail to land their prized recruits in the most marginal seats in years in which they are likely to be in the minority suggests that the success of party committees in the face of unfavorable national trends may be limited. As in previous chapters, minority party status causes ambitious politicians to pull back from electoral politics as they decide to run for a different office, remain in their current office, or leave electoral politics altogether. Finally, given that my results were generally stronger for the post-1994 Congress, the relevance of recruitment efforts continues to grow.

In the final two chapters of this book, I turn from studying the U.S. House of Representatives to examining how expected minority party status affects incumbents and candidates for the U.S. Senate and state legislatures. The first four chapters of this book demonstrate that, in a variety of circumstances, likely minority party status causes elected politicians and potential candidates to disengage from electoral politics. Conditional party government often heightens this effect. The final two chapters of this book provide a window into how minority party status affects politicians at varying levels of the political opportunity structure. The sixth chapter of this book goes up a rung to examine a body that operates more on consensus, the U.S. Senate. The seventh and final chapter goes a step down the opportunity structure to investigate state legislative bodies, which vary from containing budding ambitious politicians to having citizen legislators elected by only a few thousand of their peers.

SIX

Political Ambition, Electoral Engagement, and the U.S. Senate

The 1996 election was, as a whole, a strong showing for the Democratic Party. President Bill Clinton won reelection by a larger margin than his initial victory in 1992 in both the popular vote and the Electoral College, and Democrats gained a House seat relative to their 1994 result.[1] However, Democrats actually *lost* ground in the U.S. Senate, giving up seats in Alabama, Arkansas, and Nebraska, while gaining a seat in South Dakota. With their two-seat net gain, Republicans held a solid 55–45 seat majority in the Senate going into President Clinton's second term. The three seats Democrats lost all had something in common: a popular, longtime incumbent decided to retire and the open seat then flipped to Republicans. Democratic retirements were not limited to these three seats. In fact, eight of the 15 Democratic senators whose terms expired in 1997, or 53 percent of them, decided to retire in 1996. Many of the Democrats who retired were among the eldest senators, including Howell Heflin (D-AL) and Jim Exon (D-NE), who were both 75 years old, and Claiborne Pell (D-RI), who would be 78 on Election Day. In contrast, only five of the 19 Republicans up for reelection retired, with senior senators such as 72-year-old Ted Stevens (R-AK) and 93-year-old Strom Thurmond (R-SC) seeking additional terms.

While a number of factors were certainly at play in these retirement decisions, in this chapter I argue that the fact that Democrats were unlikely to regain the majority in 1996 may have played some role in the numerous Democratic retirements this cycle among senior Democratic senators and the relatively small number of Republican retirements. While these Democrats could still stop the Republican agenda, it would be more difficult for them to push Democratic policy goals forward. With Democrats likely to retain the filibuster and veto pivots to block the most detested Republican proposals, these senators may have seen little point in staying. In contrast, with the GOP reassuming the majority in 1994 and being likely to keep it in 1996, these senior Republicans were able to play a central role in driving policy in the upper chamber. Some strong Democratic challengers ran this year, including Representative Tim Johnson (D-SD), who unseated Senator Larry Pressler (R-SD), but the large number of retirements by senior senators hampered the party's prospects.

I begin this chapter by examining past studies of the U.S. Senate that focus on the meaning of minority party status with an eye toward understanding how scholars conceptualized minority party status in the chamber and how this varies from the House. Subsequently, I discuss the theoretical expectations that arise from this literature for the decision to run and retire from the Senate among those who are likely to be in the minority. I test my theory using data from U.S. Senate elections from 1946 to 2018, demonstrating that minority party status matters in the U.S. Senate in very specific circumstances.[2] After discussing these results, I consider their broader implications for our understanding of minority party status in the U.S. Senate.

The Value of Minority Party Status in the World's Most Deliberative Body

Previous Perspectives on the U.S. Senate

Historically, research on the U.S. Senate focused on the power of individual senators in a body steeped with norms and traditions. In his work on the post–World War II Senate, Matthews (1960, 92) focuses on the importance of "folkways" in the body, which were rules for behavior that guided the actions of individual senators. For example, new senators were to act like "apprentices" and deferred to their senior colleagues; senators were supposed to devote considerable time to a single issue area and extend courtesy to their colleagues. This meant that senators not only respected one another, but also extended reciprocity to each other by voting for one another's proposals (Matthews 1960). At first glance, it seems that the Senate in this era was not a terrible place for a member of the minority party, something Sinclair (1989, 29) corroborates. However, Sinclair also notes that the large number of liberal northern Democrats elected starting in 1958 initially experienced significant frustration in realizing their policy goals, before galvanizing support to usher in the most successful era of progressive policymaking since the New Deal. Rather than change the institutions of the Senate, these senators were able to realize their influence by shifting "the institution's ideological center of gravity" (Sinclair 1989, 49). In other words, northern Democrats were able to amass a majority for their policy goals under existing Senate structures because of their large numbers. In the years between 1959 and 1969, Democrats not only had a majority, but also controlled at least 60 seats, which dampened the influence of southern conservatives in their caucus. Additionally, filibusters were rare and northern Democrats could sometimes rely on support from northern Republicans when needed, as was the case with civil rights legislation in the mid-1960s. This allowed for an era of productive policymaking for Senate liberals.

As the style of senators changed to become more public facing and floor-debate-oriented in the 1970s (Sinclair 1989), individual senators became more influential (Den Hartog and Monroe 2011). As quoted by Den Hartog and Monroe (2011, 29), Smith (1989, 348) notes that this was a period defined by "individualism and chaos" on the floor. Senators from both parties, such as Jesse Helms (R-NC) and Howard Metzenbaum (D-OH), used their individual power to force leadership to accede to their demands (Sinclair 1989, 140). Thus, minority party senators were able to wield considerable power not as a caucus, but as individuals, and leaders had to resort to unconventional strategies in order to move legislation through the body (Sinclair 1989, 2015). Senators assumed that the majority would remain with Democrats in this era and when the party lost control in 1980 amid Ronald Reagan's landslide victory over President Jimmy Carter, Democrats were shocked (Lee 2016).

The loss of majority control in 1980 precipitated two interlinked phenomena: an increasingly partisan Senate and one where majority control was frequently competitive. Considerable attention in the literature investigating this period centers on the rise of the filibuster and obstruction by the minority party in the Senate (e.g., Binder and Smith 1997; Wawro and Schickler 2006; Koger 2010; Smith 2014). Unlike in the House, Senate institutions give the minority party the ability to block the majority's priorities. Due to increased ideological divergence between the parties as partisan issues increasingly appeared on the Senate agenda, the minority increasingly took advantage of Senate rules to stymie the other party (Lee 2011). While major policy differences between the parties have been an important driver of the increased use of obstructive tactics like the filibuster, Lee (2016) argues that the other central feature defining this era, the competitiveness of Senate majority control, has itself further driven increased polarization and obstruction. She argues that competition for reelection causes members to think about the broader goal of party control, seeking to bolster the image of their party and tarnish that of their opponents. Thus, ironically, while each party now views majority control as important, the tools that they can use to undermine the other party cause the value of majority party status in the Senate to become less valuable. As Smith (2014) notes, the expectation is that the majority leader will stop the minority from offering amendments and the minority will prevent legislation from moving forward, rendering the institution dysfunctional.

An alternative framework presented by Den Hartog and Monroe (2011) suggests that one advantage the majority holds in the Senate relates to their agenda-setting powers. Specifically, they argue that the "consideration costs" (i.e., the sacrifices made to have proposals considered) paid by the majority are lower than those paid by the minority because the majority has agenda-setting powers (Den Hartog and Monroe 2011, 9–14). Senate procedures, they argue, advantage the majority at various stages of the legislative process. Offering evidence for their theory, they find that switches in majority control predict an almost 30 percentage point shift in the proportion of final passage votes that move policy to the left (Den Hartog and Monroe 2011, 172–73). When Republicans take control of the chamber, policy moves away from liberal priorities, while the opposite happens when Democrats assume the majority. In explaining their model, Den Hartog and Monroe (2011, 7) use the analogy of a football game, where the majority party is on offense and thus "is in a much better position to score," but they do not *always* score—and sometimes, the minority party scores. This stands in contrast to the House, where the majority typically succeeds. Similarly, in the context of the Senate appropriations process, Hanson (2014) finds that the power of the majority is greater than in some previous accounts, albeit limited by institutional rules. Thus, although there is debate over the extent to which the Senate majority has an advantage over the minority, any theory about its effect should account for this advantage being less than that of the House, but should also consider the fact that some considerable benefits remain for the Senate majority.

Should Senators Fear the Minority?

At their core, senators epitomize Schlesinger's ideal of the ambitious politician seeking to rise up the opportunity structure (Schlesinger 1966). Existing below only the presidency, (arguably) the vice-presidency, and possibly some powerful large state governorships, the Senate is effectively the penultimate rung on the ladder of political ambition. Of particular relevance here is that House members seek to rise to the next level of power by winning seats in the U.S. Senate. The Senate also represents the next logical step for many governors, as a senator retains more power than a number of state executives and the Senate does not have term limits, allowing a politician with static ambition to remain in this nearly top rung position for decades. Some even skip the intervening step of the House, as many statewide row officers (e.g., attorney general, lieutenant governor) and some large city mayors run for Senate. Sometimes a state legislator is able to win a Senate seat (e.g., Iowa's Joni Ernst in 2014), but this is relatively rare, albeit somewhat more common among state legislative leaders such as Speakers of the House including current Senators Thom Tillis (R-NC) and Jeff Merkley (D-OR).

Unlike the House, minority party status is not likely to be uniformly unpleasant for minority party senators. Most importantly, minority party senators are often able to play a role in policymaking. In the less partisan historical Senate, minority party senators were able to be part of positive policymaking efforts (i.e., passing new policies they supported) by adding amendments to bills and using the norms of the Senate to make deals with their colleagues that allowed them to advance their priorities. In the more partisan Senate of recent years, minority party senators can at least stop the majority party on many agenda items by using devices like the filibuster. The Senate majority has sought to expand its powers, although the institution's march toward majoritarianism has been halting at times. The Congressional Budget Act of 1974 gave additional powers to the majority party through the simple majority reconciliation process, which the Senate first used to pass a major policy program in 1981. However, the Senate scaled back this power with the establishment of the Byrd Rule in 1986, limiting reconciliation to budget-related items for existing programs once a year on each subject related to reconciliation (Sinclair 2015).[3] The Senate used reconciliation to pass major presidential priorities including the Clinton budget (1993), Bush tax cuts (2001 and 2003), the Affordable Care Act (2009), and the Trump tax cuts (2017). In terms of executive branch and judicial appointments, the majority party gained the power to confirm nominees using a simple majority in 2014, when the Democratic majority triggered the "nuclear option" for executive branch and lower court nominees. The subsequent Republican majority then expanded this power to include Supreme Court nominees in 2017. The current Senate is a combination of majoritarianism on court nominees and reconciliation bills, but remains supermajoritarian otherwise.

If the majority has an advantage in candidate quality, it is most likely to exist when majority party status has the potential to result in the passage of policy that divides the parties. Put differently, a candidate quality differential is most likely to exist when the Senate is likely to work similarly to the House. In the post–World War II era, the main period where a party had the ability to move policy in this manner was for Democrats from 1958 to 1966. The reason that the Democrats' majority was able to push policy in this era was because they won so many seats that the influx of liberal northern Democrats drowned out the voices of southern conservatives. Furthermore, Republicans in this period still held to old Senate norms and traditions and did not actively block Democrats when the party had the 50 votes needed to pass legislation. Indeed, on the issue that provoked the most obstruction—civil rights legislation—northern Republicans often provided the votes to help overcome southern Democratic obstruction. Democrats again had a supermajority in the mid-1970s, but senators had become less deferential to one another. Indeed, the Senate in 1975–76 had almost twice as many cloture votes as the four Congresses from 1959 to 1967 combined.[4] Democrats also came close to winning a sufficiently large supermajority in the 2008 elections, falling a seat short of being "filibuster proof," and later briefly had one from mid-2009 to early 2010 after Senator Arlen Specter of Pennsylvania changed parties to become a Democrat in early 2009. This soon became a distant memory after the election of Scott Brown in the Massachusetts special election in January 2010 to replace the late U.S. Senator Ted Kennedy (D-MA). Democrats lost six more seats in the November 2010 midterm elections. Thus, all else equal, the era in which majority party status (or rather, *effective* majority party status) would be most likely to produce a differential in candidate quality is from 1958 to 1966.

Minority party status is also likely to have a different effect on retirement in the Senate than it does in the House. The ability to block most policies they dislike, combined with having a longer time horizon than House members, is likely to diminish the retirement gap between majority and minority party senators. In the years immediately following World War II, senators knew that if they stuck around long enough, they would eventually amass the seniority necessary to gain influence in the body (Sinclair 1989, 29). In the 1970s, senators from both parties were able to exert their individual prerogative to halt policies they did not care for in the Senate. After the 1980s, the content of the Senate agenda became more partisan (Lee 2011) and minority party senators were more likely to find being on the losing side of issues to be unpleasant. Increased partisanship also meant that senators who lost were frequently on the losing side for multiple issues. For example, Republicans early in the Clinton administration no doubt did not enjoy being on the losing side of the Omnibus Budget Reconciliation Act of 1993, which raised taxes and passed solely with Democratic votes. Republicans also saw the Clinton crime bill—which included a temporary assault weapons ban—pass mostly with Democratic votes in 1994.[5] At the same time, however, Republicans were able to stop the Clinton health care plan during the 103rd Congress and, given recent history, could readily expect that they might be back in the Senate majority after the 1994 elections or relatively soon thereafter. In total, the experience of a post-1980 minority party senator is unlike that of a House member in the minority: they are able to play defense and occasionally score. They can also expect to return to offense relatively soon—soon at least given the time horizon of senators, who serve longer terms than do House members.

Should the prospect of minority party status cause a senator to retire, it would be because it removes some of the optimism that senator has to play a role in positive policymaking in the near future. One such group potentially lacking this optimism are the most senior minority party senators. The time horizon shifts for senators as they age. A 40-year-old minority party senator in the post-1980 era can reasonably expect that they will be able to play a role in setting the Senate's agenda in the not too distant future. A 75-year-old minority party senator, however, cannot as easily have this expectation and may instead decide to retire rather than spend another six years on defense. All senators, majority or minority, feel the grind of constant partisanship, but—consistent with Den Hartog and Monroe (2011)—the benefits of agenda-setting power mean that the majority is more likely to be able to pass its policy objectives than is the minority. Thus, I expect that majority party status is less likely to affect incumbent retirement decisions than in the House, but when it does, it is most likely to affect senior minority party senators in the post-1980 era.

A Measure of the Likelihood of Being in the Senate Minority

Before testing whether the prospect of minority party status affects the behavior of senators, I first modify the measure introduced in chapter 2 for House elections. I again use an OLS regression where the dependent variable measures the percentage of seats held by the president's party. As with the House model, I include a measure of the president's approval in the first Gallup Poll after May 1 of that election year and the change in real disposable income from the second quarter of the year before the election to the second quarter of the election year. I modify the midterm variable so that it signifies a president's second midterm. As discussed by Mayhew (2014), a president's second midterm is likely to be far worse for them in the Senate than their first midterm due to the "Six-Year Itch," a phenomenon whereby presidents tend to lose far more Senate seats in their second midterm due to growing fatigue with the president's party. The senators who are up in this election won as the president swept to their initial victory and now may lose as presidential approval wanes. Indeed, the only post–World War II two-term president to suffer more Senate seat losses in his first midterm than his second was Bill Clinton. George W. Bush and Donald Trump actually saw Republicans *gain* seats in their first midterm election. Finally, while I include the previous overall number of seats as a variable, I also include a measure of the number of ongoing seats that the president's party holds. These variables account for the fact that a party is more likely to win the majority if they hold a relatively large number of seats that are *not* up and that the number of seats won in a Senate class by a party is likely to remain relatively constant from one election to another under normal circumstances. All of these variables attain significance and my model has an adjusted R^2 value of almost 0.86.

TABLE 6.1. OLS model of Senate outcomes

Variable	U.S. Senate (1946–2018)
Previous Seats in Class	0.379*
	(0.108)
Ongoing Seats	0.918*
	(0.084)
Approval	0.086*
	(0.039)
Change in Income	0.998*
	(0.220)
Sixth-Year Itch	−4.408*
	(1.329)
Intercept	4.491
	(3.870)
Adjusted R^2	0.859
N	37

*$p < 0.05$; dependent variable measures percentage of seats won. Summary statistics in appendix.

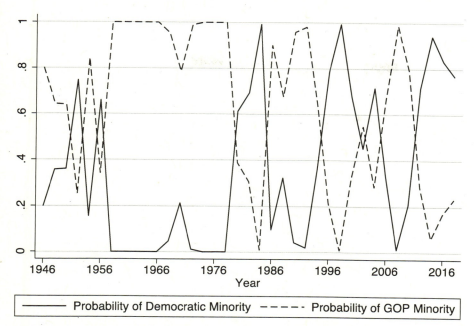

Figure 6.1. Probability of minority party status by party, 1946–2018

As with my analysis of the House, I use postregression predicted values from an OLS regression to obtain an estimate of how likely it is that the president's party will win the majority in the Senate. For incumbents from the president's party, one minus this probability serves as an estimate of how likely it is that their party will be in the minority in the next Senate. For incumbents of the party not holding the White House, this probability serves as an estimate that they will be in the minority. For the candidate quality models, I take the opposite because the unit of analysis centers on the party not currently holding the seat.[6]

In figure 6.1, I display the independent variable over time for each party. Broadly, this graph shows a competitive majority before 1956 and after 1980 and a solid hold on majority control for Democrats in between these two periods. As with the House, this measure has a stronger correlation with flips in majority control than seat margins alone, 0.70 compared to -0.22 for the seat margin measure (i.e., parties with larger majorities are slightly less likely to lose majority control than those with narrow majorities).

Assessing Candidate Emergence Patterns and Retirement Decisions for the U.S. Senate

Having constructed my key independent variable, I build my main models for this chapter. Using random effects logistic regression models, my dependent variables measure retirement decisions and candidate quality over the period from 1946 to 2018. In creating a measure of candidate quality, I look at those candidates for whom a run for Senate represents a logical next step up the ladder of political ambition. In this measure, I designate out-party candidates who have won a statewide office, a seat in Congress, or a large-city mayoral election as quality candidates.[7] I fine-tune the candidate quality measure for the Senate because 57.8 percent of out-party Senate candidates have held *some* elective office, with these contenders varying from local officeholders and state legislators to House members and statewide elected officials. My control variables in these models are consistent with those in the House chapters. Specifically, in both models I control for the presidential vote lean, number of terms served, ideological extremism, and whether the seat is located in the South. In the two candidate entry models, I control for whether the incumbent senator for the seat is retiring. Finally, I control for the senator's age in the retirement models.

TABLE 6.2. Senate candidate entry decisions

Variable	All Seats	1946–1956 and 1968–2018	1946–1956 and 1968–2018, Without South	1958–1966, Without South
Probability of Party in Minority	−0.642*	−0.351	−0.095	−1.713*
	(0.177)	(0.200)	(0.224)	(0.731)
Seat in South	−0.447*	−0.293	—	—
	(0.170)	(0.176)		
Presidential Vote Lean	−0.071*	−0.081*	−0.069*	−0.079
	(0.009)	(0.010)	(0.012)	(0.051)
Retiring	1.198*	1.199*	1.141*	1.374
	(0.172)	(0.183)	(0.205)	(0.798)
Terms	−0.159*	−0.144*	−0.120*	−0.326
	(0.049)	(0.052)	(0.059)	(0.256)
Ideological Extremism	0.869*	0.656	0.264	2.556
	(0.420)	(0.469)	(0.523)	(1.616)
Constant	−0.485	−0.620	−0.643	−0.342
	(0.422)	(0.423)	(0.434)	(0.690)
N	1,277	1,100	859	138
Log-likelihood	−735.235	−636.720	−513.837	−80.992

*$p < 0.05$, dependent variable measures whether quality candidate runs

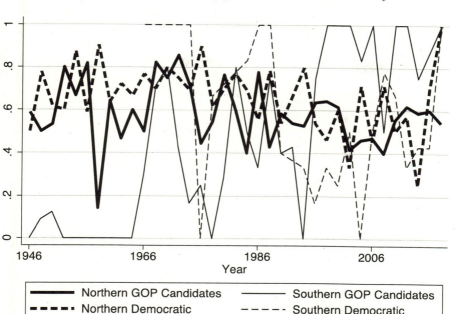

Figure 6.2. Candidate quality by region and party

I find a statistically significant relationship between the probability of minority status and the entry of a quality candidate over the entire period. However, this result does not tell the entire story. Two sets of seats are driving this finding: southern seats, particularly in the Solid South era, and, as suggested by my theory, all seats from 1958 to 1966. Consistent with my findings in chapter 4, I consider the poor state of southern Republicans' bench in the mid-20th century when examining the entry of quality candidates in the South. As one can see in figure 6.2, there is a huge gap in candidate quality in the South in the years immediately after World War II. The lack of potential Republican candidates in the offices below senator drives this finding. In most southern states, there were either no or few living current or former Republican House members, governors, row officers, or large city mayors. Thus, before the 1970s, almost *no* contest in the South featured a quality Republican out-party candidate regardless of whether the GOP looked likely to capture the Senate majority. As figure 6.2 shows, however, there was a smaller, but still consistently meaningful gap in candidate quality in the *North* between 1958 and 1966. My theory would suggest that this was driven by the fact that the confluence of large

Democratic majorities and senators' willingness to accede to Senate norms allowed liberals to dominate policymaking, making prospective Democratic candidates from the region more likely to want to run and pass what they viewed to be good public policies.

To investigate these findings further, I ran several additional models. First, I looked at all seats in years *other* than the period from 1958 to 1966. In this model, the coefficient for the minority party measure drops slightly below the standard 0.05 threshold for significance (p=0.080). Further, when one examines only northern Senate seats in this period (i.e., all years besides 1958–66), no discernable relationship exists between the minority party measure and quality candidate entry. In contrast, when one looks at entry decisions in northern Senate seats between 1958 and 1966, a significant relationship exists between the probability of minority party status and quality candidate entry decisions. A seat where the out-party candidate had a 0 percent chance of being in the minority should they win (effectively, a Republican-held seat) saw a 52.2 percent chance of featuring an out-party quality candidate. In contrast, one where the candidate from the out-party had a 100 percent chance of being in the minority (i.e., a seat held by a Democrat) had a 24.5 percent chance of having a quality candidate (see figure 6.3). Considering the substantially smaller number of observations in this period compared to the entire universe of Senate elections in this dataset (and the effect of sample size on standard errors), this result provides strong support for my theory. This result suggests that the period in which the effect of expected minority party status affected Senate candidate entry decisions most similarly to House candidates was when the Senate's ability to efficiently pass ideologically charged policy was most like that of the House. Finally, other individual years in which Democrats had the potential to gain (or keep) enough seats to substantially alter public policy in a manner that divided the parties along ideological lines, such as 1974, 1976, and 2008, also feature a substantial gap in candidate quality between the parties. For example, Democrats nominated quality candidates in 35 percent of seats they did not currently hold in 2008, compared to only 16.7 percent for Republicans. The candidate entry patterns in these years adds to the evidence provided by the 1958–66 model to demonstrate that differences in candidate quality are most likely to emergence when a majority is large enough to overcome the obstacles presented by the institutions meant to slow down policymaking in the Senate.

Next, I examine the effect of minority party status on Senate retirement decisions. Senators have a longer time horizon than House members based upon their longer terms. Additionally, party control of the Senate

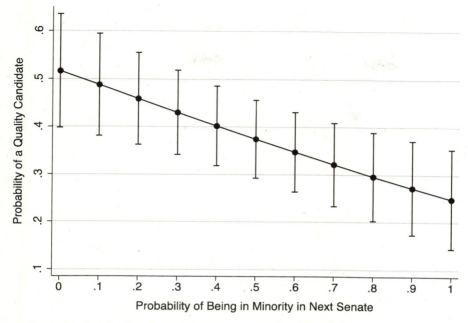

Figure 6.3. Candidate entry decisions in nonsouthern Senate seats, 1958–1966

has switched more frequently than the House, so one might not expect the prospect of minority party status to predict a retirement decision. Nevertheless, a significant relationship exists between the probability of minority status and retirement decisions (see table 6.3). Like the candidate entry result, however, a specific set of senators in a specific period drives this finding—the most senior senators late in the time series. In chapter 2, I found that the retirement of longtime Democratic members who were in a position to become committee or subcommittee chairs, as well as increased retirement among Republicans who saw committee leadership as being out of reach, powered the significant relationship between the probability of minority party status and retirement decisions in the pre-Reform Congress.

A similar dynamic is present here, but for a different period. Based upon the expectations from my theory regarding time horizons and age in the post-1980 Senate, I examine the relationship between a senator's age and retirement decisions.[8] In the pre-1980 Senate, no significant relationship exists. This is unsurprising considering that minority party senators in this era still generally had a substantial role in policymaking. After 1980,

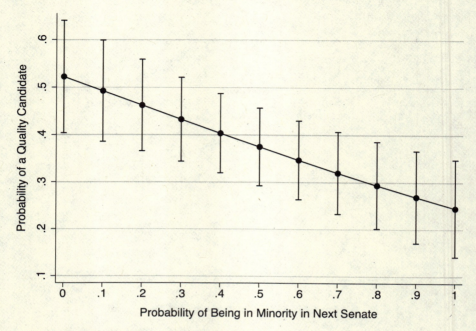

Figure 6.4. Senate retirement decisions, 1946–2018

however, the interaction between age and the probability of being in the minority has a positive relationship with retirement decisions. This relationship becomes even stronger if one narrows the period to 1994 to 2018. A 60-year-old senator, who falls just below the average age for a senator in this period, is no less likely to run for reelection as the probability of being in the minority increases, while a 40-year-old senator is actually *less* likely to retire as the probability of minority party status increases. However, the probability of a retirement for an 80-year-old senator dramatically increases as the probability of being in the minority goes up. An 80-year-old senator who is all but guaranteed to be in the majority has a 8.5 percent chance of retiring, *below* that of their younger copartisans, compared to a 55.9 percent chance of a retirement for an 80-year-old senator who is fated to the minority. Returning to the opening vignette for this chapter, this dynamic helps explain the numerous retirements by Democratic senators in 1996 and the few Republicans who retired that year. Channeling Den Hartog and Monroe (2011), senators such as Ted Stevens (R-AK) and Strom Thurmond (R-SC) knew that they would be able to not only be on offense, but that they would be able to help lead their team. Democratic senators of the

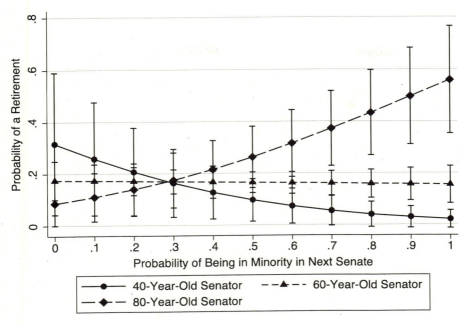

Figure 6.5. Senatorial retirement decisions and age, 1994–2018

TABLE 6.3. Senate retirement decisions

Variable	Entire Period	1946–80	1982–2018	1994–2018
Probability of Party in Minority	0.567*	−2.391	−5.826*	−9.455*
	(0.230)	(2.108)	(2.203)	(2.955)
Age	0.052*	0.059*	−0.019	−0.044
	(0.011)	(0.021)	(0.023)	(0.030)
Probability of Party in Minority *Age	—	0.043	0.101*	0.155*
		(0.033)	(0.035)	(0.045)
Presidential Vote Lean	−0.018	0.021	−0.051*	−0.051*
	(0.011)	(0.017)	(0.018)	(0.019)
Terms	0.077	−0.106	0.257	0.182
	(0.070)	(0.119)	(0.174)	(0.114)
Seat in South	0.045	−0.337	0.246	0.298
	(0.206)	(0.359)	(0.287)	(0.327)
Ideological Extremism	1.258*	0.748	2.356*	1.293
	(0.542)	(0.714)	(1.060)	(1.191)
Constant	−5.510*	−5.689*	−2.268*	1.800
	(0.805)	(1.376)	(1.640)	(1.821)
N	1,277	626	651	413
Log-likelihood	−506.671	−224.556	−267.621	−170.009

*$p < 0.05$, dependent variable measures whether a senator retires

same age did not have the same starring role and were less likely than were their younger colleagues to be able to wait things out until they returned to the majority.

A Note on 2018

Before discussing the broader implications of these results, I briefly detail how retirement and candidate entry patterns from 2018 depart somewhat from what one might expect based on results for other generally similar years. Republicans had strong, although not certain odds of keeping the Senate in 2018. In 2016, when the Democratic Party had a similar probability of minority party status, three Democratic senators who were at least 75 years old on Election Day—Harry Reid (D-NV), Barbara Boxer (D-CA), and Barbara Mikulski (D-MD)—decided to retire.[9] Thus, one might expect at least *some* retirements among older members of the party's caucus. In 2018, however, not a single Democratic senator retired, including 85-year-old Dianne Feinstein and 76-year-old Bill Nelson. (Voters later retired Nelson.) Democrats also ran a strong slate of quality Senate candidates ranging from House members like Jacky Rosen (D-NV), Kyrsten Sinema (D-AZ), and Beto O'Rourke (D-TX) to 75-year-old former Governor Phil Bredesen (D-TN). Senate Democrats' retirement and candidate entry patterns were like those of a party that was likely to have lots of power after the next election, rather than that of an underdog.

To explain this result, I turn to a comment made in an interview with a House member. Based on this interview, I believe that Donald Trump played a large role in the dynamics of these decisions in 2018. This legislator spoke of an "all hands on deck" mentality for dealing with Trump among Democratic legislators, and for the first two years of the Trump administration, the Senate was the only chamber that was able to serve as a check.[10] Thus, even though Majority Leader McConnell was able to shepherd judges and Trump administration appointees through the chamber, Democratic senators were able to stop a number of conservative legislative priorities including the repeal of the Affordable Care Act.[11] However, besides stopping run-of-the-mill conservative policies, I took the comment from this interviewee to go even further. Democrats believed that Trump represented an existential threat to American democracy and they needed to check his power. In the House, running again meant quite possibly being in the majority after 2018. In the Senate, however, it meant that one would probably be in the minority. However, Democrats believed it was still important to run in order to minimize Republicans' advantage in the chamber. For an older senator, running again (and winning) meant that they could use their expertise and ranking member position on important committees to check the administration. As a result, every Democratic senator ran for another term in 2018, regardless of age, electoral vulnerability, or other factors. In 2020, only a single Senate Democrat decided to retire, compared to three Republicans, suggesting that this dynamic may have continued into the next election cycle.

Understanding the Effects of Minority Party Status on Legislators

In this chapter, I sought not only to answer the question of *whether* minority party status affected the behavior of senators and potential Senate candidates, but *which* politicians are most affected. Broadly, it seems that likely minority party status strongly influences some politicians, while others feel little effect. The two groups of politicians who were most affected by the prospect of minority party status were candidates in the North in the period where liberals passed an array of policy goals ranging from Medicare to the Civil Rights Act and older senators in recent years. A trait shared by both of these groups is their ability to push for positive policy change. A new Democratic senator in the majority in the early 1960s and a senior majority party senator in the post-1980 Senate have greater potential to push for positive policy change than does a minority party politician opposite them. The experience of a minority party senator in either of these circumstances comes closest among senators to approximating the misery felt more broadly by minority party House members under conditional party government. The typical senator, however, does not experience the same amount of unpleasantness as does a House member, or at least knows that they will be able to get back on offense fairly soon, mitigating the effect of minority party status (Den Hartog and Monroe 2011).

The results from this chapter also have important implications for our understanding of how the prospect of minority party status affects the opportunity structure for senators and those politicians who may want to become senators. Minority party status generally distorts the opportunity structure less than it does in the House. When the Senate is most likely to be able to pass policies efficiently, there are more quality candidates from the likely majority and fewer from the likely minority than one might otherwise expect, but these circumstances are rare. A progressively ambitious House member or governor will often decide to run for the Senate if that is their next political goal. Minority party status altered the static ambition of the very oldest senators in recent years, but the typical senator over the period is generally unaffected. In total, it seems that when a politician has a latent desire to run for Senate, but for specific cases, they will act on their ambitions regardless of whether they are likely to be in the minority. As a result, more voters are given the ability to support a quality out-party Senate candidate than in House elections, leading to more competitive Senate elections overall. Ultimately, more frequent turnover in party control of the body occurs as the minority leaves fewer seats on the table in bad years, making it easier to gain the seats necessary to win the majority in the next good year. The results presented in this chapter are not entirely rosy for democratic competition—after all, several subsets of Senate seats are affected by the prospects of minority party status—but it seems that the institutions of the upper chamber cause the effects of minority party status to become less widespread across Senate seats than in the House.

SEVEN

Laboratories of Ambition? The Legislative Minority in U.S. States

I had a front row seat to the apocalypse.
—Anonymous former minority party state legislator

Ellie Kinnaird had enough. The eight-term Democratic North Carolina state senator who represented the area around progressive college town Chapel Hill decided that it was time to resign from the state legislature after suffering through the 2013 long session.[1] Among other things, this legislative session had seen the repeal of the Racial Justice Act (which had put an effective moratorium on the death penalty in North Carolina), the passage of a photo ID requirement to vote, a budget that included major cuts to the University of North Carolina system, and the nationally derided motorcycle helmet and abortion ban bill-in-one (Kinnaird 2013; Binker and Leslie 2013).[2]

In announcing her decision to resign, Kinnaird said the following:

> What led me to this decision are the actions taken by the Republican majority in the legislature that has been a shocking reversal of the many progressive measures that I and many others have worked so hard to enact: measures that over the years had made North Carolina a model of moderate-to-progressive, pro-business but also pro-people public policy in the South. From the Republicans' denial of health care security for our people to their failure

to promote a vibrant work force through support for our education systems at all levels and from their tax cuts for the wealthy and
their tax increases for the poor and middle class to their efforts to
deny people their right to vote, they have been pursuing a divisive
and, I think, immoral agenda. The needless pain and suffering the
Republicans have brought upon us that I have written about add up
to a huge setback for North Carolinians from all walks of life. My
own personal sadness is the dismantling of my environmental, social
justice and death penalty efforts. (Kinnaird 2013)

In an interview with local news station WRAL, Kinnaird elaborated
further, calling her experience in the legislative minority "heartbreaking"
and saying that while she had "done good things," she could not "do it anymore under these circumstances" (Binker and Leslie 2013). Taken at face
value, Senator Kinnaird's stated reasons for retiring are largely in keeping
with the findings from chapter 2 of this book for the U.S. House of Representatives. As a minority party member, Senator Kinnaird's experience in a
legislative body was miserable, so she decided to retire. Crucial differences
exist, however, between the U.S. Congress and the North Carolina Senate.
For one thing, being a North Carolina state legislator is not a full-time
job, and many legislators (including Senator Kinnaird) live close enough to
the state capital to commute from home when in session. Further, having
completed the "long session" in 2013, Senator Kinnaird would have had
to spend only several months at the North Carolina Capitol the following year for the 2014 "short session." Yet Senator Kinnaird had decided
that it was not worth it to continue serving, and submitted her resignation.
Instead, she said she would focus on registering voters in advance of the
competitive 2014 U.S. Senate election between Senator Kay Hagan (D-
NC) and Republican North Carolina House Speaker Thom Tillis (Binker
and Leslie 2013).

Senator Kinnaird's decision highlights the broader dynamics surrounding minority party legislators—particularly those who are white and female.
In the instance of the North Carolina Senate, many of Senator Kinnaird's
Democratic colleagues soon left the North Carolina Senate—particularly
her white colleagues. In 2013, eight of the 17 Democratic North Carolina
state senators were white and nine were Black. Of these 17 senators, only
five remained in the North Carolina Senate as of early 2020.[3] However,
four of those five who remained were Black and the fifth, Mike Woodard
of Durham, won his seat in 2012 after Democrats had already lost control
of the state legislature. One of the four Black Democrats still serving as of

early 2020, Senate Minority Leader Dan Blue, served in the North Carolina Senate when Democrats were still in the majority, and a second, Gladys Robinson of Greensboro, first won her seat in 2010 when the chamber flipped to Republicans for the first time since Reconstruction. Several of the white Democrats who left did so to pursue other offices—Josh Stein resigned for a successful run for North Carolina attorney general, while Dan Clodfelter (briefly) became mayor of Charlotte.[4]

In this chapter, I examine the effect of minority party status on state legislators and candidates. I theorize that, similar to Congress, state legislators are more likely to leave office and quality candidates are less likely to run when they can expect to serve in the minority in the next session of the legislature. I begin by discussing existing perspectives on the minority party in state legislative bodies, drawing on these perspectives to apply my theory of minority party status to the states. Next, I apply my measure of competitiveness to state legislative elections, using this measure to examine the emergence of quality candidates in the 2012 and 2014 elections. My results are surprising. I find that quality candidates are actually *more* likely to run as the probability that they will be in the minority increases. Using qualitative data from interviews, I seek to explain this surprising result and then examine the dynamics surrounding retirement decisions in these years. These interviews revealed that the prospect of minority party status at the state level affects retirement decisions to some extent, but that gender and race also play a significant role in these decisions. As one female legislator put it to me, there exists a "minority in the minority." Finally, I discuss implications of this finding for future research on the role of minority party status on elected politicians.

Minority Party Status and State Legislatures

Existing Research on the Minority Party

The status of the political minority in U.S. states has been an important concern for scholars since at least the mid-1900s, when V. O. Key wrote his landmark work on southern states (Key 1949). In this period, Republicans did not exist as an organized party in most parts of the region. As a result, ambitious politicians who sought office did not do so as Republicans, making the Democratic primary the real election. A Republican leader, Key (1949, 292) wrote, could not "entertain[s] seriously the notion that his party will during his lifetime gain control of his state government." Key's study is crucial in establishing that (seemingly) permanent minority party status is an important feature of parties in state government and that this has effects on the behavior of elected politicians. The response to perpetual minority party status can vary considerably based on how unpleasant the experience is for minority party legislators. Looking at southern parties in the 1980s, Harmel (1986, 739) finds that "perceptions of poor treatment" can cause minority party legislators to more formally organize in opposition to the majority. Despite such organizational efforts, a small minority party is unlikely to gain much traction in a legislative body to influence policy. Martorano (2004) found that the minority party tends to have more procedural rights when the majority party's seat advantage is narrow in a state legislature, granting the minority more influence in the decision-making process.

Increased polarization in the states also affects the experience of a minority party legislator, with procedural advantages for the majority heightening this gap. Kim and Phillips (2009, 135) argue that majority party status is valuable in the states, but only in legislatures that are "procedurally partisan." Similarly, Clark (2015, 9) argues that both partisanship and the "institutional prerogatives" of the majority determine the extent of the influence of the majority party. Other studies focus specifically on the role of conditional party government when looking at the role of party influence in state legislatures. Extending this theory of party influence in Congress, Aldrich and Battista (2002) show that there is substantial variation in the extent to which states exhibit the characteristics of conditional party government (also see Bianco and Sened 2005). They also find that polarized legislatures have committees that are more representative of the chamber, acting more "policy-oriented" than "distributive" (Aldrich and Battista 2002, 169). In other words, when polarization exists and parties seek to influence the process to advantage their ability to achieve policy successes, committees are more likely to reflect the overall partisan divisions of the chamber. This is costly to the minority party, as a partisan advantage on committees in a polarized chamber is likely to pass policies that favor the majority.

Party competition often breeds polarization, although there are some cases of extreme polarization in states that lack competition. Drawing on Key (1949), Aldrich and Battista (2002) argue that the extent to which there is party competition in elections is an important precursor of polarization. Similarly, Hinchliffe and Lee (2015, 172) use five different measures of party competition ranging from "the number of recent shifts in party control" to "the ratio of Republicans to Democrats in the electorate" to demonstrate a relationship between increased party competition and high polarization. Nevertheless, there are some state legislative bodies that are highly polarized and, practically speaking, not particularly competitive in terms of likely shifts in party control. In their study of state-level polarization, Shor and McCarty (2011) find that the most polarized state is—by a fair distance—California, followed by Washington, Colorado, Michigan, and Arizona. While some of these states, such as Colorado and Washington, exhibited high levels of competition for majority control in this era, nobody reasonably could expect a change in party control in California or Arizona in this period.[5] Despite this discordance, there is an important distinction between southern minority parties in the Key era and a perpetual legislative minority like 2000s-era California Republicans. In the 1960s, southern Republicans held no more than a handful of seats and left many others uncontested, while a present-day perpetual minority still usually holds *some* seats in the legislature and contests many others, despite not having any real chance at winning the majority.[6]

A Theory of Minority Party Status in State Legislatures

State legislative elections feature a combination of ambitious politicians and political amateurs, each leaving their mark on public policymaking. Some politicians run for state office because they see it as the next step on the political ladder. Local politicians such as mayors or county commissioners might seek to win a position in a state legislature because they see it as winnable, positioning them well to win a statewide office or seat in Congress in the future. State legislative offices are also low enough on the political opportunity structure that some aspiring ambitious politicians may also seek them as their initial foray into electoral politics. At the same time, some individuals may run for state legislature because they see winning a seat as a way to influence policy in their state, but they might not want to run for a higher office. With many legislatures only meeting for a few weeks to a few months in a year, these people are still able to retain much of their identity as a nonpolitician. While the motivations surrounding both sets of individuals are important and, as I argue below, minority party status may influence each group, progressively ambitious politicians are of particular interest to this study. These politicians may have experienced what it is like to be in the minority in local government, although this is less likely than for politicians in higher levels of government. More pressingly, though, the supply of these politicians is important for creating a *bench* for a political party to draw from for higher offices. Thus, there are both conceptual and normative reasons to look at the entry decisions of local politicians who have previously won an office.

As at the national level, minority party status is likely to be unpleasant for state legislative politicians, affecting their decisions to run for and remain in office. State legislators, like members of Congress, attain influence in the body when their party is in the majority. Being in the majority allows them to gain influence on committees and on the floor, giving them the opportunity to shepherd legislation through the chamber and see their policy priorities become law. Also similar to Congress, state legislators frequently cast roll call votes, with the minority often having the unpleasant experience of ending up on the losing side of votes. One crucial difference exists between state legislatures and Congress—the amount of time spent in session and voting on issues. Most state legislators in the minority party lose on far fewer votes per year than do members of Congress. Fewer total votes typically take place in state legislatures given the length of state legislative sessions compared to that of Congress, causing the feeling of losing to be less widespread and potentially reducing the urge to pull back from elective politics.

Not all states disempower the minority party to the same degree, however, so I expect minority party status to exert a stronger force on politicians when there is conditional party government. Particularly in the past, some states exhibited the "distributive" model discussed by Aldrich and Battista (2002). Indeed, in some states, minority party legislators sometimes even served as committee chairs (Hamilton and Smith 2012). As in Congress, however, polarization has generally increased at the state level, although some variation still exists (Shor and McCarty 2011). In those states where polarization is highest, I expect differences in candidate entry and retirement to be starkest. These politicians are most likely to view the experience of being in the minority as unpleasant and pull back from electoral politics.

Applying the Measure of Minority Party Prospects to the U.S. States

To analyze how likely minority party status affects state-level politicians, I use a combination of quantitative and qualitative analysis. Candidate emergence lends itself well to quantitative analysis, while qualitative interviews help provide a window into retirement decisions. Existing legislators, of course, were candidates at one point in their career; I also interviewed several unsuccessful candidates who ran for state legislature. It is difficult, however, to determine the correct population to draw from when looking at candidates who considered running, but ultimately did not run, so looking at broad emergence patterns provides the best approach to analyzing candidate entry decisions. At the federal level, publications such as *Roll Call* are helpful in identifying these individuals, but there is far less reporting on entry decisions at the state legislative level. Interviews, however, add important context to my findings on candidate entry.

At the same time, term limits make an analysis of retirement decisions at the state level less straightforward than for federal legislators. It is difficult to know if a term-limited legislator would have retired anyway if their state did not have term limits, or if the looming presence of term limits made a non-term-limited legislator decide to retire a term before they had to leave. I include a model of retirement decisions for state legislators in states without term limits that did not undergo redistricting; as a whole, however, my examination of retirement decisions focuses on first-person accounts.

Measurement of Competitiveness at the State Legislative Level

Before proceeding, I apply my measure of minority party prospects to state legislative chambers. In this chapter, I focus on state politicians in the 2012 and 2014 elections, the two elections immediately following the post-2010 redistricting. State legislative elections, particularly in this period, provide a good window into the role of likely minority party status for several reasons. First, state elections allow one to leverage the fact that the probability of minority party status varies in different state chambers across the country at the same point in time. Second, this period represents one of substantial change in state politics. These two cycles transpired in the immediate aftermath of the 2010 elections, which saw Republicans flip 20 state legislative chambers, with many of these going from either solidly Democratic or competitive to solidly Republican in a single election cycle (Ballotpedia 2010). Using these newfound gains to their advantage, Republicans were then able to draw redistricting maps in many states that cemented their majorities. Thus, an examination of these cycles allows one to examine how Democratic state legislators began to adjust to life in the minority.

Before analyzing how likely minority party status affects state politicians' decision to run for a legislative body, I construct my measure of how likely it is that a state legislative politician would be in the minority in the next legislative session. As foretold by the large number of measures used by Hinchliffe and Lee (2015), the measurement of competition at the state level has long been a central concern of state politics researchers. Historically, scholars used the folded Ranney Index, measured based on the proportion of seats held by each party in the state legislature, the closeness of the most recent gubernatorial election, and the amount of time each party controlled each of these institutions, to measure competition at the state level (Ranney 1976). However, this measure looks at the overall political climate of a state rather than the competition of a specific institution. Some states, such as Massachusetts, have seen frequent close elections for governor with repeated shifts between the parties, while exhibiting little competition for state legislative control. Other states, such as Washington, have seen just the opposite.[7] Seeking to improve upon this measure, Holbrook and Van Dunk (1993) construct a measure of district-level competition based upon the closeness of legislative elections. As discussed above, other scholars have used a wide array of other measures (see Hinchliffe and Lee 2015; also see Curiel 2019 for an inventive new measure). That the measurement of state legislative competition has received such a great degree of attention in the literature demonstrates the importance of carefully justifying the measure that one is to use.

As with federal institutions, I construct this measure by using postregression predicted values from an OLS regression where the dependent variable is the percentage of seats in a legislative body held by the president's party (i.e., for this period, Democrats). I focus on candidate entry in states with single-member first-past-the-post elections occurring in these years, so I cannot include every state chamber in my analysis.[8] For the sake of consistency, I include the chambers that I examine in my candidate entry models in these OLS regressions. I use separate models for 2012 and 2014, with the same independent variables in each model. These measures include the percentage of seats held by the president's party (i.e., Democrats) after the previous election (either 2010 or 2012), President Obama's average approval in that state as measured by Gallup in 2012 or 2014, and the state's change in personal income at the end of the second quarter from the year before the election (2011 or 2013) to the end of the second quarter in the election year (2012 or 2014, see table 7.1). The number of seats before the election and presidential approval strongly correlate with outcomes, while the change in income does not attain significance. Overall, these models are an excellent predictor of legislative outcomes with an adjusted R^2 of above 0.9 for both years. By including presidential approval, this measure improves upon only looking at previous Democratic strength. In these years, Democrats did well in states where President Obama was popular, while losing ground in states where he was less popular.[9]

Two central features define legislative chambers in this era: (1) the overall lack of competitiveness and (2) Republican dominance in terms of the percentage of all chambers that they control. As displayed in table 7.1, the vast majority of chambers in my sample (76%) in this period had either a greater than a 90 percent—or less than 10 percent—probability of having a Democratic majority after the next election. Further, in more than half of all chambers in my study (52%), Democrats had a less than 10 percent probability of winning the majority. Democrats had somewhat better prospects in 2012 than 2014, but even in the former year, which saw President Obama win reelection over Republican candidate Mitt Romney by 4 percentage points in the national popular vote, Democrats had less than a 10 percent chance of winning the majority in 45 percent of chambers. In this era, it is clear that the Republican Party is generally dominant in state legislative elections. Indeed, even after the 2018 elections—which saw Democrats win many governorships and flip a number of state legislative chambers—most swing states retained Republican majorities in both legislative chambers.

A Quantitative Analysis of the Effects of Minority Party Status in the 2012 and 2014 State Legislative Elections

To examine the effect of minority party status on candidate entry decisions in the 2012 and 2014 elections, I construct random effects logistic regression models for each election year, with random effects by state chamber (e.g., the California Assembly). In each of these models, the dependent variable measures whether the out-party candidate previously had won elective office. While originally designed for congressional elections, Van

TABLE 7.1. Models of state legislative outcomes in 2012 and 2014

Variable	2012	2014
Percentage of Seats before Election	0.789*	0.825*
	(0.056)	(0.040)
Presidential Approval	0.541*	0.344*
	(0.120)	(0.093)
Change in Income	0.110	0.810
	(0.403)	(0.674)
Intercept	−14.615*	−11.769*
	(4.912)	(3.571)
Adjusted R^2	0.909	0.945
N	64	67

*$p < 0.05$, dependent variable measures percentage of seats won by Democrats

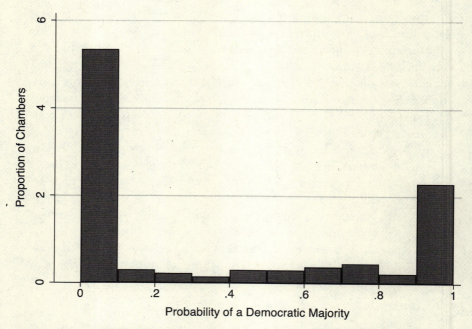

Figure 7.1. Minority party status and state legislative chambers in 2012 and 2014

Dunk (1997) used this metric in a study of candidate emergence at the state level. This is an imperfect measure for candidate quality at the state level, given that fewer offices exist below state legislator than do those below member of Congress, but it taps into the same concept of political experience as when used for higher offices. To assess further the robustness of this measure, I asked a number of state-level interviewees what characterizes a quality candidate. Previous elective office was one—but not the only—characteristic mentioned by interviewees. Other features interviewees mentioned, including being a "good public speaker" and "having emotional intelligence," are much harder to conceptualize than Jacobson's (1989) dichotomous measure. Additionally, in this context, the Jacobson measure captures those who are ambitious officeholders, seeking to move up to the next level of electoral politics after having attained some other, typically lower office.[10] Thus, I proceed with my analysis using this measure.

The independent variables in my models are similar to those for federal institutions in other chapters, modified to fit state legislative electoral politics. Like previous chapters, in both year's models I include a measure of the district's 2012 presidential vote as compared to the country as a whole, whether there is an incumbent running for the seat, if a first-term incumbent is running, and if the seat is located in the South. For 2014, I also measure whether redistricting took place for the seat since the most recent election.[11] Given the significant variation that exists across states in terms of legislative professionalism, I include Squire's (2015) updated measure of the concept. Finally, given the relative standing of state senates compared to state houses, I include a dummy variable for whether the chamber is an upper chamber.

My results here are surprising. In both years, I find a statistically significant, but *positive* relationship between a party's prospects for minority party status and the probability that they run a quality candidate. In 2012, going from all-but-assured majority party status to near-certain minority party status results in an increase in the proportion of quality candidates from 11.2 percent to 14.3 percent. A comparable change in 2014 results in a slightly larger substantive change, with the proportion of seats featuring quality candidates increasing from 9.3 percent to 13.5 percent.[12] In addition to the minority party status variable, many of the control variables attain significance. Open seats, those with first-term incumbents, and upper chambers have more quality candidates run, while those located in

TABLE 7.2. State legislative candidate entry in the 2012 and 2014 elections

Variable	2012	2014
Probability of Minority Party Status	0.314*	0.496*
	(0.137)	(0.130)
Presidential Vote Lean	−0.062*	−0.069*
	(0.005)	(0.005)
Incumbent Not Running	0.914*	1.120*
	(0.128)	(0.133)
First-Term Incumbent	0.572*	0.629*
	(0.123)	(0.119)
Located in South	−0.536*	−0.791*
	(0.238)	(0.252)
Redistricted Seat	—	0.346*
		(0.263)
Legislative Professionalism	1.731*	0.316
	(0.864)	(0.674)
Upper Chamber	0.424*	0.440*
	(0.190)	(0.183)
Constant	−2.403*	−2.294*
	(0.285)	(0.228)
N	3,885	4,331
Log-Likelihood	−1328.022	−1361.508

*$p < 0.05$, dependent variable measures whether candidate from party not holding seat is quality candidate

the South and those that lean more heavily to the in-party in terms of presidential vote are less likely to feature a quality candidate. In 2012, legislative professionalism relates positively to candidate quality, as does the redistricting variable in 2014.

The results for the minority party measure become even more unexpected when examining the effect of conditional party government on candidate quality. To carry out this analysis, I divide each year into two groups based upon whether the chamber has above or below average polarization, as measured by Shor and McCarty (2011). In 2012, the minority party variable does not attain significance for low-polarization chambers, but does for high-polarization ones. In 2014, the variable reaches significance for both groups, but the substantive effect is larger for high-polarization chambers (see table 7.3). This suggests that quality candidates may even be *more* likely to run as the probability that they will be in the minority increases in high-polarization contexts than when polarization is low. In sum, the quantitative results for this chapter are far from my expectations. To explain these surprising results, I next turn to a series of interviews I completed during the summer of 2019. These interviews focused on retirement decisions, but I also interviewed several unsuccessful quality candidates whose accounts are helpful in exploring this finding.

State Legislatures' Permanent Minority? A Qualitative Analysis of Race, Age, and Minority Party Status in the Post-2010 Era

To investigate further the unexpected results in the previous section, I turn to first-person accounts from interviews with current legislators, retired members, and unsuccessful candidates from three different states that I conducted in the summer of 2019. I designed these interviews to allow

TABLE 7.3. Conditional party government and candidate entry

Model	Significance	Change in Percentage of Quality Candidates, Majority to Minority
2012 Low Polarization	NS	12.7 to 13.9
2012 High Polarization	**	9.7 to 15.3
2014 Low Polarization	**	9.2 to 12.5
2014 High Polarization	**	9.7 to 14.6

Dependent variable measures whether candidate from party not holding seat has held office **p < 0.05, *p < 0.10, NS = Not Significant; controls were the same as overall models.

these politicians to share their experiences with minority party status and how being in the minority affected their decision-making process. I selected these interviewees through a combination of quota sampling and purposive sampling. I actively sought to include legislators to approximate the racial and gender demographics of Democratic legislators nationwide.[13] I specifically focused on Democratic legislators here for several specific reasons. First, in this era, the vast majority of state legislators who experience minority party status are Democrats. Second, not only do these state legislators experience minority party status, but this minority party status may come close to approximating the experience of national Republicans in the 1955–95 era in terms of its seeming permanence. As a result, the title of this section is an homage to Connelly and Pitney's 1994 work. Many Democratic state legislators have no reasonable expectation of *ever* being in the majority. Permanent minority status also has important implications for national electoral politics, as these legislators' departure from state legislatures may sap Democrats' bench. Third, many state legislatures flipped party control in the 2010 elections, resulting in many Democratic legislators suddenly being thrust into the minority after having had the ability to shape public policy in the majority. Fourth, as noted by Connelly and Pitney (1994, 2), Democratic politicians are typically more willing to speak to academics, making a study of Democratic legislators more practical. I believe that these results should generalize to minority party legislators of either party, as I did not find strong differences between Republicans and Democrats in my federal interviews. Nonetheless, it is possible that there are party differences in state-level service, so the reader should interpret the generalizability of these results with some caution.

Minority Party Status and the Decision to Run

I first draw upon these interviews to explore why quality candidates might be more likely to enter when their party is likely to be in the minority. When asked about the role of minority party status, few interviewees cited it as an obstacle to their initial decision to run, although some did mention that candidate recruitment efforts could be harder in years where their party is likely to be in the minority. As a group, however, those I spoke to seemed relatively unaware of what it was like to be in the minority party before they got to the legislature. Indeed, even those who had served in other political bodies seemed optimistic about their prospects for bipartisanship in legislatures, citing previous experience working with Republicans as a reason for hope once they got to the state legislature. These politicians expected that their ability to work with others at the substate level would translate to state government.

While this belief in bipartisanship may seem far-fetched, it is common for people to impute their current experiences into future situations, even when such an expectation is unreasonable, due to what scholars refer to as "future is now" bias (Givi and Galak 2019). While many of the quality candidates who run for Congress draw their experience from state or big city politics, a large number of the state legislative quality candidates in my dataset served as small city or town councilmembers, mayors, or special district representatives. Their experience may not be as imbued with partisan politics as the typical congressional candidate, so potential state legislative candidates may believe in an ability to work across the aisle in the state legislature. Further, as Madison noted in "Federalist 10," opinions are more likely to be homogenous the smaller the geographic constituency, so a potential candidate's day-to-day contact with politicians from the other party may also be somewhat limited in their current job, further biasing their expectations for work in the legislature (Madison, Hamilton, and Jay [1787–88] 2003a).

Others may run because they are upset at current circumstances and think they can change things by winning a seat in the legislature. One unsuccessful candidate knew that her party would be in the minority, but said she felt that there needed to be more Democratic voices in the legislature and that her role was to bring forward Democratic ideals. This response may help explain why minority party status has an even stronger effect under conditional party government. A potential candidate, holding office in their community, sees their state legislature doing things that they dislike. Given their office, they feel that they could potentially win a seat and become a voice of reason in the legislature, not quite understanding the reality of what it means to be in the political minority.

Members of the political minority, particularly Democrats, had good reason to be angry. In this period, Republicans enacted a number of policies that angered progressives ranging from union busting laws across the Midwest to new restrictions on abortion that Democrats strongly opposed. By running for the legislature, these quality candidates may have felt they could serve as a bulwark against these proposals. Even if they did not win, these candidates may have also felt a desire to run for expressive reasons so that their party's political views were articulated (Hamlin and Jennings 2011).[14] Further, psychological research has shown that those who are angry tend to have altered risk perceptions, often engaging in risk seeking-behavior and lashing out against those at whom they are mad (Lerner and

Keltner 2001; Achterberg et al. 2001; Garfinkel et al. 2016). For those who win and enter the legislature as a minority party member, reality may set in, and some might decide to depart once they realize that they cannot effectively push back against this agenda. First-person accounts of how legislators' conceptions of minority party status changed once they took office are particularly useful in looking at how these notions changed over time.

How Does Minority Party Status Affect Retirement Decisions?

While retirement decisions lend themselves to first-person accounts for the reasons detailed previously, I ran a model for legislators in nonredistricted states without term limits in 2014 to get an initial look at whether a relationship between likely minority party status and retirement might exist. There was a slightly positive relationship between these two variables, but it fell far short of statistical significance.[15] Thus, I turned to my interviews for a more fine-grained look at the decision to retire. These interviews demonstrated that the effect of minority party status varies widely in terms of pushing state legislators toward retirement. Of the three former state legislators with whom I spoke, two said that minority party status played a role in their decision to retire. These two who retired varied in the strength to which minority party status prompted their decision. One legislator, who represented a safe seat, described minority party status in the starkest terms, saying that it felt like a "kick in the teeth" when she entered the legislative minority. This legislator said that she had thought that her experience with compromise in a county prosecutor's office would prepare her to serve in the state legislative minority, but "nothing prepares you to have your ass handed to you every day," as she felt happens in the legislative minority. Unprompted, this legislator spoke of her experience in the legislature in psychological terms that approximated the theory I presented in chapter 1. The experience in the legislature was deeply demoralizing for this legislator. She said that the experience not only made her mad but also sad, and that "no amount of self-care" could fully mitigate these feelings. Thus, when an opportunity in county bureaucracy came up, she decided to leave the legislature. It is worth noting that this legislator had some success in policymaking, at least as much as can be expected for someone in the minority. She was able to see a bill she cosponsored with a Republican become law early in her first term. However, even this experience had costs related to minority party status. As this bill was making its way through the legislature, her Republican colleagues forced her to "pipe down" on other matters she cared about if the partnership on the bill was to continue. In sum, consistent with Lee (2016), she felt that there were two ways to approach minority status: one can either be a member of the "vocal opposition" and not get anything done or keep one's mouth shut and "beg for crumbs." She said she left because she was not suited to the second of these, but party leadership preferred this second strategy. In her new county position, she felt she was able to get more done to help everyday people, even though the scope of the job covered many fewer people.

Minority party status played a different role in the retirement decisions of the other two retired state legislators with whom I spoke. One former legislator, who went into the minority after a long career where he was in the majority more than the minority, stated that minority party status made running for another term an immediate nonstarter. He might have retired anyway because he said that there were other things he wanted to do in life, but minority party status obviated any further need for consideration. While he had served in the minority before, this new stint was incredibly unpleasant because he felt that the majority tried to "inflict as much indignity as possible." Further, this legislator had played an important role in many policy successes in the state for Democrats and he now saw many of these being undone. He clearly felt that minority party status was unpleasant, saying that "everyone in the minority feels mistreated" and that it was "just a matter of degree."

The third legislator with whom I spoke, despite also having the experience of going from the majority to the minority, did not attribute her decision to leave the legislature to minority party status. This legislator, despite having frustrations in the minority, claimed to enjoy the strategy involved with countering the majority and spoke of the importance of the "loyal opposition." While this legislator left, she attributed her decision to another career opportunity arising rather than being due to minority party status.

Two of the five current legislators with whom I spoke considered retiring at some point due to minority party status. One of these legislators said that, should Democrats not win a majority in their chamber in 2020, he plans to "concede defeat" and allow someone else to run for his seat. When asked about minority party status, he said "it sucks," and, not unlike the first legislator described above, described the experience as being more unpleasant than he expected. Saying that he was "bright-eyed and bushy-tailed" when he entered the legislature, he soon learned that he could not "talk sense" into the majority. Like the first legislator, this legislator described the experience in psychological terms, saying it was "emotionally draining" and that he had not anticipated how hard it would be to lose on

votes that directly impacted those he loved and cared about. This legislator has decided to stay for the time being because he views the majority as
being "within arm's length," but already is making plans to leave should
that not materialize.

Another legislator almost retired due to minority party status, but
decided not to after personal reflection. This legislator described his experience in the minority as being "depressing" and stated that his first several
terms were rough because Republicans "treated us poorly" as retribution
for how they had been treated in the minority. He came to hate his experience in the legislature and decided he either needed to find a different way
of doing things or leave the legislature altogether. This legislator stated
that he had a realization that, while he had disagreements with those in
the majority, they were people who meant well, even if they disagreed on
policy mechanisms. Like the first legislator above who decided to retire,
he described two possible paths for service in the minority: becoming a
"flamethrower" and not have much chance of passing bills or being a "col-
laborator" when possible in order to pass bills. This legislator chose the
second option and had some success, describing himself as "threading the
needle of not selling out principles, but being nice to the majority." This
approach is not for every legislator, but it has allowed this legislator to
continue serving while in the minority and see some meaningful success
on legislation. Overall, these interviews showed that minority party status
plays a role in retirement decisions for some legislators, but that the extent
of this reaction is not universal. Additionally, these interviews revealed how
different factors can prompt legislators at different ages to retire. For older
legislators, age can be a factor if they want to retire from public life altogether, while younger legislators might have frustration in the minority,
but decide they want their career to take a different direction.

Nonretirement Decisions: Strategies for Making the Most of Minority Party Status

Several current legislators, despite the unpleasant experience of minority party status, have not retired nor seriously contemplated leaving due
to their being in the minority. One commonality among these legislators
was having specific colleagues in the majority whom they knew they could
work with on specific issues, bringing up specific Republican members by
name during our interviews. One legislator spoke specifically of having
received private information about budget negotiations from a contact on
the other side of the aisle. These legislators also spoke of going to Repub-

licans and getting them to serve as a primary sponsor in order to get a bill they supported through the legislature. For one legislator, working with Republicans to achieve policy goals in county elective government presaged this collaboration. These legislators spoke of being in the minority as unpleasant—or "oppressive," as one legislator described it—but they had specific strategies that enhanced their effectiveness and made them willing to remain in the body.

One of these legislators also attributed her anger at the direction of policymaking as playing a role in her decision not to retire. This legislator said she was "pissed" at the direction of the state and angry at Republicans for destroying democracy at the state and national level. This reaction suggests that anger and sadness may sometimes provoke opposite reactions in terms of engagement in electoral democracy. While legislators who described themselves as being sad or depressed tended to leave or consider leaving, anger seemed to prompt this legislator to want to stay and fight. These divergent reactions are unsurprising if one considers perspectives from psychology comparing these two emotions, which tend to show that those who are angry often strike back at the object of their feelings, while those who are sad more often instead pull back from life (Achterberg et al. 2001; Ekman 2003; Rivers et al. 2007).

Term Limits and Retirement Decisions

When looking solely at the decision to retire, it is difficult to determine the role of term limits in those states in which they are in place. A state legislator facing term limits may have decided to retire anyway, while the shadow of term limits may also cause a legislator to retire a cycle in advance. One state legislator spoke directly of the effect of term limits on a perpetual minority party. For perpetual minority party legislators, term limits can interact with the inability of minority party legislators to get anything done in office and cause them to leave if an opportunity opens up. This legislator spoke of how term limits cause members to look for a way out, wishing that "someone would offer [me] a life raft" when a colleague finds a path out. With few or no policy successes to show for their time in the legislature, minority party members might have difficulty finding a good job once their time is up. This member, who had a law degree, said it might be tough to go back to practicing after a long period of time out of practice. Finally, term limits also have the effect of not allowing a legislator to wait it out if they think long-term trends or other changes in their state might favor their party, shortening their time horizon and thus pushing them toward retirement.

"The Minority in the Minority":
Race, Gender, and Minority Party Status

Numerous minority party legislators shared how gender or race affected their or other legislators' experience in the minority. Gender plays an important role in the experiences of state legislators, with one female interviewee describing her experience of being in "a minority within a minority." This legislator said that her experience in the legislature made her come to believe that there was a "war on women" and that "the patriarchy looms large" in both the majority *and* the minority party. She felt that her party focused on recruiting (mostly white) male candidates to run for office and did not care about diversifying the caucus. Not all female interviewees shared these feelings, but one interviewee spoke of how female members in the caucus had lacked support from the party in their initial run for office, leaving them disenchanted.

Interestingly, the Black legislators with whom I spoke were among those who spoke most of working with Republicans to achieve policy goals. One of these legislators said that her experience in elective county government prepared her to work with Republicans; despite being in the majority party in that decision-making body, she felt ignored by the other Democrats who were white. To achieve success, she went to a Republican and was able to get his help, convincing him to engage in logrolling so they both could realize policy goals. When this politician got to the legislature, she sat back and read the other legislators, approaching those whom she thought could be trustworthy partners on legislation. This legislator was rather sanguine about prospects for winning the majority and wanted Republicans to be included in the policymaking process should the majority flip. Another Black legislator spoke of the need to work hard in the minority, but that his previous experiences as a person of color prepared him to have to work hard regardless of circumstances.

At the same time, several white interviewees spoke of tensions that existed between white and Black legislators related to majority control. One legislator spoke somewhat negatively about the perceived unwillingness among some Black legislators to pay party dues to try to win back the majority. This legislator said that their caucus spoke openly about the need for diversity, actively trying to manage tensions. Other Black legislators may be willing to pay party dues, but not go beyond that, as one Black legislator characterized their approach. This legislator did not see a benefit to going beyond paying standard party dues. Another white legislator spoke with frustration about party leadership's unwillingness to whip or primary several Black legislators who frequently voted with Republicans on important issues. Speaking broadly of caucus politics, one legislator pointed out that the diversity of the Democratic caucus makes internal agreement especially difficult as the party includes so many groups that each have specific priorities (also see Grossmann and Hopkins 2016). In contrast, Republicans are almost monolithically white (and predominantly male), making internal agreement easier.

In sum, these interviews raised important questions about the extent to which majority control is an equally valuable collective goal for members. Importantly, feelings of marginalization by female and Black legislators may not depend on whether they are in the majority to the same degree as for male and white legislators. As Hawkesworth (2003, 529) notes in her study of the 103rd (1993–95) and 104th (1995–97) Congresses , legislative practices can "structure hierarchies on the basis of race and gender." In this period, Black female members of Congress frequently felt excluded even when they attained seniority or leadership positions in the body. Indeed, even though Democrats held the majority during the 103rd Congress and held the Senate and White House at the same time, Black female legislators saw themselves at odds with many others in the party, including President Clinton, on welfare reform. While conditions deteriorated once Republicans won the majority in 1994, they had already been bad for Black female legislators even when Democrats had the majority. While Hawkesworth's study focused on national politics, white males have traditionally dominated legislative institutions at all levels, suggesting that these findings may also translate to state politics. Feelings of marginalization may have a variety of effects ranging from efforts to change the party from within to working with the other party when beneficial to one's group. Indeed, during the redistricting process following the 2010 census, some Black Democrats voted with Republicans in order to preserve or expand descriptive representation for Black Democrats, even when it cost Democrats seats. In explaining her vote to help Republicans override Democratic Governor Jay Nixon's veto of the Missouri redistricting map, State Representative Jamilah Nasheed (D-MO) said "I'm black before I'm a Democrat" (Berg 2011; also see Lublin 1999). Thus, it may be the case that the Black legislators I interviewed had strategies for working with Republicans because of the need to work with *anyone* who could help their constituents.

Party Dues

Another topic relevant to minority party status that came up in interviews pertained to legislators' engagement in party fundraising efforts. Enforcement of party dues varied widely based on the state. In one state where Democrats are in a particularly bad position, an interviewee spoke of the fact that the party tries to get members to contribute dues, but it was not well received by the caucus and did not achieve much success. In this same state, several former candidates I spoke to said that they had received promises of financial help from the party that never materialized. In another state, legislators spoke of an increasingly well-run party dues operation where most members were compelled to pay dues. While Democrats are also in a poor position in this state, it is marginally more conceivable that they could attain the majority relatively soon. A legislator in a state with relatively low legislative professionalism commented on the fact that, in part due to the need to fundraise for the party, the job of a legislator was full-time, despite still having part-time pay.

Conclusion

In total, the findings of this chapter suggest that minority party status plays a different role at the state level than in national politics. Unlike their national counterparts, quality candidates at the state level become more likely to run for office when their party is likely to be in the minority. My interviews revealed that these individuals are relatively ignorant about their ability to achieve their goals before entering the legislature. Others may feel a sense of duty to run when they see their state moving in a direction with which they strongly disagree. Some politicians who win election to a legislative body then realize that the reality of service in the minority is untenable and they decide to retire, but this effect is far from universal. The focus of this book is to examine the overall effect of minority party status on electoral engagement, but the interviews I conducted revealed important findings that suggest that individuals from different groups may not perceive and react to minority party status in the same way. Future research should examine the conditional effects of minority party status on individuals from different groups.

My findings also have important implications for the quality of democratic governance. Institutional memory is important for the success of legislative bodies, and when substantial turnover takes place after a switch in majority control, a party can lose some of its most effective leaders. One interviewee said that she was the only legislator with a particular area of expertise who had served in the body when Democrats last had the majority and party leaders asked her not to retire in case the majority flipped. In some cases, particularly in states with term limits, no members may remain from the last time a party held the majority, potentially leading to rookie mistakes, should the majority flip. Although the findings for this chapter are not as universal as for the national chapters, they suggest that at least some legislators consider minority party status when deciding whether to remain. Further, when a party's numbers in a state legislature decline, it becomes less likely that they are able to run quality candidates for Congress. Thus, the decision of an incumbent legislator to leave electoral politics has the potential to reverberate upward to national politics.

Conclusion

Now that Democrats are in the majority, there's a lot more I can do here.

—Representative Scott Peters (D-CA), as quoted by Rudell (2019)

In the aftermath of the 2018 election, the patterns of electoral engagement by politicians of both parties demonstrated the continued relevance of the findings presented in this book. Already as of early 2020, a retirement gap has begun to develop between the parties. Democrats like Representative Scott Peters (D-CA), who had considered leaving to run for mayor of San Diego in 2020, have decided to remain in Congress, while there has been a cavalcade of Republican retirements (Rudell 2019; Davis 2019). Of these retirements, two that particularly stand out Representatives Susan Brooks (R-IN) and Will Hurd (R-TX).[1] Both of these members had legislative effectiveness scores in the top quintile of the Republican caucus in the most recent Congress. Further, their retirements make their seats in Congress more likely to flip to Democrats, making the task of winning the House even more difficult for Republicans in 2020. The DCCC also has a substantial fundraising advantage over its Republican counterpart and a number of sought-after Democratic candidates announced they would run for the remaining swing seats held by Republicans. These include former State Representative Christina Hale (D-IN) for Susan Brooks's seat and Gina Ortiz Jones, who lost by fewer than 1,000 votes in 2018, for Will Hurd's seat (Barrón-López 2019; Montellaro 2019). These patterns of retirement, fundraising, and candidate entry and recruitment are likely to continue in future congressional elections. Thus, after briefly summarizing the findings of each chapter, I conclude by discussing the implications of my findings for American democratic politics.

Summary of Findings

In each chapter, I examined the effect of minority party status in a different context. As the title of this book suggests, the experience of minority party legislators is truly miserable and has meaningful consequences for their electoral engagement. The findings presented in this book were well encapsulated by a quote from former Representative David Jolly (R-FL), who explained the large number of Republican retirements for the 2020 cycle by explaining that minority party status, "can be a miserable personal experience, particularly for members in the minority without leadership prospects" (Shabad 2019).[2] Jolly continued by noting that "there is little opportunity to be effective legislatively, but [there are] always increasing demands on fundraising and time away from family. Throw in the daily rage cycle created by the president, and a lot of members are simply ready to walk away." As this quote shows, minority party status is a deeply unpleasant experience that touches upon various aspects of daily life for a member of Congress and continues to increase for Republicans in the age of Trump.

This book began by looking at the effects of minority party status on congressional incumbents. The results presented in chapter 2 showed that minority party status affects retirement decisions, with House members who are likely to be in the minority choosing to depart Congress sooner. This effect is stronger under conditional party government. I also demonstrated that both safe *and* marginal seat incumbents choose to retire when it is likely that their party will be in the minority, demonstrating that those members who are most likely to lose their seat in a bad year for their party are not solely driving this effect. The wide variety of districts from which Republican members retired in 2018 further showed that both marginal and safe seat members retire when it is likely that their party will be in the minority in the next session of Congress. Retirement is not the only behavior of incumbents affected by likely minority party status. In chapter 3, data on party fundraising patterns demonstrated that incumbents from the likely minority party are less likely to contribute to party fundraising efforts. Members dislike these efforts under the best of conditions and their seeming futility makes them even more dismal. Both of these results show that minority party status can compound upon itself, as a party that has to defend a larger number of open seats with fewer financial resources is likely to win fewer seats than it may have otherwise.

Next, I focused on the effect of minority party status on potential candidates and the parties that recruit them. In chapter 4 I found that—as with incumbents—quality candidates are less likely to emerge when a party is doomed to the minority. In the Solid South era, a wide disparity in candidate quality existed below the Mason-Dixon Line because Republicans lacked a bench of potential candidates to draw from, while a smaller disparity existed in the North. After conditional party government came to dominate the House, a wider disparity existed in both regions. Since 1994, candidate quality differences have existed most in electorally marginal seats because quality candidates struggle to win seats that lean strongly to the other party even under the best of conditions. In chapter 5, I examined candidate entry from the perspective of parties, which seek to recruit strong candidates to run in as many winnable races as possible. Parties have to redouble their efforts to recruit strong candidates when they are unlikely to win the majority because strong candidates are less likely to run without encouragement when conditions are bad for their party. However, these efforts are less likely to be successful as the probability that their party will be in the minority rises.

Finally, I looked at how minority party status affects politicians' electoral engagement in American political institutions beyond the U.S. House of Representatives. In chapter 6, I looked at how minority party status in the U.S. Senate affects candidate entry and retirement decisions. As with the House, the lack of a Republican bench in the South resulted in Democrats retaining an overall recruitment advantage in the region in this era. However, Democrats also had an advantage in the North from 1958 to 1966, where the intersection of a supermajority and Republican deference to Senate customs allowed for the passage of an array of progressive policy programs. Senior senators have largely driven retirement disparities between the Senate majority and minority in recent years. Senior senators from the majority seek to stay on as they retain more influence in the body, while senior minority party senators who do not want to spend the rest of their careers fighting against majority party proposals leave the body at higher rates. Overall, these results showed that minority party status exerts its strongest effect on senators when conditions most closely approximated those in the House. Finally, in chapter 7 I considered the effect of minority party status in the American states. Since the 2010 elections, many state legislative chambers have been uncompetitive and Democrats have been at a disadvantage in a disproportionate number of bodies. Using data on candidate entry from 2012 and 2014, I found that minority party candidates are actually slightly *more* likely to run when their party is likely to be in the minority, perhaps due to ignorance about the realities of minority party status and an impetus to fight back against majority party policies they strongly oppose. Next, using qualitative interviews with current and former state legislators, I looked at the conditions under which minority party Democrats in recent years have decided to retire from state legislative bodies. I found that some—but not all—state legislators consider minority party status when deciding whether to run for another term. However, this effect may not be uniform across all legislators. A female legislator decided to retire due to minority party status and her feelings of dissatisfaction within her caucus, while several Black legislators expressed that adversity exists regardless of whether their party is in the majority. In total, the results from these two chapters demonstrate that the effect of majority party status is not isolated to the U.S. House of Representatives.

Implications for Electoral Democracy and Public Policymaking

The findings from this study have important implications for voters, public policymaking, and democratic politics as a whole in the United States. These results suggest that James Madison was right to worry about what a unified majority can do to limit the rights of the minority, but that he was overly optimistic about the extent to which American political institutions could constrain such a majority. The feelings of sadness caused by continuously losing that interviewees expressed are a direct result of the majority constantly trampling the minority. Madison's ideal of government spreads out these feelings among all legislators, limiting them for each individual representative. Everyone would lose sometimes, but few legislators would be on the losing side as frequently as is the reality for the minority party today. The negative consequences for American democracy that result from the same people always being on the losing side are numerous.

For voters, the electoral disengagement of minority party politicians means that a smaller share of the electorate has the opportunity to experience a campaign where the likely minority party offers them a credible option. With fewer quality candidates, fewer incumbents, and less money, the likely minority party's efforts to gain seats focus on a smaller set of districts. For voters, this means that more contests are a choice between a strong candidate from the likely majority and a weaker minority party candidate. When the existing majority party is favored, their numbers increase beyond what they may otherwise have been. When a flip in majority control becomes extremely likely, however, the current majority recognizes the warning sign, experiencing many retirements and running few quality candidates. As a result, the outgoing minority does better than expected, surging into the majority with more seats than they may have otherwise won. In both cases, perception becomes reality as voters' decks are stacked against the party that is likely to lose the election.

Strong challengers, even those who ultimately lose, may affect the thinking, actions, and representational style of incumbent legislators or shape how incumbents position themselves for the next campaign. Legislators who fear a tough challenge are likely to be more responsive to the concerns of voters. If the democratic goal is to have a healthy opposition squaring off against a robust party in power, the negative effects of minority party status pull us further away from that goal.

As minority party politicians pull back, the quality of public policymaking in the United States is also likely to suffer. As shown by the results in chapter 2, effective and ineffective minority party politicians alike are likely to retire when minority party status is likely. Further, given their small numbers and inherent disadvantage, the loss of electorally effective members is likely to hurt the minority disproportionately. When the minority party loses its most effective leaders, it is less able to counter the majority and to advance its own policy proposals. However, the minority may not fully recognize the true cost of retirements until they eventually claw their way back to the majority. When minority party members retire, institutional memory is lost, making effective governance more difficult to achieve. Experts in policy areas may retire, with novices replacing them. While it is unlikely that many minority party Republicans would have made it through the entire 40 years of Democratic control even without this effect, it is reasonable to expect politicians in shorter periods of minority party status to make it back to the majority someday. When conditions become so unpleasant that members are not willing to wait it out for four or eight years, the leaders running a party or chairing a committee are likely to be less experienced when they do eventually return to the majority.

The results of this book also suggest that members care about more than just winning reelection to Congress. If members simply cared about reelection, we would expect minority party status not to have a substantial effect on either retirement or party fundraising patterns because a member would not care much if their party were in the minority (Mayhew 1974a). However, these findings suggest that members think about other concerns such as amassing power in the institution and enacting good public policy (Fenno 1978; Rohde 1991; Aldrich and Rohde 2001). My interviews further attested to the role of policy considerations; interviewees frequently brought up policy concerns when asked about the effects of minority party status. Thus, while it is easy to dismiss politicians as self-concerned seekers of reelection, they also care about enacting their view of good public policy. The ambition that voters so often disdain is an important vehicle to having politicians in office who have the skill to deliver on their promises.

Some potential solutions exist to mitigate the problems that result from electoral disengagement due to minority party status, although it is important that such efforts focus on constructive policymaking. If one simply empowers the minority's ability to slow down the policy process, as with the filibuster in the Senate, the result is likely to be gridlock. Instead, efforts should focus on empowering the minority, while still seeking to move forward the policy process. Legislative institutions could privilege a small number of motions from the minority, so long as a set number of majority party members have agreed to serve as cosponsors. By involving the majority, this institution prevents the minority from offering "messaging votes" meant to make the majority look bad (see Lee 2016, 142). It is unlikely that majority party members will want to cosponsor many proposals offered by minority party members from swing districts, as such an action may help these marginal seat members win reelection. If my interviews are any guide, however, there may be some willingness to join proposals offered by safe district members of the majority if there is mutual agreement. As these members, due to the political makeup of their districts, are least likely to lose reelection and thus remain in the institution long enough to one day be in the majority, such a reform would accomplish the important task of furthering institutional memory. By involving these legislators in policymaking efforts, this reform might remove some of the sting of losing, encouraging them to remain in the institution longer. Further, by giving them a role in policymaking, they would have valuable experience in governing that they could put to good use once their party eventually wins the majority. Admittedly, such a reform is unlikely, but until something makes the experience of minority party members less miserable, ambitious politicians from the likely minority party will try to avoid service in a legislative chamber where the indignity of losing to the majority party is an everyday occurrence.

Appendixes

Appendix A

Notes on Interview Subjects and Methods

During the summer of 2019, I conducted 17 interviews for this book. The Duke Institutional Review Board (IRB) determined that the research was exempt from IRB review and approved an amendment to my protocol when I sought to interview more interviewees than was initially planned.[1]

Summary of Interviews

Table A1 provides a description of the most important characteristics pertaining to the individuals I interviewed. At the national level, I perfectly balanced the sample between Democrats and Republicans at three apiece, with an additional subject for whom party labels were not relevant. At the state level, I interviewed 10 Democratic legislators and unsuccessful candidates with the hope of learning more about the status of minority party Democrats in an era where the party is disproportionately in the minority at the state level. My state level interviews focus on potential, current, or former officeholders; I split my national interviews between legislators and staff, with an additional interviewee fitting neither category. State level interviewees came from three different states, including those from states with relatively high and low levels of legislative professionalism.

Interview Process

In reaching out to interview subjects, I used a combination of quota interviews and prepositive interviews (see Kapiszewski, MacLean, and Read

2015). At the national level, I sought to balance the sample between Democrats and Republicans, while at the state level, I focused on Democrats, but sought to include female and African American legislators in my sample.

To recruit subjects to my interview pool, I drew upon my own contacts, those of people I know, and through a quasi-snowball approach. When I thought an interview subject could help recruit subjects who would further the study and I felt comfortable asking, I asked for recommendations on additional subjects I could recruit to the study. In some cases, it was not relevant or necessary to ask for additional interviewees or the rapport did not exist to do so.

When I recruited subjects to the study, I used one of two IRB-approved emails, which I provide here. I used the first with prior contacts and the second with those whom other contacts helped me reach out to or recommended I contact.

- Dear (Name), I hope that all is well with you. I am currently writing a book on the topic of minority party status and electoral engagement in politics. For this book, I am conducting some interviews with people with direct experience with the topic of the book and I was wondering if you would be willing to speak with me about your experiences.
- Dear (Name), My name is Jacob Smith and I am a Lecturing Fellow at Duke University. I am currently working on a book on the topic of minority party status and electoral engagement in politics. For this book, I am conducting some interviews with people with direct experience with the topic of the book. (Contact name) suggested that you might be a good person to interview and I was wondering if you might be willing to speak with me about your experiences. I am happy to provide a more detailed description of the project upon request and look forward to hearing your response.

Interviews were open-ended, although I prepared questions in advance that I thought were of particular relevance for that interviewee. Most interviews lasted around 30 minutes, although several lasted for more than an hour. Some interviewees were clearly more comfortable sharing their experiences with the minority than others were, and these interviews lasted longer than did others. Some interviews with sitting legislators were limited in length and scope by their responsibilities and duties.

APPENDIX TABLE A.1. Summary statistics about interview subjects

Party	N
Democrat	13
Republican	3
Unspecified/Irrelevant	1
Level	
National	7
State	10
Role	
Legislators/ Candidates	13
Staff	3
Other	1
For State Legislators: Current Status	
In Office	5
Out of Office	3
Unsuccessful Candidate	2
For State Legislators: Race	
White	8
Black	2
For State Legislators: Gender	
Male	5
Female	5

Appendix B

Discussion of Data Collection for
Campaign Finance Data in Chapter 3

To collect the party fundraising variable used in chapter 3, in April 2019 I downloaded the Federal Election Commission's list of primary campaign committees associated with candidates in each election cycle from 1990 to 2018. This list labeled some incumbents as nonincumbents and vice versa, so I used a list of incumbents and copied the nine-digit code beginning "C00" associated with each incumbent into an Excel file (e.g., Speaker Pelosi's campaign committee has the code C00213512). I then downloaded the FEC files for "contributions to candidates and independent expenditures" and "any contribution from one committee to another" for each year. I extracted contributions to any *House* candidate from the first file and to a House party committee (the DCCC or NRCC) from the second file.[2] Then, using the nine-digit codes for candidate committees, I was able to use Excel formulas to determine the amount each member gave to other candidates and to their party committee. Next, to determine the amount given from leadership PACs, I began by forming a list of these organizations from *Open Secrets*, which has a list of active leadership PACs by cycle on their website. I copied the nine-digit code associated with that leadership PAC for each incumbent who had an active leadership PAC that cycle into the Excel file and again used an Excel formula to determine how much they gave to other candidates in that cycle. In a few rare cases, a candidate had two leadership PACs listed, so I added these totals. Further, in some cases *Open Secrets* listed two incumbents for a leadership PAC, so I divided the total evenly between them. Finally, after calculating the amount given to other candidates from leadership PACs, I added this amount to the candidate-to-candidate and party committee giving from a candidate's primary campaign committee to arrive at a value of total party fundraising efforts. Before using this value in my models, I converted it into real 2018 dollars using the CPI calculator from the Bureau of Labor Statistics.[3]

Appendix C

Detailed Discussion of Methods for Content Analysis

I used LexisNexis Academic to collect stories on party recruitment from 1990 to 2014 from the *New York Times*, the *Washington Post*, and *Roll Call*, *NexisUni* for the *New York Times* and *Washington Post* in 2016–18, *ProQuest* for *Roll Call* in 2016–18, and the *CQ Weekly* website for all years. To carry out the content analysis, I designed a search string to find the articles that were most likely to discuss party recruitment.[4] I designed this search string to capture mentions of active party recruitment by including as many synonyms of "recruit" as possible to capture a wide array of articles that could potentially contain useful information. This search string captured a relatively large number of articles that did not relate to the topic, but it was beneficial to include a broad search string of terms to limit the exclusion of relevant articles as much as possible.

While my search string was wide ranging, my standards for coding an article as relaying a recruitment attempt were strict. Using the typology put forward by Kazee and Thornberry (1990) that classifies candidates into three groups based on how involved the party was in their decision to run, I focused on "party recruits" and "mixed" cases that clearly leaned toward "party recruits." I did not want to include "self-starters" in my cases because these decisions to run were not because of party recruitment efforts. Thus, I coded races as having party recruitment from the party that did not currently hold the seat when there was an *active* party attempt to convince a candidate to run. I did not include a seat as having a recruitment effort if the party simply added a candidate to a party list, but it was not apparent that the party asked the candidate to run. Importantly, the word "recruit" is both a noun and a verb, which affected my coding decisions.[5] As a noun, the term refers to one who has recently enlisted, typically in reference to the military. As a verb, the term has an active meaning focused on seeking to ask individuals to join some cause or institution. When articles used the term "recruit," I looked for verb usages, unless other evidence in the article suggested that there was an active recruitment attempt.

This method does not pick up every case of recruitment, but it does a good job of approximating the amount of recruitment taking place in a cycle. To examine further the robustness of my method, I asked an interviewee who worked closely with a party committee how well the coverage of recruitment in publications such as *Roll Call* approximated the reality of what happened behind the scenes. This interviewee responded that, generally speaking, the discussion closely corresponded to what went on behind the scenes. As he pointed out, when a party really wants to recruit someone, a story could end up leaking to the press in many potential ways. First, the party may want to leak it in order to get a positive story about the candidate. Second, the candidate themselves may share it with reporters in an effort to get some good press coverage and build their image. Third, the party is likely to enlist incumbent members from the House delegation to try to get their help recruiting the potential candidate, and the House member—or their staff—may divulge the story. In other words, the more serious the recruitment attempt, the greater the number of people who will know about it, and the more likely that someone will leak it to someone in the press. Finally, using public data on which candidates ran in the election, I was able to code whether the desired recruit, if mentioned by name, actually decided to run to analyze whether or not a recruitment attempt succeeded, allowing me to test the second part of my theory.

Notes

Introduction

1. See Hohmann, James. 2015. "Washington Democrats are popping champagne to celebrate Heidi Heitkamp's decision to stay in the Senate" Twitter/@jameshohmann. https://twitter.com/jameshohmann/status/641641272755781632.

2. In West Virginia, Democrats had the ability to sustain vetoes on budget-related items, but nothing else.

3. However, Jones does not offer data on the longevity of House and Senate Democrats as a point of comparison.

4. The last Republican to have served in the House majority in the 1950s, John Jacob Rhodes (R-AZ), retired in 1982.

5. Smith (2014) also discusses how the rise of an attainable Senate majority following the 1980 election contributed to the development of the dysfunctional "Senate Syndrome" that characterizes the modern Senate.

6. The second point here seems to contradict Lee (2016), although it covers a different period.

Chapter One

1. Henceforth, when I refer to the minority party, I mean the party that is likely to be in the minority after the next election.

2. Another interpretation of this quote could be that Quayle was an uncommonly unqualified figure for high office.

3. *The Missoulian* later rescinded its endorsement after Greg Gianforte body slammed *Guardian* reporter Ben Jacobs the day before the election. (See https://missoulian.com/opinion/editorial/missoulian-rescinds-gianforte-endorsement/article_ab947a9d-9220–5dc5–9193-f1ae9ef03c60.html.)

4. Indeed, part of why Nancy Pelosi remained Democratic leader even after the party fell into the minority for four terms starting in 2010 was likely because of her success at fundraising for Democrats even as minority leader (Pearson 2019).

5. This does not have to be another federal office or another legislative office.

6. While Nancy Pelosi again became Speaker of the House in 2018, she confirmed that she would have stepped aside as Democratic leader if Hillary Clinton had won the 2016 presidential election (McPherson 2018). Furthermore, although Democrats won the 2018 House election, before Donald Trump won the 2016 election Democrats did not expect to assume majority status for years to come, with a number of factors including gerrymandering making winning the majority extremely difficult without an unpopular president of the other party in the White House.

7. Edwards later lost a primary for Prince George's County executive in 2018 (Vitka 2018).

8. Additionally, a certain baseline level of recruitment action may exist even when a party faces long odds to win the majority.

9. See Werner, Erica. 2017. "Martha McSally stood up in GOP conference meeting and said let's get this 'f[-]ing thing' done. Yes, direct quote—per members and aides." Twitter.com/@ericawerner. https://twitter.com/ericawerner/status/860138281064943617.

10. In addition, one can reasonably assume that Democrats did not offer some proposals in this period supported by the majority of Democrats because of almost assured failure on the floor.

11. Negative agenda power refers to the ability of the majority to prevent legislation from coming to a vote.

12. A final passage minority party roll is when a final passage vote passes and a majority of the minority party voted against the bill. Roll rates per Congress calculated using data presented by Gary Cox and Mathew McCubbins. I made this division between the two periods so that an equal number of years were in both periods.

13. Similarly, the concept of loss aversion in economics suggests that people prefer to avoid losses than obtain gains of a similar amount (e.g., Kahneman and Tversky 1979).

14. In this formula, p is the probability of success, B represents the benefits received by a political actor by achieving a goal, C represents costs and D represents civic duty. While R usually relates to personal benefits, one can also consider it as relating to all benefits, including goals such as the ability to enact good public policy.

Chapter Two

1. See https://twitter.com/jamesfallows/status/986405763211022336.

2. For example, the Cook Political Report rated Ryan's seat as solidly Republican.

3. See figure 2.2 for the retirement rate by Congress.

4. See Kondik, Kyle. 2018. "CRYSTAL BALL RATINGS CHANGE: Retirement of Rep. Rodney Frelinghuysen (R, NJ-11) moves his district from Leans Republican to Toss-up. Another bad one for the Rs." Twitter.com/@kkondik. https://twitter.com/kkondik/status/958015092154658817.

5. See Crass, Scott. 2018. "I got it! Iowa's Second Congressional District

in 1990. Dukakis had won with 56% there in '88 as Tom Tauke(R) was re-elected. In '90, Tauke gave it up to challenge Harkin&Jim Nussle—against all expectations, edged Eric Tabor by fewer than 2,000 votes." Twitter.com/@Crass Political. https://twitter.com/CrassPolitical/status/956780715156361216.

6. See Highton (2011) for a good discussion of strategic retirement in the context of its implications for measuring the incumbency advantage.

7. Another member also agreed, offering the 2016 presidential election as the rare example where elected politicians were completely surprised by a result.

8. Interviewees from both parties noted that these negative feelings can set in during the previous lame duck session once the writing is on the wall and little more can be accomplished before the change in party control.

9. Economic data from the St. Louis Federal Reserve Bank; for 1946, data are from the start of the year before election to the start of the election year because quarterly data were not collected. Gallup data from Presidential Approval Center.

10. The exceptions are 1948, 1980, and 2008, when the winning presidential party made substantial House gains.

11. Data on seat margins comes from official House records on the opening day of Congress http://history.house.gov/Institution/Party-Divisions/Party-Divi sions/. Correlation varies from -1 to 1. A correlation closer to either pole is stronger while ones close to 0 are weak.

12. Data shared generously by Gary Jacobson and Jamie Carson. Some observations for more recent elections collected by author.

13. For Democrats—where DW-Nominate scores are almost always negative—this measure is calculated by subtracting the individual member's DW-Nominate score from the party mean, while for Republicans this measure is calculated by subtracting the party mean from the individual member's DW-Nominate score. DW-Nominate scores available from voteview.com; data on year of member birth also available here. Age was calculated by subtracting year of birth from year of election. Data on terms served available from Congressional Biographical Directory (http://bioguide.congress.gov/biosearch/biosearch.asp).

14. I do not include year dummy coefficients in this table and other tables for space considerations, but they are available upon request. I also conducted an analysis where I ran a Weibull fixed effects parametric survival model and obtained similar results to the random effects logit. A member who is likely to be in the minority is just under 1.5 times more likely to retire than a member who is likely to be in the majority. Specific results of survival model available in online appendix.

15. See the online appendix for regression tables. The result for 1946–54 may also be in part due to the relatively smaller sample size in this period.

16. For this model, I use decade dummies, with 2010s dummy left out, due to estimation issues with year dummies.

17. It is worth noting that a legislator may have a low effectiveness score because they cannot overcome obstacles put in place by other legislators or the institution, or because they are shirking their duties. Wiseman and Volden calculate these scores using bill introductions, actions in committee, action beyond the committee, passage from the institution, and by looking at whether the bill becomes law (Wiseman and Volden 2014, 27). The first of these metrics can most readily allow one to determine if shirking is present.

18. Summary statistics for the retiring Republicans in 2018 are available in the appendix.

19. See Schlesinger (1966, 10) for an in-depth discussion of these forms of ambition.

Chapter Three

1. DCCC stands for the Democratic Congressional Campaign Committee; NRCC stands for the National Republican Congressional Committee.

2. Technically speaking, a retiring member could become Speaker of the House, but a nonmember has never assumed this position.

3. Also see http://www.cfinst.org/pdf/federal/2016Report/pdf/CFI_Federal-CF_16_Table3–06.pdf.

4. The *Roll Call* article that Nir (aka "DavidNYC") links to has a broken link.

5. See the second story listed on the page; the link for the story is broken on the *Swing State Project* page."

6. Nir is referring to the fact that Representative Debbie Wasserman-Schultz (D-FL) did not help the Democratic Party in their 2008 efforts to defeat three of her South Florida Republican colleagues in the House, Ileana Ros-Lehtinen, Mario Diaz-Balart, and Lincoln Diaz-Balart (Clark 2008).

7. See Ocasio-Cortez, Alexandria. 2019a. "Spending a few hours today doing calltime. But instead of calling donors, I'm calling constituents to personally follow up on casework they've brought to our office, and give them progress updates myself. Getting big money out of politics means your Reps can do more of this. Twitter.com/@AOC. https://twitter.com/AOC/status/1101573021020631041.

Ocasio-Cortez, Alexandria. 2019b. "The more you chip in to fund Reps who don't take corp money (even if it's $5, $10, or $27) that's less time they spend dialing for dollars & more time they spend in committee. I sit through committee hearings in full. They often last hours—but that's hours each day *learning.*" Twitter.com/@AOC. https://twitter.com/AOC/status/1101283777823850496.

Ocasio-Cortez, Alexandria. 2019c. "Update: Calling the @USPS to figure out why my Morris Park constituents are only getting mail once every 2–3 days! This look like a systemic issue. We're on the case y'all" Twitter.com/@AOC. https://twitter.com/AOC/status/1101579908747329543.

8. I include incumbents who were in office on Election Day and (in a few cases) members who had died or resigned within a month of the election.

9. See appendix for a detailed discussion of how I collected this data.

10. I code chamber or party leader variable as "1" if a member is Speaker, party leader, or whip and "0" if otherwise.

11. I round to the nearest month here.

12. A Hausman Test indicates a fixed effects model is preferable to a random effects model. An unbiased fixed effect tobit estimator does not exist (STATA N.d.).

13. I do not include year dummy results in the table for space reasons, but I can provide these results upon request.

14. Mean value for this variable is 0.476 and the standard deviation is 0.346. I held all other variables at their means.

15. Another way to conceptualize the party fundraising process is in two steps:

the decision to give and then the decision of how much to give. To capture this process, I also ran a two-step model, using a logit to model the decision to give and a log-normal model for the decision of how much to give. For the second part of this model, logging the amount of dollars limits the effect of each additional dollar for large positive values of the dependent variable. In this model, the minority party variable fell just short of significance in the logit (p=0.068) and easily attained significance in the log-normal model. For the first part, it is worth noting that 86 percent of members gave some amount of money to party efforts—and 93 percent after 1994—suggesting that for most members the decision is more one of how much to give than whether to give.

Chapter Four

1. Unlike the presidential race, Bloom did not take her case to the Florida Supreme Court and conceded in November.

2. In this chapter I use Gary Jacobson's definition of quality candidates being those who have previously held political office.

3. Offices of successful candidates available from House biographical directory at http://bioguide.congress.gov/biosearch/biosearch.asp.

4. This number counts Bernie Sanders (I-VT) as a Democrat and Virgil Goode (I-VA) as a Republican, based upon their Speaker votes and the party with whom they caucused.

5. Stork's name remained on the ballot, but votes for him counted for Rorapaugh. Jacobson codes this seat as not having a quality Democratic candidate in 2004.

6. Again, see Congressional Biographical Directory for previous offices for those who won seats in Congress.

7. For example, State Representative John Salazar (D-CO), Athens-Clark County Commissioner John Barrow (D-GA), State Representative Charlie Melancon (D-LA), and State Assembly Member Brian Higgins (D-NY) won competitive House races in seats formerly held by Republicans in 2004. Political amateur Melissa Bean (D-IL) also won a House seat in this election.

8. For example, Senators Thom Tillis (R-NC) and Jeff Merkley (D-OR) were state house Speakers when they won seats to the U.S. Senate.

9. Anchorage's 291,826 people represented 41.09 percent of Alaska's population in 2010; New York's 8,175,133 people represented 42.19 percent of the state's population in 2010. (See https://factfinder.census.gov/faces/nav/jsf/pages/community_facts.xhtml?src=bkmk).

10. In 2019, two mayors of cities with populations between 100,000 and 200,000, Pete Buttigieg of South Bend, IN and Wayne Messam of Miramar, FL, announced their intentions to run for president in 2020. This, however, is a rare next step for a mayor.

11. Rarely, a governor or other statewide executive officer runs for Congress. They have experience with the minority from their interactions with the legislative branch while in office.

12. My findings in chapter 7 suggest that this assumption may apply more strongly for quality candidates holding state offices where partisan confrontation is more common.

13. In chapter 7, I examine candidate entry decisions for state legislatures using a similar framework as in this chapter.

14. Gary Jacobson and Jamie Carson generously shared this data. Data on candidate quality since 2012 was collected by the author using Politics1.com descriptions of candidate biographies and Google searches.

15. Jacobson and Carson (2016) note that, due to the declining incumbency advantage, first-term incumbents are not as vulnerable as in the past, although the data shows that they still attract the most quality challengers, even when compared to second-term incumbents.

16. As a robustness check, given the relatively weak correlation between presidential and House outcomes in this era, I also ran a model with the percentage of vote received by the winning House candidate as a control. The focal independent variable remains significant.

17. See http://www.alabamasheriffs.com/pages?id=41 (accessed May 14, 2019.) Hillary Clinton carried 13 counties in Alabama (New York Times 2017a).

18. Data on 1966 quality of Alabama candidates from Jacobson-Carson dataset.

19. See https://www.nytimes.com/elections/2016/results/president. Row offices are county executive offices such as controller and coroner.

20. The most Republican-leaning seat that Democrats won from Republicans in 2018 was New York's 22nd Congressional District, where Republican Donald Trump received a 9.34 percentage point higher vote share than in the country as a whole in 2016. This seat was won by Democrat State Assemblyperson Anthony Brindisi in 2018.

21. Sarah Treul and Rachel Porter are doing excellent work on this topic at UNC-Chapel Hill.

Chapter Five

1. Illinois' 12th District had long been held by Democrat Jerry Costello before Republican Mike Bost defeated first-term Democrat Bill Enyart in 2014.

2. See https://www.nytimes.com/interactive/2018/upshot/elections-polls.html.

3. Wexton won while Davis narrowly lost.

4. Later in this chapter, I explain my method for collecting this data.

5. Or, if an incumbent, win reelection.

6. Reed (2009) also studied this recruitment process in the context of Japan's multimember districts.

7. Notably, Democrat Jesse Sbaih alleged that Senator Harry Reid (D-NV) encouraged him to get out of the race because a Muslim could not win the district (Farenthold 2016).

8. See https://www.dailykos.com/stories/2012/11/19/1163009/-Daily-Kos-Elections-presidential-results-by-congressional-district-for-the-2012–2008-elections.

9. In this case "the party" is being used broadly. While the DCCC would have incentive to be involved, other party apparatuses at the state and national level may well have also been involved.

10. Barzee Flores was ultimately unsuccessful at defeating Diaz-Balart. Javier Rodríguez would have had to resign his Florida Senate seat under a new "resign-

to-run" law, creating a potentially costly special election for Florida Democrats (Caputo 2018b).

11. This falls into Kazee and Thornberry's (1990) category of "mixed."

12. This search string was "Democratic Congressional Campaign Committee" OR "DCCC" OR "National Republican Congressional Committee" OR "NRCC" AND (persuade* OR convince* OR encourage* OR recruit* OR draft* OR nudge* OR coax* OR urge* OR push* OR prompt* OR lure* OR entice*).

13. In appendix C, I provide a more in-depth description and justification of my coding method.

14. Specifically, I control for a district's presidential vote lean compared to the country as a whole, whether the incumbent member is in their first term, the total number of terms they have served, their ideological extremity compared to their party caucus, if the seat is located in the South, whether the seat is open because of a retirement, and if the seat has been redistricted since the last election. I also include time fixed effects.

15. Cases from 1992 were excluded from analysis because the 1992 year dummy predicted failure perfectly. Results do not substantially change with exclusion of year dummies to include 1992 cases.

16. That is, those seats in which the other party's presidential candidate would have received under 60 percent of the vote in a tied election.

17. See appendix table 5.2 for results of this analysis.

18. In the cases where multiple potential favored nominees were mentioned in the first article for a seat, this variable measures if any of these potential recruits ended up running. A joint test indicated that year dummies were not necessary for these models. Results remain largely constant if year dummies are included.

Chapter Six

1. Due to a number of party switches of conservative southern Democrats, this number downplays the magnitude of Democrats House gains.

2. I include all regularly scheduled Senate elections as well as special elections occurring in November of even numbered years (i.e., midterms and presidential years).

3. These subjects are spending, revenues, and the debt limit (Reich and Kogan 2016).

4. See https://www.senate.gov/legislative/cloture/clotureCounts.htm.

5. See 103rd Senate 1st Session Roll Call #190 and 103rd Senate 2nd Session Roll Call #295 (https://www.senate.gov/legislative/votes_new.htm).

6. I subtract one from the original probability for seats not held by the president's party to capture how likely a challenging candidate from the president's party is to be in the majority should they win election to Congress. For seats held by the president's party, I use the probability obtained in the postregression predicted values since the challenging party does not currently hold the White House.

7. I classify mayors of cities with a larger population than the mean congressional district as quality candidates.

8. Practically speaking, given the number of senators, older majority party senators are generally going to chair some committee (freshman Utah Republican U.S.

Senator Mitt Romney aside). Results are similar if I interact seniority with the minority party variable.

9. As discussed in the opening vignette, Democrats took great pleasure in preventing Senators Heitkamp, McCaskill, and Manchin from retiring to run for governor in 2016. This suggests both that there is some value in a Senate majority and that things were not so hopeless in 2016 as to push these senators to leave.

10. While this representative spoke of the House Democrats, this dynamic should translate to the Senate.

11. The Trump phenomenon also makes it difficult to determine the extent to which the Senate's march toward majoritarianism causes senators to have a similarly negative experience in the minority to the House, resulting in a retreat from electoral politics. Senate Democrats had help from Senators Susan Collins (R-ME), Lisa Murkowski (R-AK), and John McCain (R-AZ) in defeating health care repeal efforts.

Chapter Seven

1. North Carolina has a long legislative session in odd years and a shorter session in even years.

2. For a list of what passed in the 2013 North Carolina legislative session, see https://www.wral.com/news/state/nccapitol/asset_gallery/11997682/.

3. See https://ballotpedia.org/North_Carolina_State_Senate for a list of senators and their start date of service.

4. Two of the senators in 2013 died in office: Martin Nesbitt of Asheville, who was white, died in 2013, while Earline Parmon of Winston-Salem, who was Black, died in 2016. Democrat Gene McLaurin, who was white, lost his seat when he sought reelection in 2014.

5. Since then, the Arizona legislature has become more competitive, with a switch in party control in 2020 within reasonable expectations.

6. A rare exception is the Hawaii Senate. Republican have had either zero or one seat in the body in recent years (Blair 2018).

7. Washington has seen some close recent gubernatorial elections (especially the 2004 contest where Democrat Christine Gregoire defeated Republican Dino Rossi by only 129 votes), but Democrats have held the seat since 1985 and have won a number of these elections by wide margins.

8. Additionally, presidential vote by state legislative district, which I use in a variable in the candidate entry models, is not available from Daily Kos Elections for every state legislative chamber.

9. The postregression predicted value that Democrats will be in the majority equals the probability that Republicans will be in the minority, while one minus the postregression predicted value corresponds to the probability that Democrats will be in the minority. When pairing values to seats, it is important to remember that the party being examined for candidate quality models is not the same as in retirement models, so this variable will equal 1- the value for the other scenario.

10. There are some rare cases of members of Congress running for state legislatures, either after having lost or after being redistricted out of their seat (e.g., Michigan's Jim Barcia ran for the Michigan Senate in 2002 after he was redistricted from his House seat).

11. In advance of the 2012 election, redistricting took place across the country. Several states, including Maine and Alaska, had redistricting after 2012 and before 2014, either due to court decisions or—in the case of Maine—a quirk in state law where redistricting for state legislative districts occurred before the year ending in "4" instead of the year ending in "2" in the 2010s (Levitt 2013.d.). This dummy variable measures whether redistricting occurred for that district.

12. The overall proportion of quality candidates is likely higher in 2012 because it is a redistricting year.

13. See appendix A for a more in-depth discussion of my process of recruiting interviewees.

14. The candidate I mention in this paragraph felt she could win and, given the seat's demographics, was not incorrect in believing that; however, others may run for this reason, using this reason. I believe her goal of bringing forth Democratic ideals applied to both the settings of the election and in the legislature, but one could run to do this in just the first setting.

15. The full model is available in the online appendix. It is more difficult to match incumbent legislators with newly drawn districts than for members of Congress because, with rare exception (the California and Texas state senates), states have more populous congressional districts than state legislative districts. This results in more incumbent state legislators having their seats divided between numerous other districts so it is sometimes difficult to assign an incumbent a district.

Conclusion

1. On the day that Susan Brooks retired, I broke the news of her retirement to one of her colleagues who expressed both surprise and disappointment that she was leaving Congress.

2. Jolly served as a Republican in the House majority from 2014 to 2017, but is now an independent.

Appendices

1. I drew upon Lee (2016) in writing this appendix.

2. I removed contributions to Senate and presidential candidates as these have no direct bearing on which party controls the House.

3. See https://data.bls.gov/cgi-bin/cpicalc.pl.

4. This search string was "Democratic Congressional Campaign Committee" OR "DCCC" OR "National Republican Congressional Committee" OR "NRCC" AND (persuade* OR convince* OR encourage* OR recruit* OR draft* OR nudge* OR coax* OR urge* OR push* OR prompt* OR lure* OR entice*).

5. See https://www.merriam-webster.com/dictionary/recruit.

Works Cited

Achterberg, Michelle, Anna C. K. van Duijvenvoorde, Marian J. Bakermans-Kranenburg, and Eveline A. Crone. 2001. "Control Your Anger! The Neural Basis of Aggression Regulation in Response to Negative Social Feedback." *Journal of Cognitive and Affective Neuroscience* 11 (5): 712–20.

Advocate. 2004. "Openly Gay Stork to Drop Out of Congressional Race." *Advocate*, September 16. https://www.advocate.com/news/2004/09/16/openly-gay-stork-drop-out- congressional-race-13716

Akin, Stephanie. 2019. "Alexandria Ocasio-Cortez's Call for a 'Living Wage' Starts in Her Office." *Roll Call*, February 22. https://www.rollcall.com/news/congress/alexandria-ocasio-cortezs-call-living-wage-starts-office

Aldrich, John H. 2000. "Presidential Address: Southern Parties in State and Nation." *Journal of Politics* 62 (3): 643–70.

Aldrich, John H. 2011. *Why Parties? A Second Look*. Chicago: University of Chicago Press.

Aldrich, John H., and William T. Bianco. 1992. "A Game-Theoretic Model of Party Affiliation of Candidates and Office Holders." *Mathematical and Computer Modelling* 16 (8–9): 103–16.

Aldrich, John H., and John S. Coleman Battista. 2002. "Conditional Party Government in the States." *American Journal of Political Science* 46 (1): 164–72.

Aldrich, John H., and John D. Griffin. 2018. *Why Parties Matter: Political Competition and Democracy in the American South*. Chicago: University of Chicago Press.

Aldrich, John H., and David W. Rohde. 2001. "The Logic of Conditional Party Government: Revisiting the Electoral Connection." In *Congress Reconsidered*, 7th ed., edited by Lawrence C. Dodd and Bruce I. Oppenheimer. Washington, DC: CQ Press.

Allen, Jared. 2010. "House Democratic Leaders to Push Members for Dues." *The*

Hill, February 25. https://thehill.com/homenews/campaign/83537-house-dem-leaders-to-push-members-for-dues-payments

Archer, John. 2006. "Testosterone and Human Aggression: An Evaluation of the Change Hypothesis." *Neuroscience and Biobehavioral Reviews* 30 (3): 319–45.

Associated Press. 2000. "Clay Shaw Declares Victory over Elaine Bloom in House Race." Associated Press State and Local Wire. Retrieved from https://advance-lexis-com.proxy.lib.duke.edu/api/document?collection=news&id=urn:contentItem:41MF-3BM0–009F-S2RT-00000–00&context=1516831

Associated Press. 2004. "Reps. Harris, Boyd Win Heated Battles for House Seats." *Gainesville Sun*, November 3. https://www.gainesville.com/article/LK/20041103/News/604166566/GS

Atkinson, Mary Layton, John Lovett, and Frank Baumgartner. 2014. "Measuring the Media Agenda." *Political Communication* 31 (2): 355–80.

Ballotpedia. 2010. "State Legislative Elections Results, 2010." *Ballotpedia*. https://ballotpedia.org/State_legislative_elections_results,_2010

Banks, Jeffrey, and D. Roderick Kiewiet. 1989. "Explaining Patterns of Candidate Competition in Congressional Elections." *American Journal of Political Science* 33 (4): 997–1015.

Barber, Michael. 2016. "Donation Motivations: Testing Theories of Access and Ideology." *Political Research Quarterly* 69 (1): 148–59.

Barrón-López, Laura. 2019. "DCCC Outraises NRCC in May." *POLITICO*, June 20. https://www.politico.com/story/2019/06/20/dccc-raises-88m-in-may-1373020

Baumgartner, Frank, Suzanna De Boef, and Amber E. Boydstun. 2008. *The Decline of the Death Penalty and the Discovery of Innocence*. New York: Cambridge University Press.

Bendetto, Richard. 2006. *Politicians Are People, Too*. Lanham, MD: University Press of America.

Berg, Rebecca. 2011. "Legislature Overrides Nixon Veto of Redistricting Map." *St Louis Post Dispatch*, May 5. https://www.stltoday.com/news/local/metro/legislature-overrides-nixon-veto-of-redistricting-map/article_6995ad6c-813a-5d55-b094- eed9ef306c8e.html

Bernhardt, Paul C., James M. Dabbs Jr., Julie A. Fieldan, and Candice D. Lutter. 1998. "Testosterone Changes during Vicarious Experiences of Winning and Losing among Fans at Sporting Events." *Physiology and Behavior* 65 (1): 59–62.

Bianco, William T., and Itai Sened. 2005. "Uncovering Evidence of Conditional Party Government: Reassessing Majority Party Influence in Congress and State Legislatures." *American Political Science Review* 99 (3): 361–71.

Bierman, Noah. 2016. "'Senator, You're No Jack Kennedy' Almost Didn't Happen: How It Became the Biggest VP Debate Moment in History." *Los Angeles Times*, October 4. https://www.latimes.com/politics/la-na-pol-debate-quayle-bentsen-20161004-snap-story.html

Binder, Sarah A., and Stephen S. Smith. 1997. *Politics or Principle? Filibustering the United States Senate*. Washington, DC: Brookings Institution Press.

Binker, Mark, and Laura Leslie. 2013. "Sen. Kinnaird Resigns from Legislature." *WRAL*, August 21. https://www.wral.com/sen-kinnaird-resigns-from-legislature-/12792527/

Birnbam, Jeffrey. 1987. "House Republicans, Frustrated in Minority Role, Often Ask Themselves Whether It's Time to Leave." *Wall Street Journal*, June 5.

Black, Gordon. 1972. "A Theory of Political Ambition: Career Choices and the Role of Structural Incentives." *American Political Science Review* 66 (1): 144–59.

Blair, Allyson. 2018. "After a Two-Year Dry Spell, Hawaii Once Again Has a Lone Republican in the State Senate." *Hawaii News Now*, November 8. https://www.hawaiinewsnow.com/2018/11/08/after-two-year-dry-spell-hawaii-once-again-has-lone-republican-state-senate/

Bowman, Bridget. 2018. "Targeting a Blue Texan: Will National Democrats Pay a Price?" *Roll Call*, May 17. https://www.rollcall.com/news/politics/laura-moser-texas-dccc-intervention

Box-Steffensmeier, Janet. 1996. "A Dynamic Analysis of the Role of War Chests in Campaign Strategy." *American Journal of Political Science* 40 (2): 352–71.

Brady, David W., Morris P. Fiorina, and Arjun S. Wilkins. 2011. "The 2010 Elections: Why Did Political Science Forecasts Go Awry?" *PS: Political Science and Politics* 44 (2): 247–50.

Broockman, David E. 2014. "Mobilizing Candidates: Political Actors Strategically Shape the Candidate Pool with Personal Appeals." *Journal of Experimental Political Science* 1 (2): 104–19.

Brune, Tom. 2014. "Steve Israel Goes from DCCC to a New Leadership Party Job." *Newsday*, November 17. https://www.newsday.com/news/nation/steve-israel-goes-from-dccc-to-a-new-leadership-party-job-1.9627439

Bullock, Charles S. 1972. "House Careerists: Changing Patterns of Longevity and Attrition." *American Political Science Review* 66 (4): 1295–1300.

Bushouse, Kathy, and Anthony Man. 2002. "McBride Provided Scant Boost." *Sun-Sentinel*, November 17. https://www.sun-sentinel.com/news/fl-xpm-2002-11-17-0211170166-story.html

Bustos, Joseph. 2017. "Brendan Kelly Might Be Running for Congress, Would Be 'Formidable Candidate.'" *Belleville News-Democrat*, June 23. https://www.bnd.com/news/local/article157847039.html

Cahn, Emily. 2015a. "Rep. Janice Hahn to Run for County Supervisor (Updated)." *Roll Call*, February 18. http://www.rollcall.com/news/home/rep-janice-hahn-to-run-for-l-a-supervisor

Cahn, Emily. 2015b. "Senate Democrats Nearly Run Table in Recruitment." *Roll Call*, October 5. https://www.rollcall.com/2015/10/05/senate-democrats-nearly-run-table-in-recruitment-2/

Cahn, Emily, and Nathan Gonzales. 2015. "Illinois Democrat Hesitant on House

Race." *Roll Call*, February 3. https://www.rollcall.com/news/house-races-2016-sheila-simon-illinois-mike-bost

Cain, Bruce, John Ferejohn, and Morris Fiorina. 1987. *The Personal Vote*. Cambridge: Harvard University Press.

Campbell, James. 1993. *The Presidential Pulse of Congressional Elections*. Lexington: University of Kentucky Press.

Canes-Wrone, Brandice, David W. Brady, and John F. Cogan. 2002. "Out of Step, Out of Office: Electoral Accountability and House Members' Voting." *American Political Science Review* 96 (1): 127–40.

Cann, Damon M. 2008. *Sharing the Wealth: Member Contributions and the Exchange Theory of Party Influence in the U.S. House of Representatives*. Albany: State University of New York Press.

Caputo, Marc. 2018a. "Democrats Fear Shalala Campaign Is in 'Sleep Mode' While Challenger Surges." *POLITICO*, September 19. https://www.politico.com/story/2018/09/19/florida-2018-elections-miami-27th-828642

Caputo, Marc. 2018b. "Rodríguez Drops Out of Miami Congressional Race, Boosts Democratic Chances of Capturing State Senate." *POLITICO*, April 11. https://www.politico.com/states/florida/story/2018/04/11/rodriguez-drops-out-of-miami-congressional-race-boosts-democratic-chances-of-capturing-state-senate-359611

Cardosi, Mandi. 2015. "With an Eye on Joe Manchin, WV Senate Passes Bill to Change Way Vacancies Are Filled in U.S. Senate." *State Journal*. https://www.wvnews.com/statejournal/news/with-an-eye-on-joe-manchin-wv-senate-passes-bill/article_fedac794-142c-5487-96d9-55cfc7eb691a.html

Carnes, Nicholas. 2018. *The Cash Ceiling: Why Only the Rich Run for Office—and What We Can Do about It*. Princeton: Princeton University Press.

Carsey, Thomas M., and William Berry. 2014. "What's a Losing Party to Do? The Calculus of Contesting State Legislative Elections." *Public Choice* 160 (1): 251–73.

Carson, Jamie L. 2005. "Strategy, Selection, and Candidate Competition in U.S. House and Senate Elections." *Journal of Politics* 67 (1): 1–28.

Carson, Jamie L., Michael H. Crespin, Carrie P. Eaves, and Emily Wanless. 2011. "Constituency Congruency and Candidate Competition in U.S. House Elections." *Legislative Studies Quarterly* 36 (3): 461–82.

Carson, Jamie L., and Aaron A. Hitefeld. 2018. "Donald Trump, Nationalization, and the 2018 Midterm Elections." *Forum: A Journal of Applied Research in Contemporary Politics* 16 (4): 531–49.

Caygle, Heather. 2018. "Luján Taps Experienced Team for Assistant Speaker's Office." *POLITICO*, January 8. https://www.politico.com/story/2019/01/08/ben-ray-lujan-house- democrats-1086125

CBS Sunday Morning. 2013. "The Psychology of Winning—and Losing." *CBS News*, February 3. http://www.cbsnews.com/news/the-psychology-of-winning-and-losing/

Cheney, Kyle. 2015a. "Manchin Won't Run for West Virginia Governor." *POLIT-ICO*, April 19. http://www.politico.com/story/2015/04/joe-manchin-wont-run-for-wva-governor-117119

Cheney, Kyle. 2015b. "McCaskill Won't Run for Mo. Governor." *POLITICO*, January 12. https://www.politico.com/story/2015/01/claire-mccaskill-will-not-run-for-governor-missouri-114179

Chenoweth, Erica, and Jeremy Pressman. 2017. "This Is What We Learned by Counting the Women's Marches." *Washington Post*, February 7. https://www.washingtonpost.com/news/monkey-cage/wp/2017/02/07/this-is-what-we-learned-by-counting-the-womens-marches/?utm_term=.c126098c3551

Clark, Jennifer Hayes. 2015. *Minority Parties in U.S. Legislatures: Conditions of Influence*. Ann Arbor: University of Michigan Press.

Clark, Lesley. 2008. "Democrats Torn between Party, GOP Friends." *McClatchy Newspapers*, March 9. https://www.mcclatchydc.com/news/politics-government/article24478039.html

Condon, Stephanie. 2011. "Jane Harman Expected to Resign from Congress." *CBS*, February 7. https://www.cbsnews.com/news/jane-harman-expected-to-resign-from-congress

Congressional Research Service. 2019. "Congressional Careers: Service Tenure and Patterns of Member Service, 1789–2019." Congressional Research Service. https://fas.org/sgp/crs/misc/R41545.pdf

Connelly, William F., Jr., and John J. Pitney Jr. 1994. *Congress' Permanent Minority? Republicans in the U.S. House*. Lanham, MD: Rowman and Littlefield.

Connolly, Griffin. 2018. "Florida Rep. Dennis Ross Retiring after 8 Years." *Roll Call*, April 11. https://www.rollcall.com/news/politics/florida-rep-dennis-ross-retiring-8-years

Cook Political Report. 2018. "2018 House Race Ratings. April 6, 2018." *Cook Political Report*. https://www.cookpolitical.com/ratings/house-race-ratings/183822

Cooper, Joseph, and William West. 1981. "Voluntary Retirement, Incumbency, and the Modern House." *Political Science Quarterly* 96 (2): 279–300.

Copeland, Gary W. 1989. "Choosing to Run: Why House Members Seek Election to the Senate." *Legislative Studies Quarterly* 14 (4): 549–65.

Cottle, Michelle. 2018. "How Trump Made Special Elections Great Again." *Atlantic*, January 1. theatlantic.com/politics/archive/2018/01/how-trump-made-special-elections-great-again/549317/

Cox, Gary, and Mathew D. McCubbins. 1993. *Legislative Leviathan: Party Government in the House*. Berkeley: University of California Press.

Cox, Gary, and Mathew D. McCubbins. 2005. *Setting the Agenda: Responsible Party Government in the U.S. House of Representatives*. New York: Cambridge University Press.

Curiel, John. 2019. "Tripartite Redistricting Cartels and Overlapping Ambition." PhD diss., University of North Carolina at Chapel Hill.

Currinder, Marian L. 2003. "Leadership PAC Strategies and House Member Contributions." *Legislative Studies Quarterly* 28 (4): 551–77.

Daily Kos Elections. N.d. "Daily Kos Elections Statewide Results by LD (public) IL_ Upper." *Daily Kos Elections*. https://docs.google.com/spreadsheets/d/1YZRfFiC DBEYB7M18fDGLH8IrmyMQGdQKqpOu9lLvmdo/edit#gid=1094557625

Daugherty, Alex. 2018. "Democrat Mary Barzee Flores Switches Races to Challenge Republican Mario Diaz-Balart." *Miami Herald*, May 3. https://www. miamiherald.com/news/politics-government/article210394744.html

Davis, Julie Hirschfield. 2019. "Deprived of Power, House Republicans Head for the Exits." *New York Times*, August 2. https://www.nytimes.com/2019/08/02/us/ politics/house-republicans-retirement.html

DeBonis, Mike. 2015. "Joe Manchin Waves Off Governor Run with a Swipe at Harry Reid." *Washington Post*, April 20. http://www.washingtonpost.com/news/ post-politics/wp/2015/04/20/joe-manchin-waves-off-governor-run-with-a- swipe-at-harry-reid/

Deering, Christopher J., and Paul J. Wahlbeck. 2006. "Determinants of House Committee Chair Selection: Republicans Play Musical Chairs in the 107th Congress." *American Journal of Political Science* 34 (2): 1–21.

Den Hartog, Chris, and Nathan W. Monroe. 2011. *Agenda Setting in the U.S. Senate: Costly Consideration and Majority Party Advantage*. New York: Cambridge University Press.

Dominguez, Casey B. K. 2011. "Does the Party Matter? Endorsements in Congressional Primaries." *Political Research Quarterly* 64 (3): 534–44.

Draper, Robert. 2013. "The Future Mr. Speaker." *New Republic*, February 23. https://newrepublic.com/article/112487/chris-van-hollen-democrats-next- speaker-house

Edmondson, Catie. 2019. "House Democratic Campaign Arm Nears War with Liberals over Primary Fights." *New York Times*, April 7. https://www.nytimes. com/2019/04/07/ us/politics/democrats-liberals-tension.html

Egar, William T. 2016. "Tarnishing Opponents, Polarizing Congress: The House Minority Party and the Construction of the Roll Call Record." *Legislative Studies Quarterly* 41 (4): 935–64.

Eilperin, Juliet. 2000. "For Women, a Crucial Role." *Washington Post*, August 15. https://www.washingtonpost.com/archive/politics/2000/08/15/for-women- a-crucial-role/43289290-d8cc-47ac-b5a3–8b92d5c09f47/%3Futm_ term=.5d57fa5e16b2

Eilperin, Juliet, and Helen Dewar. 2000. "House GOP Has Slim Edge as More Races Are Decided." *Washington Post*, November 18. https://www.washing- tonpost.com/archive/politics/2000/11/18/house-gop-has-slim-edge-as-more- races-are-decided/bd7d44a6–7253-4415-b85d-1e4425882405/

Eilperin, Juliet, and Matthew Vita. 2000. "House Race Recounts Also May Be Crucial." *Washington Post*, November 10. https://www.washingtonpost.com/archive/ politics/2000/11/10/house-race-recounts-also-may-be-crucial/d080101b- aefb-4332-b23d- a925ccd19a42/

Ekman, Paul. 2003. *Emotions Reveled: Recognizing Faces and Feelings to Improve Communication and Emotional Life.* New York: Henry Holt and Company.

Ellis, John. 2015. "Valley Democrats Frustrated with National Party Leaders Running Local Campaigns." *Fresno Bee,* December 27. https://www.fresnobee.com/news/politics-government/politics-columns-blogs/political-notebook/article49382455.html

Everett, Burgess, and Glenn Thrush. 2016. "McConnell Throws Down Gauntlet: No Scalia Replacement under Obama." *POLITICO,* February 13. https://www.politico.com/story/2016/02/mitch-mcconnell-antonin-scalia-supreme-court-nomination-219248

Farenthold, David. 2016. "Nev. Candidate Says Reid Urged Him to Quit, Because 'a Muslim Cannot Win This Race.'" *Washington Post,* March 28. https://www.washingtonpost.com/politics/nev-candidate-says-reid-urged-him-to-quit-because-a-muslim-cannot-win-this-race/2016/03/28/7ebbffea-f2ce-11e5-89c3-a647fcce95e0_story.html

Fenno, Richard. 1978. *Homestyle: House Members in Their Districts.* New York: Little Brown.

Ferraro, Thomas, and Richard Cowan. 2010. "Speaker Pelosi Running for House Minority Leader." *Reuters,* November 5. https://www.reuters.com/article/us-usa-congress-pelosi/speaker-pelosi-running-for-house-minority-leader-idUSTRE6A443I20101105

Fisher, Samuel H., III, and Rebekah Herrick. 2002. "Whistle While You Work: Job Satisfaction and Retirement from the U.S. House." *Legislative Studies Quarterly* 27 (3): 445–57.

FiveThirtyEight. 2018. "Forecasting the Race for the House." *FiveThirtyEight,* November 6. https://projects.fivethirtyeight.com/2018-midterm-election-forecast/house/

Fowler, Linda. 1979. "The Electoral Lottery: The Decision to Run for Congress." *Public Choice* 34 (3–4): 399–418.

Francia, Peter L., John C. Green, Paul S. Herrnson, Clyde Wilcox, and Lynda W. Powell. 2003. *The Financiers of Congressional Elections: Investors, Ideologues, and Intimates.* New York: Columbia University Press.

Frantzich, Stephen E. 1978. "Opting Out: Retirement from the U.S. House of Representatives, 1966–1974." *American Politics Quarterly* 6 (3): 251–73.

Garfinkel, Sarah N., Emma Zorab, Nakulan Navaratnam, Miriam Engels, Núria Mallorquí-Bagué, Ludovico Minati, Nicholas G. Dowell, Jos F. Brosschot, Julian F. Thayer, and Hugo D. Critchley. 2016. "Anger in Brain and Body: The Neural and Physiological Perturbation of Decision-Making by Emotion." *Journal of Cognitive and Affective Neuroscience* 11 (1): 150–58.

Gimpel, James G., Frances E. Lee, and Shanna Pearson-Merkowitz. 2008. "The Check Is in the Mail: Interdistrict Funding Flows in Congressional Elections." *American Journal of Political Science* 52 (2): 373–94.

Givi, Julian, and Jeff Galak. 2019. "The 'Future Is Now' Bias: Anchoring and (Insufficient) Adjustment When Predicting the Future from the Present." *Journal of Experimental Social Psychology* 84. https://doi.org/10.1016/ j.jesp.2019.103830

Golshan, Tara, and Ella Nilsen. 2018. "How a 21-Year-Old College Senior Became the Breakout Star of 2018 Election Forecasting." *Vox*, June 1. https://www.vox.com/2018/6/1/17164960/ midterms-2018-forecast-projection-g-elliott-morris

Gordon, Sanford C., Gregory A. Huber, and Dimitri Landa. 2007. "Challenger Entry and Voter Learning." *American Political Science Review* 101 (2): 303–20.

Green, Donald P., and Jonathan S. Krasno. 1988. "Salvation for the Spendthrift Incumbent: Reestimating the Effects of Campaign Spending in House Elections." *American Journal of Political Science* 32 (4): 884–907.

Green, Matthew N. 2008. "The 2006 Race for Democratic Majority Leader: Money, Policy, and Personal Loyalty." *PS: Political Science & Politics* 41 (1): 63–67.

Green, Matthew. 2015. *Underdog Politics: The Minority Party in the U.S. House of Representatives*. New Haven: Yale University Press.

Grim, Ryan, and Sabrina Siddiqui. 2013. "Call Time for Congress Shows How Fundraising Dominates Bleak Work Life." *Huffington Post*, January 8. http://www.huffingtonpost.com/2013/01/08/call-time-congressional-fundraising_n_2427291.html

Grossmann, Matt, and David A. Hopkins. 2016. *Asymmetric Politics: Interest Group Republicans and Group Interest Democrats*. New York: Oxford University Press.

Hagen, Lisa. 2017. "Dems Land Top Recruit for Ros-Lehtinen's Florida District." *The Hill*, June 28. https://thehill.com/homenews/campaign/339946-fla-dem-officially-enters-crowded-race-to-replace-retiring-gop-rep

Halbfinger, David. 2011. "L.I. Congressman Leads Uphill Charge toward a Democratic House." *New York Times*, March 19. https://www.nytimes.com/2011/03/19/ nyregion/19steveisrael.html

Hall, Richard L., and Robert P. Van Houweling. 1995. "Avarice and Ambition: Representatives' Decision to Run or Retire from the U.S. House." *American Political Science Review* 89 (1): 121–36.

Hamilton, Reeve, and Morgan Smith. 2012. "Dewhurst Shuffles Senate Committee Chairs." *Texas Tribune*, October 4. https://www.texastribune.org/2012/10/04/lt-gov-dewhurst-shuffles-senate-committee-chairs/

Hamlin, Alan, and Colin Jennings. 2011. "Expressive Political Behaviour: Foundations, Scope and Implications." *British Journal of Political Science* 41 (3): 645–70.

Hanson, Peter. 2014. *Too Weak to Govern: Majority Party Appropriations in the U.S. Senate*. New York: Cambridge University Press.

Hare, Christopher, Keith T. Poole, and Howard Rosenthal. 2014. "Polarization in Congress Has Risen Sharply: Where Is It Going Next?" *Washington Post*, February 13. http://www.washingtonpost.com/blogs/monkey-cage/wp/2014/02/13/polarization-in-congress-has-risen-sharply-where-is-it-going-next/

Harmel, Robert. 1986. "Minority Partisanship in One-Party Predominant Legislatures: A Five-State Study." *Journal of Politics* 48 (3): 729–40.

Hassell, Hans. 2016. "Party Control of Party Primaries: Party Influence in Nominations for the US Senate." *Journal of Politics* 78 (1): 75–87.

Hassell, Hans. 2018. *The Party's Primary: Control of Congressional Nominations.* New York: Cambridge University Press.

Hawkesworth, Mary. 2003. "Congressional Enactments of Race-Gender: Toward a Theory of Raced-Gendered Institutions." *American Political Science Review* 97 (4): 529–50.

Heberlig, Eric. S., Marc J. Hetherington, and Bruce A. Larson. 2006. "The Price of Leadership: Campaign Money and the Polarization of Congressional Parties." *Journal of Politics* 68 (4): 992–1005.

Heberlig, Eric S., and Bruce A. Larson. 2005. "Redistributing Campaign Contributions by Members of Congress: The Spiraling Costs of the Permanent Campaign." *Legislative Studies Quarterly* 30 (4): 597–624.

Heberlig, Eric S., and Bruce A. Larson. 2007. "Party Fundraising, Descriptive Representation, and the Battle for Majority Control: Shifting Leadership Appointment Strategies in the U.S. House: 1990–2002." *Social Science Quarterly* 88 (2): 404–21.

Heberlig, Eric S,. and Bruce A. Larson. 2010. "Congressional Parties and the Mobilization of Leadership PAC Contributions." *Party Politics* 16 (4): 451–75.

Heberlig, Eric S., and Bruce A. Larson. 2012. *Congressional Parties, Institutional Ambition, and the Financing of Majority Control.* Ann Arbor: University of Michigan Press.

Heberlig, Eric S., and Bruce A. Larson. 2014. "U.S. House Incumbent Fundraising and Spending in a Post–Citizens United and Post-McCutcheon World." *Political Science Quarterly* 129 (4): 613–42.

Helderman, Rosalind. 2012. "In Retirement, GOP Moderate LaTourette Bemoans Rise of Extremes." *Washington Post*, July 31. https://www.washingtonpost.com/blogs/2chambers/post/retiring-rep-steve-latourette-you-have-to-hand-over-your-wallet-and-your-voting-card-to-extremes/2012/07/31/gJQA1XtqMX_blog.html

Hernandez, Raymond. 2007. "Republican Congressman in New Jersey Will Retire." *New York Times*, November 20. https://www.nytimes.com/2007/11/20/us/politics/20ferguson.html

Herrnson, Paul. 1988. *Party Campaigning in the 1980s.* Cambridge: Harvard University Press.

Herrnson, Paul. 2009. "The Roles of Party Organizations, Party-Connected Committees, and Party Allies in Elections." *Journal of Politics* 7 (4): 1207–24.

Hershey, Marjorie. 2009. *Party Politics in America.* New York: Pearson Longman.

Hetherington, Marc J., Bruce Larson, and Suzanne Globetti. 2003. "The Redistricting Cycle and Strategic Candidate Decisions in U.S. House Races." *Journal of Politics* 65 (4): 1221–34.

Hibbing, John. 1992. "Voluntary Retirement from the U.S. House of Representatives: Who Quits?" *American Journal of Political Science* 26 (3): 467–84.

Highton, Benjamin. 2011. "The Influence of Strategic Retirement on the Incumbency Advantage in U.S. House Elections." *Journal of Theoretical Politics* 23 (4): 431–47.

Hinchliffe, Kelsey L., and Frances E. Lee. 2015. "Party Competition and Conflict in State Legislatures." *State Politics and Policy Quarterly* 16 (2): 172–97.

Holbrook, Thomas M., and Emily Van Dunk. 1993. "Electoral Competition in the American States." *American Political Science Review* 87 (4): 955–62.

Hook, Janet. 1986. "House GOP: Plight of a Permanent Minority." *Congressional Quarterly Weekly Report,*. June 21.

Hopkins, Daniel. 2018. *The Increasingly United States: How and Why American Political Behavior Nationalized.* Chicago: University of Chicago Press.

House, Billy. 2015. "Steny Hoyer: Don't Bet on Democrats Retaking House Majority." *Bloomberg Politics*, January 29. https://www.bloomberg.com/news/articles/2015-01-29/steny-hoyer-don-t-bet-on-democrats-retaking-majority

House Oversight and Reform Committee. 2019. "Cummings Announces Subcommittee Chairs and Full Committee Vice Chair." https://oversight.house.gov/news/press-releases/cummings-announces-subcommittee-chairs-and-full-committee-vice-chair

Hulse, Carl. 2016. "Steve Israel of New York, a Top House Democrat, Won't Seek Reelection." *New York Times,* January 6. https://www.nytimes.com/2016/01/06/us/politics/steve-israel-house-democrat-new-york.html

Hulse, Carl. 2018. "'You Control Nothing': House Republicans Brace for Life in the Minority." *New York Times*, December 29. https://www.nytimes.com/2018/12/29/us/ politics/house-republicans-minority.html

Hundsdorfer, Beth. 2017. "Brendan Kelly Is for Congress: This Is Why." *Belleville News- Democrat,* July 5. https://www.bnd.com/news/local/article159824559.html

Hunt, Kasie. 2010. "Earl Pomeroy Loses." *POLITICO*, November 2. https://www.politico.com/blogs/ house-races-2010/1110/Earl_Pomeroy_loses.html

Hyde, David, and Gil Aegerter. 2017. "Why Is Rep. Dave Reichert Leaving Congress? Trump Is One Possibility." *KUOW*, September 6. https://www.kuow.org/stories/why-rep-dave-reichert-leaving-congress-trump-one-possibility

Jacobs, Ben. 2013. "Earl Pomeroy Doesn't Regret the Obamacare Vote That Ended His Career." *Daily Beast*, November 12. https://www.thedailybeast.com/earl-pomeroy-doesnt-regret-the-obamacare-vote-that-ended-his-career

Jacobson, Gary C. 1978. "The Effects of Campaign Spending in Congressional Elections." *American Political Science Review* 72 (2): 469–91.

Jacobson, Gary C. 1989. "Strategic Politicians and the Dynamics of U.S. House Elections, 1946–1986." *American Political Science Review* 83 (3): 773–93.

Jacobson, Gary. 2019. "Extreme Referendum: Donald Trump and the 2018 Midterm Elections." *Political Science Quarterly* 134 (1): 9–38.

Jacobson, Gary C., and Jamie L. Carson. 2016. *The Politics of Congressional Elections.* New York: Rowman and Littlefield.

Jacobson, Gary C., and Samuel Kernell. 1983. *Strategy and Choice in Congressional Elections.* New Haven: Yale University Press.

Johnson, Bertram. 2012. *Political Giving: Making Sense of Individual Campaign Contributions*. Boulder, CO: Lynne Rienner.

Jones, Charles O. 1970. *The Minority Party in Congress*. Boston: Little, Brown and Co.

Kahneman, Daniel, and Amos Tversky. 1979. "Prospect Theory: An Analysis of Decision under Risk." *Econometrica* 47 (2): 263–92.

Kane, Paul. 2016. "Steve Israel, Former Democratic Campaign Leader, to Retire from House after 16 Years." *Washington Post*, January 5. https://www.washington post.com/news/powerpost/wp/2016/01/05/steve-israel-former-democratic-campaign-leader-to-retire-from-house-after-16-years/?noredirect=on&utm_term=.46693a553015

Kapiszewski, Diana A., Lauren M. MacLean, and Benjamin L. Read. 2015. *Field Research in Political Science: Practices and Principles*. Cambridge: Cambridge University Press.

Kazee, Thomas A., and Mary C. Thornberry. 1990. "Where's the Party? Congressional Candidate Recruitment and American Party Organizations." *Western Political Quarterly* 43 (1): 61–80.

Kenney, Patrick J., and Tom W. Rice. 1987. "The Relationship between Divisive Primaries and General Election Outcomes." *American Journal of Political Science* 31 (1): 31–44.

Key, V. O., Jr. 1949. *Southern Politics in State and Nation*. Knoxville: University of Tennessee Press.

Key, V. O., Jr. 1964. *Politics, Parties, and Pressure Groups*. New York: Thomas Y. Crowell.

Kiewiet, D. Roderick, and Langche Zeng. 1993. "An Analysis of Congressional Career Decisions, 1947–1986." *American Political Science Review* 87 (4): 928–41.

Kim, Henry A., and Justin H. Phillips. 2009. "Dividing the Spoils of Power: How Are the Benefits of Majority Party Status Distributed in U.S. State Legislatures?" *State Politics and Policy Quarterly* 9 (2): 125–50.

Kinnaird, Eleanor. 2013. "Ellie Kinnaird State Senate: Your Senator in Orange and Chatham Counties." http://elliekinnaird.org/

Kliff, Sarah. 2018. "Seattle's Radical Plan to Fight Big Money in Politics." *Vox*, November 5. https://www.vox.com/2018/11/5/17058970/seattle-democracy-vouchers

Kloner, Robert A., Scott McDonald, Justin Leeka, and W. Kenneth Poole. 2009. "Comparison of Total and Cardiovascular Death Rates in the Same City during a Losing versus Winning Super Bowl Championship." *American Journal of Cardiology* 15 (12): 1647–50.

Koff, Stephen. 2009. "White House Flies Sen. Brown in for Vote." *Cleveland Plain Dealer*, February 14. https://www.cleveland.com/nation/index.ssf/2009/02/white_house_flies_sen_brown_in.html

Koger, Gregory. 2010. *Filibustering: A Political History of Obstruction in the House and Senate*. Chicago: University of Chicago Press.

Kolodny, Robin. 1998. *Pursuing Majorities: Congressional Campaign Committees in American Politics*. Norman: University of Oklahoma Press.

Kolodny, Robin, and Diana Dwyre. 1998. "Party-Orchestrated Activities for Legislative Party Goals." *Party Politics* 4 (3): 275–95.

Kolodny, Robin, and Diana Dwyre. 2006. "A New Rule Book: Party Money in the Post-BCRA World." In *Financing the 2004 Election*, edited by David B. Magleby, Kelly Patterson, and Quin Monson. Washington, DC: Brookings Institution Press.

Koziatak, Mike. 2016. "Schimpf Takes 58th State Senate Race, Says Economy Will Be His Priority." *Belleville News-Democrat*, November 8. https://www.bnd.com/news/local/ article113482668.html

Kurtzleben, Danielle. 2017. "Female Retired Marine with Viral Campaign Ad Hopes to Bridge Gap in Democratic Party." *NPR*, August 3. https://www.npr.org/2017/08/03/541223715/female-retired-marine-with-viral-campaign-ad-hopes-to-bridge-gap-in-democratic-p

La Raja, Ray. 2008. *Small Change: Money, Political Parties, and Campaign Finance Reform*. Ann Arbor: University of Michigan Press.

Law, Tara. 2019. "Rep. Ocasio-Cortez Becomes Youngest Woman Ever to Preside Over the House of Representatives." *Time*, May 11. https://time.com/5587669/ocasio-cortez-youngest-woman-preside-house/

Lawless, Jennifer L., and Richard L. Fox. 2010. *It Still Takes a Candidate: Why Women Don't Run for Office*. New York: Cambridge University Press.

Lawless, Jennifer L., and Sean M. Theriault. 2005. "Will She Stay or Will She Go? Career Ceilings and Women's Retirement from the U.S. Congress." *Legislative Studies Quarterly* 30 (4): 581–96.

Lawrence, John. 2018. *The Class of '74: Congress after Watergate and the Roots of Partisanship*. Baltimore: Johns Hopkins University Press.

Lazarus, Jeffrey. 2005. "Unintended Consequences: Anticipation of General Election Outcomes and Primary Election Divisiveness." *Legislative Studies Quarterly* 30 (3): 435–61.

Lazarus, Jeffrey. 2008. "Why Do Experienced Challengers Do Better Than Challengers?" *Political Behavior* 30 (2):185–98.

Lee, Frances. 2009. *Beyond Ideology*. Chicago: University of Chicago Press.

Lee, Frances. 2011. "Agreeing to Disagree: Agenda Content and Senate Partisanship, 1981–2004." *Legislative Studies Quarterly* 33 (2): 199–222.

Lee, Frances. 2016. *Insecure Majorities: Congress and the Perpetual Campaign*. Chicago: University of Chicago Press.

Levitt, Justin. 2013. "Maine." *All About Redistricting*. http://redistricting.lls.edu/states-ME.php

Liesman, Steve. 2018. "Majority of Americans Approve of Trump's Handling of the Economy for the First Time: CNBC survey." *CNBC*, June 25. https://www.cnbc.com/2018/06/25/majority-of-americans-approve-of-trumps-handling-of-the-economy.html

Lerner, Jennifer S., and Dacher Keltner. 2001. "Fear, Anger, and Risk." *Journal of Personality and Social Psychology* (1): 146–59.

Levy, Adam. 2019. "Pennsylvania Republican Congressman Resigns." *CNN*, January 17. https://www.cnn.com/2019/01/17/politics/tom-marino-announces-resignation/index.html

Long, J. Scott. 1997. *Regression Models for Categorical and Limited Dependent Variables*. Thousand Oaks, CA: SAGE Publications.

Lublin, David. 1999. *The Paradox of Representation: Racial Gerrymandering and Minority Interests in Congress*. Princeton: Princeton University Press.

Madison, James, Alexander Hamilton, and John Jay. [1787–88] 2003a. "Federalist 10." In *The Federalist Papers*, edited by Clinton Rossiter. Washington, DC: Signet Classics.

Madison, James, Alexander Hamilton, and John Jay. [1787–88] 2003b. "Federalist 51." In *The Federalist Papers*, edited by Clinton Rossiter. Washington, DC: Signet Classics.

Maestas, Cherie, Sarah Fulton, L. Sandy Maisel, and Walter J. Stone. 2006. "When to Risk It? Institutions, Ambition, and the Decision to Run for the U.S. House." *American Political Science Review* 100 (2): 195–208.

Maestas, Cherie, and Cynthia Rugeley. 2008. "Assessing the 'Experience Bonus' through Examining Strategic Entry, Candidate Quality, and Campaign Receipts in U.S. House Elections." *American Journal of Political Science* 52 (3): 520–35.

Magleby, David B., and Candice J. Nelson. 2010. *The Money Chase: Congressional Campaign Finance Reform*. Washington, DC: Brookings Institution Press.

Maisel, L. Sandy. 1986. *From Obscurity to Oblivion: Running in the Congressional Primary*. Knoxville: University of Tennessee Press.

Martin, Jonathan, and Alexander Burns. 2017. "High-Stakes Referendum on Trump Takes Shape in a Georgia Special Election." *New York Times*, June 18. https://www.nytimes.com/2017/06/18/us/politics/high-stakes-referendum-on-trump-takes-shape-in-a-georgia-special-election.html

Martin, Jonathan, and Alexander Burns. 2018. "Ryan Upends Republican Hopes and Plans for Midterm Elections." *New York Times*, April 11. https://www.nytimes.com/2018/04/11/us/politics/paul-ryan-midterms-republicans.html

Martorano, Nancy. 2004. "Cohesion or Reciprocity? Majority Party Strength and Minority Party Procedural Rights in the Legislative Process." *State Politics and Policy Quarterly* 4 (1): 55–73.

Matthews, Donald R. 1960. *U.S. Senators and Their World*. Chapel Hill: University of North Carolina Press.

Matthews, Donald R. 1984. "Legislative Recruitment and Legislative Careers." *Legislative Studies Quarterly* 9 (4): 547–85.

Mayhew, David. 1974a. *Congress: The Electoral Connection*. New Haven: Yale University Press.

Mayhew, David. 1974b. "Congressional Elections: The Case of the Vanishing Marginals." *Polity* 6 (3): 295–317.

Mayhew, David. 2014. "Is the Six-Year Itch Just a Senate Thing?" *Mischiefs of Faction*, January 13. http://mischiefsoffaction.blogspot.com/2014/01/is-six-year-itch-just-senate-thing.html

McPherson, Lindsey. 2018. "Pelosi Suggests 2020 Outcome Will Help Her Decide Whether to Stay in Congress." *Roll Call*, October 22. https://www.rollcall.com/news/politics/pelosi-suggests-2020-outcome-will-help-her-decide-whether-to-stay-in-congress

Mehta, Pranjal H., and Robert A. Josephs. 2006. "Testosterone Change after Losing Predicts the Decision to Compete Again." *Hormones and Behavior* 50 (5): 684–92.

Meinke, Scott. 2016. *Leadership Organizations in the House of Representatives: Party Participation and Partisan Politics*. Ann Arbor: University of Michigan Press.

Missoulian. 2017. "Missoulian Editorial: Our Endorsement in the Special Election (with Some Reservations)." *Missoulian*, May 14. https://missoulian.com/opinion/editorial/ missoulian-editorial-our-endorsement-in-the-special-election-with-some/article_4624d844–77b5–5239-a7c5–82629063e0c9.html

Mistler, Steve. 2017. "With an Eye on the House, Democrats Turn to Veterans for 2018 Races." *NPR*, September 8. https://www.npr.org/2017/09/08/549172533/with-an-eye-on- the-house-democrats-turn-to-veterans-for-2018-races

Mondak, Jeffrey. 1995. "Competence, Integrity, and the Electoral Success of Congressional Incumbents." *Journal of Politics* 57 (4): 1043–69.

Montellaro, Zach. 2019. "Biden Tries to Set the Stage in Detroit." *POLITICO*, July 25. https://www.politico.com/newsletters/morning-score/2019/07/25/biden-tries-to- set-the-stage-in-detroit-694022

Moore, Michael K., and John R. Hibbing. 1992. "Is Serving in Congress Fun Again? Voluntary Retirements from the House since the 1970s." *American Journal of Political Science* 36 (3): 824–28.

Moore, Michael K., and John R. Hibbing. 1998. "Situational Disaffection in Congress: Explaining Voluntary Departures." *Journal of Politics* 60 (4): 1088–1107.

Morita, Kenji, Mieko Morishima, Katsuyuki Sakai, and Yasuo Kawaguchi. 2013. "Dopaminergic Control of Motivation and Reinforcement Learning: A Closed-Circuit Account for Reward-Oriented Behavior." *Journal of Neuroscience* 33 (20): 8866–90.

Murakami, Michael H. 2009. "Minority Status, Ideology, or Opportunity: Explaining the Greater Retirement of House Republicans." *Legislative Studies Quarterly* 34 (2): 219–44.

New York Times. 2017a. "Alabama Results." *New York Times*. https://www.nytimes.com /elections/2016/results/alabama

New York Times. 2017b. "Illinois U.S. House 12th District Results: Mike Bost Wins." *New York Times*, August 1. https://www.nytimes.com/elections/results/illinois-house-district-12-bost-baricevic

Nir, David. 2008. "House Dems $14m behind in DCCC Dues." *Swing State Project*, October 4. http://swingstateproject.com/diary/3298/house-dems-14m-behind-in-dccc-dues

Nir, David. 2009. "Safe House Incumbents Need to Pay Their DCCC Dues." *Swing State Project.* http://swingstateproject.com/?s=dues

Nir, David. 2010. "Dems STILL Lagging on DCCC Dues; D-Trip: 'Everything's Fine.'" *Swing State Project*, June 17. http://swingstateproject.com/diary/7093/dems-still-lagging- on-dccc-dues-dtrip-everythings-fine

Nowatzki, Mike. 2015. "Senate Passes Bill Requiring Special Election to Fill U.S. Senate Vacancies." *Dickinson Press.* https://web.archive.org/web/20150707061629/http://www.thedickinsonpress.com/news/legislature/3716092-senate-passes-bill- requiring-special-election-fill-us-senate-vacancies

Nyhan, Brendan, Eric McGhee, John Sides, Seth Masket, and Steven Greene. 2012. "One Vote Out of Step? The Effects of Salient Roll Call Votes in the 2010 Election." *American Politics Research* 40 (5): 844–79.

https://twitter.com/AOC/status/1101579908747329543

Oliveira, Tânia F., Maria J. Gouveia, and Rui F. Oliveira. 2009. "Testosterone Responsiveness to Winning and Losing Experiences in Female Soccer Players." *Psychoneuroendocrinology* 34 (7): 1056–64.

Olsen, Peter, John M. Elliott, Christopher Frampton, and Paul S. Bradley. 2015. "Winning or Losing Does Matter: Acute Cardiac Admissions in New Zealand during Rugby World Cup Tournaments." *European Journal of Preventive Cardiology* 22 (10): 1254–60.

Open Secrets. N.d. "Illinois District 12 2016 Race." *Open Secrets.* https://www.opensecrets.org/races/summary?cycle=2016&id=IL12

Ornstein, Norman. 2011. "Fixing Congress: Ending the Permanent Campaign." *Boston Review*, May 3. http://bostonreview.net/ornstein-permanent-campaign

Pathé, Simone. 2015a. "Democrats Considering Female Comstock Challengers." *Roll Call*, April 9. https://www.rollcall.com/news/barbara-comstock-jennifer-wexton-virginia-10

Pathé, Simone. 2015b. "Heitkamp Opts to Stay in Senate, Won't Run for Governor." *Roll Call*, September 9. https://www.rollcall.com/2015/09/09/heitkamp-opts-to-stay-in-senate-wont-run-for-governor/

Pathé, Simone. 2016. "Democrats Land Reid Recruit in Competitive Nevada District." *Roll Call*, January 26. https://www.rollcall.com/news/home/democrats-land-reid-recruit-competitive-nevada-district

Pathé, Simone. 2018. "Florida Candidate Goes All-In on Impeachment Message." *Roll Call*, August 6. https://www.rollcall.com/news/politics/florida-house-candidate-goes-all-in-on-impeachment-message

Pearson, Kathryn. 2019. "Nancy Pelosi Victorious—Why the California Democrat Was Reelected Speaker of the House." *The Conversation*, January 3. https://theconversation.com/nancy-pelosi-victorious-why-the-california-democrat-was-reelected-speaker-of-the-house-107333

Polsby, Nelson. 2004. *How Congress Evolves: Social Bases of Institutional Change.* New York: Oxford University Press.

Porter, Rachel, and Sarah Treul. 2018. "The Increasing Value of Inexperience in

Congressional Primaries." Paper presented at the 2018 Meeting of the Midwest Political Science Association.

Preece, Jessica R., and Olga B. Stoddard. 2015. "Does the Message Matter? A Field Experiment on Political Party Recruitment." *Journal of Experimental Political Science* 2 (1): 26–35.

Rakich, Nathaniel. 2018. "Here Are All the Republicans Retiring from Congress in 2018." *FiveThirtyEight*, July 26. https://fivethirtyeight.com/features/here-are-all-the-republicans-retiring-from-congress-in-2018/

Ranney, Austin. 1976. "Parties in State Politics." In *Politics and the American States*, edited by Herbert Jacob and Kenneth Vines. Boston: Little, Brown and Co.

Reed, Stephen R. 2009. "Party Strategy or Candidate Strategy: How Does the LDP Run the Right Number of Candidates in Japan's Multi-Member Districts?" *Party Politics* 15 (3): 295–314.

Reeve, Elisabeth. 2013. "Bay Buchanan Refuses to Be Angry on TV Anymore." *Atlantic*, February 1. https://www.theatlantic.com/politics/archive/2013/02/bay-buchanan-quits-punditry/318782/

Reich, David, and Richard Kogan. 2016. "Introduction to Budget 'Reconciliation.'" Center on Budget and Policy Priorities. https://www.cbpp.org/research/federal- budget/introduction-to-budget-reconciliation

Rellahan, Michael. 2017. "Chesco Dems Celebrate 'Unbelievable' Victory." *Daily Local News*. https://www.dailylocal.com/news/national/chesco-dems-celebrate-unbelievable-victory/article_8b90d162-fd3d-5682-8bb5-f7fb2af19045.html

Riker, William, and Peter Ordeshook. 1968. "A Theory of the Calculus of Voting." *American Political Science Review* 62 (1): 25–42.

Riley, Gavin L., and Jacob F. H. Smith 2018. "The Trump Effect: Filing Deadlines and the Decision to Run in the 2016 Congressional Elections." *Forum: A Journal of Applied Research in Contemporary Politics* 16 (2): 193–210.

Rivers, Susan E., Marc A. Brackett, Nicole A. Katulak, and Peter Salovey. 2007. "Regulating Anger and Sadness: An Exploration of Discrete Emotions in Emotion Regulation." *Journal of Happiness Studies* 8 (3): 393–427.

Roberts, Jason M., Jacob F. H. Smith, and Sarah A. Treul. 2016. "Party Committee Targeting and the Evolution of Competition in U.S. House Elections." *Journal of Elections, Public Opinion, and Parties* 26 (1): 96–114.

Robertson, Ian. 2012. *The Winner Effect: The Neuroscience of Success and Failure*. New York: Thomas Dunne Books.

Rohde, David. 1979. "Risk Bearing and Progressive Ambition: The Case of Members of the United States House of Representatives." *American Journal of Political Science* 23 (1): 1–26.

Rohde, David. 1991. *Parties and Leaders in the Postreform House*. Chicago: University of Chicago Press.

Rovner, Julie. 2019. "John Dingell, 'Dean of the House,' Remembered as a Force in Health Policy." *Kaiser Health News*, February 7. https://khn.org/news/former-rep-john-dingell-dies-longest-serving-congressman-was-a-force-in-health-policy/

Rudell, B. J. 2019. "U.S. Rep. Scott Peters on Whether the New Democratic Majority Can Unify the Country." Polis: Duke's Center for Political Leadership, Innovation, and Leadership, September 21. https://polis.duke.edu/2019/02/21/u-s-rep-scott-peters-on-whether-the-new-democratic-majority-can-unify-the-country/

Ryan, Kelsey. 2015. "Democratic Poll Finds Nearly Even Support if Paul Davis Challenged Lynn Jenkins in U.S. House Race." *Wichita Eagle*, August 22. https://www.kansas.com/news/politics-government/article31908552.html

Sanchez, Luis. 2018. "GOP Congressman Says He's Leaving Congress Because 'All I Do Is Answer Questions about Donald Trump.'" *The Hill*, May 27. https://thehill.com/homenews/house/389597-gop-congressman-says-hes-leaving-congress-because-all-i-do-is-answer-questions

Schlesinger, Joseph A. 1966. *Ambition and Politics: Political Careers in the United States.* Chicago: Rand McNally and Company.

Schneider, Elena. 2017. "The Top 10 House Races to Watch in 2018." *POLITICO*, December 25. https://www.politico.com/story/2017/12/25/house-races-2018-midterms- republicans-democrats-316207

Selverstone, Marc J. 2014. *A Companion to John F. Kennedy.* West Sussex, UK: John Wiley and Sons.

Shabad, Rebecca. 2019. "House Republicans Face Reckoning as Retirement Fever Spreads." *NBC*, August 5. https://www.nbcnews.com/politics/congress/house-republicans-face-reckoning-retirement-fever-spreads-n1038816

Shepard, Steven. 2015. "Democrats Face Narrow Path to Retake Senate in 2016." *POLITICO*, July 6. http://www.politico.com/story/2015/07/senate-2016-election-democrats-119778

Shepard, Steven. 2018. "Gallup Ends Daily Presidential Approval Tracking Poll." *POLITICO*, January 3. https://www.politico.com/story/2018/01/03/gallup-ends-presidential-approval-tracking-poll-322280

Shor, Boris, and Nolan McCarty. 2011. "The Ideological Mapping of State Legislatures." *American Political Science Review* 105 (3): 530–51.

Silver, Nate. 2018. "Another Special Election, Another Really Bad Sign for the GOP." *FiveThirtyEight*, April 25. https://fivethirtyeight.com/features/arizona-8-special-election-result/

Simon, Scott. 2009. "Politicians Are People, Too." *NPR*, July 4. https://www.npr.org/templates/ story/story.php?storyId=106268787

Sinclair, Barbara. 1989. *The Transformation of the U.S. Senate.* Baltimore: Johns Hopkins University Press.

Sinclair, Barbara. 2015. *Unorthodox Lawmaking: New Legislative Processes in the U.S. Congress.* Washington, DC: CQ Press.

Smith, Jacob F. H., and Neil I. Weinberg. 2016. "The Elevator Effect: Advertising, Priming, and the Rise of Cherie Berry." *American Politics Research* 44 (3): 496–522.

Smith, Steven S. 1989. *Call to Order: Floor Politics in the House and Senate.* Washington, DC: Brookings Institution Press.

Smith, Steven S. 2014. *The Senate Syndrome*. Norman: University of Oklahoma Press.

Smith, Steven S., and Gerald Gamm. 2001. "The Dynamics of Party Government in Congress." In *Congress Reconsidered*, 7th ed., edited by Lawrence C. Dodd and Bruce I. Oppenheimer. Washington, DC: CQ Press.

Sorauf, Frank. 1964. *Political Parties in the American System*. Boston: Little, Brown.

Squire, Peverill. 2015. "A Squire Index Update." *State Politics and Policy Quarterly* 17 (4): 361–71.

Stanton, Steven J. Center for Cognitive Neuroscience, Duke University, Durham, North Carolina, United States of America , Jacinta C. Beehner, Ekjyot K. Saini, Cynthia M. Kuhn, and Kevin S. LeBar. 2009. "Dominance, Politics, and Physiology: Voters' Testosterone Changes on the Night of the 2008 United States Presidential Election." *Plos One* 4 (10): e7543.

STATA. N.d. "xttobit- Random-effects tobit models." *STATA*, https://www.stata.com/manuals13/xtxttobit.pdf

Stimson, James, Michael MacKuen, and Robert Erickson. 1995. "Dynamic Representation." *American Political Science Review* 89 (3): 543–65.

Stone, Walter J., Sarah A. Fulton, Cherie D. Maestas, and L. Sandy Maisel. 2010. "Incumbency Reconsidered: Prospects, Strategic Retirement, and Incumbent Quality in U.S. House Elections." *Journal of Politics* 72 (1): 178–90.

Stone, Walter J., and L. Sandy Maisel. 2003. "The Not-So-Simple Calculus of Winning: Potential U.S. House Candidates' Nomination and General Election Prospects." *Journal of Politics* 65 (4): 951–77.

Stone, Walter J., L. Sandy Maisel, and Cherie D. Maestas. 2004. "Quality Counts: Extending the Strategic Politician Model of Incumbent Deterrence." *American Journal of Political Science* 48 (3): 479–95.

Theriault, Sean. 1998. "Moving Up or Moving Out: Career Ceilings and Congressional Retirement." *Legislative Studies Quarterly* 23 (3): 419–33.

Thomas, Lucas M. 2017. "Senate Hopeful Jesse Sbaih Visits Mesquite." *St. George News*, July 21. https://www.thespectrum.com/story/news/local/mesquite/2017/07/21/senate-hopeful-jesse-sbaih-visits-mesquite/497989001/

Thomsen, Danielle M. 2017. *Opting Out of Congress: Partisan Polarization and the Decline of Moderate Candidates*. New York: Cambridge University Press.

Treul, Sarah, and Rachel Porter. 2018. "Inexperienced Candidates Are Becoming More Common, but Only in One Party." *Vox*, April 20. https://www.vox.com/mischiefs-of-faction/2018/4/20/17261870/inexperienced-candidates-republicans

Van Dunk, Emily. 1997. "Challenger Quality in State Legislative Elections." *Political Research Quarterly* 50 (4): 793–807.

Vitka, Will. 2018. "Alsobrooks Wins Dem Nod for Prince George's County Executive." *WTOP*, June 10. https://wtop.com/local-politics-elections-news/2018/06/10-fight-to-be-next-prince-georges-county-executive/

Voorhees, Josh. 2018. "Laura Moser's Anti-Establishment Campaign Fizzles Out in

Houston." *Slate*, May 22. https://slate.com/news-and-politics/2018/05/laura-moser-opposed-by-dccc-loses-texas-runoff-to-lizzie-pannill-fletcher.html

Wasserman, Dave. 2017. "The Congressional Map Has a Record-Setting Bias against Democrats." *FiveThirtyEight*, August 7. https://fivethirtyeight.com/features/the-congressional-map-is-historically-biased-toward-the-gop/

Watkins, Eli. 2018. "Ocasio-Cortez to Be Youngest Woman Ever Elected to Congress." *CNN*, November 6. https://www.cnn.com/2018/11/06/politics/ocasio-cortez-youngest-woman- ever/index.html

Wawro, Gregory J., and Eric Schickler. 2006. *Filibuster: Obstruction and Lawmaking in the U.S. Senate*. Princeton: Princeton University Press.

Whitt, Ward. 2006. "The Impact of Increased Employee Retention on Performance in a Customer Contact Center." *Manufacturing & Service Operations Management* 8 (3): 235–52.

Wilson, Chris. 2018. "See How Trump's Approval Rating Stacks Up against Other Presidents after One Year." *Time*, January 17. https://time.com/5103776/donald-trump-approval-rating-graph/

Wise, Roy A. 2004. "Dopamine, Learning and Motivation." *Nature Reviews: Neuroscience* 5 (6) (June): 483–94.

Wiseman, Alan, and Craig Volden. 2014. *Legislative Effectiveness in the United States Congress*. New York: Cambridge University Press.

Wolak, Jennifer. 2007. "Strategic Retirements: The Influence of Public Preferences on Voluntary Departures from Congress." *Legislative Studies Quarterly* 32 (2): 285–308.

Zhou, Li. 2019. "Kirsten Gillibrand's Plan to Get More Small Donors into Politics: Give Every Voter $600." *Vox*, May 4. https://www.vox.com/policy-and-politics/2019/5/4/18526808/kirsten-gillibrand-democracy-dollars-2020-campaign-finance-reform

Index

1974 election, 114; as a cut-point for models, 45–46, 48, 80–81, 97–98; availability of campaign finance data, 57; resulting reforms of Congress, 22, 35

2010 election, 14, 26, 38–39, 52, 61, 63, 108, 123, 127–128; implications for minority party status for Democrats in state legislatures, 132–141, 145–146; implications for structure of Democratic House leadership, 17, 157n4; role of Affordable Care Act, 20

Affordable Care Act (Obamacare), 20, 49, 107, 118
Aldrich, John H., 10, 12, 72, 126; conditional party government, 21, 76, 124, 148; southern politics, 81–82; party structure, 90
Atkinson, Mary Layton, 96

Banks, Jeffrey, 74, 87
Battista, John S. Coleman, 76, 124, 126
Baumgartner, Frank, 96
Begich, Mark, 75
Bendetto, Richard, 24
Bentsen, Lloyd, 16
Berg, Rick, 16
Berry, William, 11
Bianco, William T., 10, 72, 124

Binder, Sarah, 2, 105
Bipartisan Campaign Reform Act (BRCA), 58, 65–66
Bloom, Elaine, 70
Boehner, John, 9, 26
Bost, Mike, 88, 162n1
Boxer, Barbara, 118
Box-Steffensmeier, Jan, 56
Boydstun, Amber, 96
Brady, David, 20, 79
Bredesen, Phil, 118
Broockman, David, 94
Brooks, Susan, 143, 165n1
Brown, Scott, 108
Brown, Sherrod, 24–25
Bryce, Randy, 29
Buchanan, Bay, 21
Bush, George H.W., 32
Bush, George W., 38, 49, 71, 110; policy achievements, 107
Buttigieg, Pete, 161n10
Byrd Rule, 107. *See also* Congressional Budget Act of 1974: budget reconciliation process

Cain, Bruce, 74
calculus of political decision-making process: Black's extension, 10, 72; Riker and Ordeshook's formulation, 9–10, 27, 72; Rohde and progressive ambition, 10, 72

call time, 7, 14–15, 55, 59. *See also* party fundraising

candidate entry, 11, 17, 86–90, 97, 144–146; after the 1994 House elections, 83–86; effect of minority party on entry of U.S. House candidates, 75–82; existing literature, 72–75; filing deadlines, 96; in early 2000s House elections, 70–72; in state legislatures, 126–135, 141, 146, 162n13, 164n8; in the U.S. Senate, 12, 75, 112–115, 118, 145

Carsey, Thomas, 11

Carson, Jamie, campaign finance, 19, 58; dataset with Gary Jacobson, 11, 159n12, 162n14, 162n15, 162n18; forecasting congressional elections, 35, 83; state legislators running for Congress, 73–74; quality candidates running for Congress in 2018, 86

Carter, James E., 105

case study, 11–12, 30; of retirement decisions in the 2018 election, 48–51

Castro, Julián, 16

Cheney, Richard, 32

civil rights legislation, 105, 108, 119

Clark, Jennifer Hayes, 9, 124

Clinton, Bill, 103, 110; agenda in Congress, 107, 109, 140

Clinton, Hillary, 51, 81, 83, 92, 93, 158n6, 162n17

Clyburn, James, 17

Coelho, Tony, 57, 63

Cole, Tom, 26

Collins, Susan, 24, 164n11

Comstock, Barbara

conditional party government, 12; and the U.S. Senate, 119; as a precondition for my theory, 21–24, 26–28; effect on candidate entry decisions, 76–77, 80, 82–83; effect on congressional retirement, 30, 35, 40, 42–43, 46, 144–145; effect on party recruitment efforts, 95–96, 102; engagement in party fundraising, 60–64; in U.S. state legislatures, 124, 126, 132, 134

Congressional Budget Act of 1974, 107; budget reconciliation process, 107–109 (*see also* Byrd Rule)

Connelly, William F., Jr.; campaign finance, 6, 58, 61, 63; party recruitment, 9, 91; permanent Republican minority, 5–6, 8, 18, 21–22, 32–34, 52, 133

content analysis, 11–12, 96, 155–156, 163n12, 165n4

Cook Political Report, 29–30, 158n2

Costello, Ryan, 50–51

Cotton, Tom, 16

Cox, Gary, 23, 35, 46, 77, 158n12

CQ Weekly: content analysis of articles, 96, 155–156. *See also* content analysis

Crowley, Joe, 54

Cruz, Ted, 16

Curiel, John, 3, 90, 128

Currinder, Marian, 7, 55, 59

Daines, Steve, 16

De Beof, Suzanna, 96

Deering, Christopher J., 7, 55, 59

Democratic Congressional Campaign Committee (DCCC), 14, 17, 19, 160n1; methods for data collection of party fundraising, 153–156, 165n4; party fundraising, 57, 63, 64, 68, 143; party recruitment efforts, 89–90, 92, 93, 162n9, 163n12

Democratic Party: 40-year era of control of Congress, 8, 10, 20–23, 32, 35–39, 43–44, 46, 51–52, 60–63, 77, 80–83, 91, 147, 158n10; and the 2017–2018 elections, 18, 26, 30, 34, 48–52, 83–89, 94, 118–119, 143, 158n6, 162n20, 164n10; as a House minority party after the 2010 elections, 11, 14–15, 17, 19, 26, 52, 76, 90, 94–95 (*see also* 2010 election); as a Senate minority party after the 2014 elections, 1–3, 157nn1–2, 164n9; as the "party of government," 5–6, 91; candidate recruitment efforts (*see* Democratic Congressional Campaign Committee (DCCC): party recruitment efforts); control of government after the 2008 election, 24–25, 38, 160n6; efforts to win back the House majority after the 1994 election, 33, 61, 70–72, 77, 161n5; engagement in party fundraising, 55,

57–58, 61, 63, 68, 157n4 (*see also* party fundraising); feelings of isolation of Black and female members, 139–140; historic strength in the South, 81, 123, 145, 163n1 (*see also* Solid South); ideology (*see* DW-Nominate scores); interviews of (*see* interview research); loss of Senate majority in 1980, 105; progressives in the U.S. Senate, 105–109, 114; quality of Senate nominees, 113–114; retirements of senators, 103–104, 115–116; selection of interviewees, 149; state legislative Democrats after the 2010 elections, 121–123, 127–129, 133–134, 136, 141, 145–146

Den Hartog, Chris, 2, 105–106, 109, 116, 119

Dent, Charlie, 29

Diaz-Balart, Mario, 93, 160n6, 162–163n10

Dominguez, Casey B. K., 94

DW-Nominate scores, 40, 159n13

Dwyre, Diana, 58

Edwards, Chet, 61

Edwards, Donna, 19, 158n7

Ellsworth, Brad, 72

Emanuel, Rahm, 62

Ernst, Joni, 107

Exon, Jim, 103

Federal Election Commission (FEC), 64; data collection from, 153–154; Federal Election Campaign Act of 1974 (FECA), 57–58

Feinstein, Dianne, 118

Fenno, Richard: member goals beyond reelection, 5, 12, 20, 33, 52, 148; reelection goal, 15

Ferejohn, John, 74

Fiorina, Morris, 20, 74

Fletcher, Lizzie Pannill, 93

Flores, Mary Barzee, 93, 162n10

Franken, Al, 24

Frantzich, Stephen, 41

Frelinghuysen, Rodney, 29–30, 158n4

Frenzel, Bill, 8

Gallup Poll, 35, 50, 110, 128, 159n9

gerrymandering, 50, 158n6; *See also* redistricting

Gianforte, Greg, 18, 157n3

Gillibrand, Kirsten, 69

Gimpel, James, 19, 56

Gingrich, Newt, 6, 8

Globetti, Suzanne, 73

Gradison, William, 34

Green, Matthew: minority party power, 8–9; party fundraising and majority control, 7, 55, 59

Great Recession, 49

Green New Deal, 54

Griffin, John, 81–82

Grim, Ryan, 7, 54–55

Grossmann, Matt, 140

Hagan, Kay, 122

Hahn, Janice, 34

Harman, Jane, 34–35, 71

Harris, Kamala, 16

Hassell, Hans, 92

Hawkesworth, Mary, 140

Heberlig, Eric, 7, 12, 64; engagement in party fundraising, 55, 58–60, 62; modelling strategy, 65–66; party fundraising and institutional advancement, 7, 59–60, 64

Heflin, Howell, 103

Heitkamp, Heidi, 1–3, 164n9

Helms, Jesse, 105

Hensarling, Jeb, 29

Herrnson, Paul, 57–58, 90–92

Hershey, Marjorie, 90

Hetherington, Marc, 59, 73

Hill, Katie, 18

Hinchcliffe, Kelsey L., 3, 124, 128

Hitefeld, Aaron, 86

Hohmann, James, 1

Holbrook, Thomas, 3, 128

Hopkins, Daniel, 83

Hopkins, David, 140

Houlahan, Chrissy, 86

House of Cards (television show), 24

Hulse, Carl, 15, 18, 21, 26, 54

Hurd, Will, 143

incumbency advantage, 52, 79, 159n6, 162n15; personal vote, 74 interview research, 13, 91–92, 126–127, 146, 156; accounts from, 59, 92, 94–95, 101, 118, 123, 130, 132–141, 148, 159n8; methods used in this book; 11, 133, 149–151

Israel, Steve, 14–15, 21, 54, 71

Jacobson, Gary: campaign finance, 19, 56, 58; forecasting congressional elections, 35, 83; dataset with Jamie Carson, 11, 159n12, 162nn14–15, 162n18; strategic politicians, 10, 31, 42, 46, 73–74; quality candidates, 70–71, 74–75, 86–87, 96–97, 101, 130, 161n2, 161n5

Johnson, Sam, 51

Johnson, Timothy, 104

Jolly, David, 144, 165n2

Jones, Charles O., 4–8, 143

Kazee, Thomas A., 91, 94, 155, 163n11

Kennedy, Edward M., 24–25, 108

Kennedy, John F., 16

Kernell, Samuel: strategic politicians, 10, 3, 42, 46, 73; quality candidates, 74

Key, V.O., Jr., 87, 90, 123–125

Kiewiet, D. Roderick, 32, 74

Kinnaird, Eleanor, 122–123

Kirkpatrick, Ann, 3

Klein, Ron, 71

Koger, Gregory, 105

Kolodny, Robin, 58, 90

Krishnamoorthi, Raja, 18

Larson, Bruce, 7, 12, 64; engagement in party fundraising, 55, 58–60, 62; modelling strategy, 65–66; party fundraising and institutional advancement, 7, 59–60, 64

Lawless, Jennifer, 32, 73

Lazarus, Jeffrey, 74, 90

leadership PAC, 7, 64, 153–154

Lee, Frances, 6–9, 22, 25, 105–106, 109, 136, 148, 157n6; inter-district contributions, 19, 56; measure of competitiveness, 3, 37, 124, 128; interview research appendix design, 165n1; partisan messaging votes, 7–8,

148; research design for interviews, 149–151, 165n1

legislative effectiveness, 138; scores by Wiseman and Volden, 21, 48, 51–52, 143, 159n17

legislative professionalism, 131–132, 141, 149

Lessig, Lawrence, 69

logistic regression, 38, 40–41, 78–79, 97, 112, 129–131, 159n14, 161n15

Lott, Trent, 32

Lovett, John, 96

Lublin, David, 140

Lujan, Ben Ray, 17

Madison, James: *Federalist 10*, 4, 134; *Federalist 51*, 1, 3–4; implications for the minority party, 3–4, 146

Maestas, Cherie, 10, 73–74, 91,

Magleby, David, 57–58, 60

Maisel, L. Sandy, 73; political amateurs, 74

majority party status: and minority party status (*see* minority party status); candidate entry, (*see* candidate entry: effect of minority party entry of U.S. House candidates); Democrats as permanent majority (*see* Democratic Party: 40-year era of control of Congress); desire to win majority, 6–7, 11–12, 15, 33; electoral benefits of serving in majority, 18–19; leadership positions, 17–18, 62; majority factions (*see* Madison, James); opportunities for first term members, 76; policy-making role, 7–9, 26, 34–35, 146–148, 158nn10–11 (*see also* legislative effectiveness); recruitment attempts (*see* minority party status: effect on recruitment attempts); Republican House majority and 2018 elections, (*see* Republican Party: retirements in 2018); role of party fundraising in advancement, 62; state legislative majority (*see* state legislatures); tools to disempower the minority party, 20–28; U.S. Senate majority (*see* U.S. Senate); willing to put up with party fundraising, 59, 61–68

Manchin, Joe, 2–3, 164n9
marginal seats. *See* swing seats
Marino, Thomas, 34
Matthews, Donald, 90, 104
Mayhew, David A.: ambition theory, 30–31; reelection goal, 5, 10, 12, 15, 19–20, 30–31, 46, 52, 147–148; Six-Year Itch, 110; the vanishing marginals, 46–48, 50–51
McCain, John, 25, 27, 164n11
McCarty, Nolan, 125–126, 132
McCaskill, Claire, 2–3, 164n9
McConnell, Mitch, 118
McCubbins, Mathew, 23, 35, 46, 77, 158n12
McGrath, Amy, 86
McSally, Martha, 20, 158n9
Meinke, Scott, 8
Merkley, Jeffrey, 107, 161n8
Metzenbaum, Howard, 105
Michel, Robert, 18
Mikulski, Barbara, 19, 118
minority party status: access to campaign finance, 19; as the opposition party, 6, 23, 28, 52–53, 124, 136, 147; effect on candidate entry decisions, (*see* candidate entry: effect of minority party on entry of U.S. House candidates); effect on party fundraising, (*see* party fundraising); effect on recruitment attempts, 88–89, 97–102, 144; effect on retirement decisions (*see* retirement decisions); feelings of frustration, powerlessness, and anger, 3, 24, 26–27, 30, 69, 74, 121–123, 134–135, 144; implications for democratic governance and public policymaking, 13, 120, 141–142, 144, 146–148; implications for electoral competition, 87, 146–147; interaction with race and gender, 123, 139–140, 146; in state legislatures (*see* state legislatures); in the U.S. Senate (*see* U.S. Senate); measurement of probability of minority party status, 30, 35–38, 59, 78, 109–111, 123–125, 127–129, 163n6, 164n9; political ambition and opportunities, 15, 17, 19, 34–35, 76, 126; rights and influence of the minority party on

policymaking, 4–8, 20–23, 26–28, 35, 82, 126, 135–138; state of mind, 5–6, 15; typology of minority party status and conditional party government, 23–24
Monroe, Nathan W., 2, 105–106, 109, 116, 119
Moser, Laura, 92–94
Murkowski, Lisa, 164n11
Murphy, Patrick, 3

National Republican Congressional Committee (NRCC), 160n1; methods for data collection of party fundraising, 153–156, 165n4; party fundraising, 57, 64; party recruitment, 89–90, 163n12
Negrete McLeod, Gloria, 34
Nelson, Bill, 118
Nelson, Candice J., 57–58, 60
neurotransmitters, 25
New Deal, 105
New York Times, content analysis of articles, 96, 155–156; live polls in 2018, 88
Nir, David, 61–62, 160n4, 160n6
Nixon, Jerimiah W. "Jay," 140
North Carolina General Assembly: 2013–15; legislative session, 121–123, 164nn1–3

Obama, Barack, 1–2, 16, 92, 128–129; Obama administration, 9, 25–26
Oberstar, Jim, 63
Ocasio-Cortez, Alexandria, 54–55, 62, 68, 160nn6–7
OLS regression, 40; model to predict outcome of U.S. House elections, 35–36; model to predict outcome of U.S. Senate elections, 110–111; model to predict outcome of U.S. state legislative elections, 128–129
Ornstein, Norman, 69
O'Rourke, Beto, 118

party fundraising, 6, 12, 15, 144, 147; access-driven donors, 18–19; accounts from interviewees, 140–141; collection of data for chapter three, 153–154;

party fundraising (*continued*)
    conditional party government (*see*
    conditional party government:
    engagement in party fundraising)
    member distaste of, 54–55, 59, 63, 67;
    factors predicting level of activity in,
    55–56; party committees (*see* Demo-
    cratic Congressional Campaign Com-
    mittee (DCCC): party fundraising and
    National Republican Congressional
    Committee (NRCC): party fundrais-
    ing); party dues, 61, 139–141. *See also*
    Heberlig, Eric; Larson, Bruce
party roll, 23, 158n12
Pearson-Merkowitz, Shanna, 19, 56
Pell, Claiborne, 103
Pelosi, Nancy, 9, 14, 61, 153, 157n4,
    158n6
Peters, Scott, 143
Pitney, John F., Jr., campaign finance, 6,
    58, 61, 63; party recruitment, 9, 91;
    permanent Republican minority, 5–6,
    8, 18, 21–22, 32–34, 52, 133
Political Action Committees (PACs), 7,
    57–58, 63–64, 137, 153–154
political ambition, 11, 15–19, 24, 86,
    148; ambition in the Solid South, 81–
    82; ambition theory, 17, 27; candidate
    entry decisions, 73–74, 86; interaction
    with minority party status, 17–19, 26,
    34, 51–52; party fundraising efforts,
    59–60; party recruitment, 95; state
    legislative candidates, 101, 121, 125;
    the U.S. Senate, 103, 107, 112, 119–
    120; types of ambition, 10, 16, 19, 31,
    34, 51–52, 60, 107, 119, 160n19
political bench, 91, 113, 125, 133, 145
political party committee, 3, 28, 69;
    campaign finance, 7, 57–58, 60–61,
    153–154; recruitment efforts, 12, 15,
    27, 86–87, 89–95, 97–99, 101–102,
    156, 162n9
political party theory, 17, 90; and mid-
    1970s U.S. Congress, 31; gatekeeping
    function of parties, 90. *See also* Aldrich,
    John H.
political polarization: and campaign
    finance, 63; and retirement decisions,
    32, 40; competitiveness of congressio-
    nal elections, 83; high and low polar-
    ization state legislative bodies, 132;
    increased polarization in Congress,
    6–8, 15, 22, 63, 83, 106, 124–126. *See
    also* conditional party government
Pomeroy, Earl, 20
Preece, Jessica, 94
psychology of winning and losing, 12,
    34; anger and altered risk percep-
    tions, 134–135; accounts from former
    legislators, 135–138; connection to
    minority party status, 21–27; sports
    and losing, 25–26; "future is now"
    bias, 134

Quayle, Dan, 16, 157n2
Quist, Rob, 18

Ranney, Austin, 3; Ranney index, 128
Raskin, Jamie, 18
Reagan, Ronald, 6, 21, 73, 105; agenda,
    60
redistricting, 131–132, 135, 140, 164n10,
    165nn11–12; after the 2010 elec-
    tion, 127, 140, 165n11; as a potential
    cause of retirement, 40–41, 131–132,
    163n14, 164n10; as a variable in mod-
    els, 41, 79, 98–99, 131, 163n14; candi-
    date entry decisions, 78–79, 112–113;
    gerrymandering (*see* gerrymandering)
Republican Party: 2020 election, 143–
    144; as a minority party, 5–8, 32–33,
    37, 39, 63, 73, 114; as a Senate major-
    ity, 106–107, 109, 110, 118–119, 147,
    157n4; candidate recruitment efforts,
    88–91 (*see also* National Republican
    Congressional Committee (NRCC):
    party recruitment efforts); coalition
    with southern Democrats in mid-
    20th century Congress, 22–23, 35,
    60–61, 80, 105, 108; control of the
    Senate after the 2014 elections, 1–3;
    dominance in state legislatures in
    the 2010s, 121–123, 125, 127, 129,
    133–135, 137–140, 164n6; effect
    of Donald Trump nomination, (*see*
    Trump, Donald J.); ideology (*see*
    DW-Nominate scores); interviews of
    Republicans (*see* interview research);

lack of bench in the South in the 20th century (*see* Solid South: lack of Republican bench); lack of consensus in House after 2012 election, 9, 26; non-retirement of senators in 1996, 103–104, 116; obstruction of Obama administration agenda, 2, 24; party fundraising (*see* National Republican Congressional Committee (NRCC): party fundraising), quality of Senate nominees, 113–114; response to efforts by Democrats to win the majority in the early 2000s, 70–73; engagement retirements in 2018, 29–30, 34, 48–51, 135–138 (*see also* retirement decisions: Republican members who retired in 2018); retirement of senior Republicans after 1954 election, 42–43, 115; struggles with candidate recruitment before 1994 election, 91 (*see also* minority party: effect on recruitment attempts); winning the majority in 1994, (*see* Republican Revolution and the 1994 election)

Republican Revolution and the 1994 election, 7, 10, 39, 58, 61, 72, 77, 83, 109, 145; implications for candidate recruitment in subsequent elections, 83–86

Reichert, Dave, 50, 52

Reid, Harry, 25, 118, 162n7

retirement decisions, 11–12, 15, 163n14; House banking scandal as a cause, 39; from U.S. House, 5–6, 14, 29–35, 38–53, 143–148, 158n3, 159n6, 165n1; from U.S. Senate, 103–104, 108–109, 112, 114–118; from U.S. state legislatures, 121–123, 126–127, 132, 135–138, 164n9; Republican members who retired in 2018, 29–30, 50–51; role of age/health, 31–32, 40–41; similarity to candidate entry decisions, 78

Rhodes, John Jacob, 157n4

Ribble, Reid, 54

Richardson, David, 93

Riley, Gavin, 12, 85

Rohde, David: conditional party government, 12, 21–22, 35; member goals

beyond reelection, 5, 20, 33, 52, 148; reelection goal, 15; progressive ambition, 10, 79

Roll Call (publication), 61, 93, 160n4; content analysis of articles, 96, 127, 155–156

Roberts, Jason, 62

Robertson, Ian, 12, 25, 34, 76

Rodriguez, Ciro, 72

Rodríguez, Jose Jávier, 93, 162–163n10

Romney, Mitt, 21, 83, 92, 129, 163–164n8

Rosen, Jacky, 16, 90, 118

Ros-Lehtinan, Ileana, 51, 93, 160n6

Ross, Dennis, 29–30

Rouda, Harley, 18

Rubio, Marco, 16

Rugeley, Cynthia, 74

Ryan, Paul, 29–30, 158n2

Sabato's Crystal Ball, 30

Sanders, Bernie, 161n4

Scalia, Antonin, 2

Schickler, Eric, 105

Schiff, Adam, 71

Schlesinger, Joseph: ambition theory, 12–13, 16–17, 28, 31, 52, 75, 106–107, 160n19

Sened, Itai, 168

seniority, 108, 140, 163n8; age and Senate retirement decisions, 103–104, 109, 115–118; committee chairs, 22, 40; retirement decisions, 5, 31–32, 40–46

September 11th attacks, 38, 71

Shalala, Donna, 93

Shaw, E. Clay, 70

Sherrill, Mikie, 86

Shor, Boris, 125–126, 132

Siddiqui, Sabrina, 7, 54–55

Silver, Nate, 49–50

Simon, Sheila, 76–77, 88

Sinclair, Barbara, 20–21, 104–105, 108

Sinema, Kyrsen, 118

Skelton, Ike, 63

Smith, Howard, 22

Smith, Jacob, 62, 74, 85

Smith, Steven S., 2, 105

Snowe, Olympia, 24

soft money, 58, 65–66
Solid South, 40,145; lack of Republican
  bench, 81, 113, 125; Richard Nixon's
  Southern Strategy, 81
Sorauf, Frank, 90
special elections, 2, 51, 65, 108, 162–
  163n10, 163n2; before the 2018 elections, 18, 49–50
Specter, Arlen, 24, 108
Squire, Peverill, 131
state legislatures, 3, 11–13, 116, 162n13,
  164n8, 165n15; candidate recruitment,
  10–12, 91–92, 101–102; competitiveness of state legislative bodies in the
  2010s, 127–129, 145; fundraising ban
  while in session, 69; interviews with
  legislators, 132–141; members of
  Congress running for state legislature,
  164n10; polarization of legislative
  bodies, 125, 132; redistricting of, (*see*
  redistricting); retirement from, 121–
  123, 145–146; quality of candidates,
  165n12; running for Congress, 74–77,
  86–87; running for the U.S. Senate,
  110, 112, 161n8; role of minority
  party, 9; Senate replacement process,
  2–3; time horizon of state legislators,
  138
Stevens, Haley, 86
Stevens, Theodore, 103, 116
Stoddard, Olga, 94
Stone, Walter, J., 31, 73
Supreme Court of the United States, 2,
  65, 107
survival model, 159n14
swing seats, 68, 71–72, 129, 143, 148;
  marginal seats, 19, 46–47, 50–51, 67,
  89, 91, 95, 98–101, 144–145, 148

Taylor, Gene, 63
term limits, 127, 135, 138, 141; of
  Republican committee chairs, 51; not
  existing for U.S. Congress, 107
Thomsen, Danielle, 32, 40, 73
Thornberry, Mary C., 91, 94, 155,
  163n11
Thurmond, J. Strom, 103, 116
Tillis, Thom, 107, 122, 161n8
tobit model, 65–67, 160n12

Treul, Sarah, 62, 162n21
Trott, David, 51
Trump, Donald J., 110; approval rating,
  49–50; effect on Republican retirements from Congress, 50, 144; election of, 49, 158n6, 164n20; protests
  against and reactions to, 49–50, 81, 85,
  118, 144; rise of amateur candidates,
  83–84, 86–87; Trump administration,
  18, 49–50, 107, 118, 164n11

U.S. House: 40 years of Democratic
  control (*see* Democratic Party: 40-year
  era of control of Congress); candidate
  entry (*see* candidate entry); candidate
  recruitment (*see* reform of rules (esp.
  after 1974 election), 22, 62, 80, 82;
  minority party (*see* minority party
  status); oversight role, 18; party fundraising (*see* party fundraising); polarization of (*see* political polarization:
  increased polarization in Congress);
  redistricting of (*see* redistricting);
  retirement (*see* retirement decisions);
  recruitment of candidates, 15 (*see also*
  Democratic Congressional Campaign
  Committee [DCCC]: party recruitment efforts; National Republican
  Congressional Committee [NRCC]:
  party recruitment efforts); Rules
  Committee, 22; structure of party
  leadership, 17, 32–33
U.S. Senate, 12–13, 57, 71, 102, 122,
  140, 144, 148, 163n2, 163nn4–5;
  1996 Senate elections, 103–104; 2018
  Senate elections, 118–120; candidate
  entry (*see* candidate entry: in the
  U.S. Senate); changes in 1970s, 105;
  competitiveness of majority in late
  2010s, 1–3, 6; defining candidate quality, 112; Democratic supermajority
  after 2008 election, 24; filibuster, 2,
  24, 104–105, 107–108, 148; influence
  of minority party, 5, 107; location
  on political ambition structure, 107,
  119–120; norms and traditions,
  104–105; replacement process, 2–3,
  108; retirement decisions of senators,
  103–104, 108–109, 118–120, 144,

164n10; *Senate Syndrome*, 157n5; state legislators running for the Senate (*see* tate legislatures: running for the U.S. Senate); supply of quality candidates, 16 (*see also* political ambition: the U.S. Senate); time horizon of senators, 108–109, 114–115; use of budget reconciliation process to pass major agenda items, 107, 109 (*see also* Byrd Rule); value of majority, 1–3, 106, 157n1, 164n9, 164n11

Van Dunk, Emily, 3, 128–130
Van Hollen, Chris, 14, 19, 62

Wahlbeck, Paul J., 7, 55, 59
Washington Post, 1; content analysis of articles, 96, 155–156
Wasserman, David, 50
Wasserman-Schultz, Debbie, 62, 160n6
wave elections, 26, 29, 52, 84
Wawro, Gregory, 105
Waxman, Henry, 8
Weinberg, Neil, 74
Wexton, Jennifer
Wilkins, Arjun, 20
Women's March, 49

Zinke, Ryan, 18